Rural Policy Research Alternatives

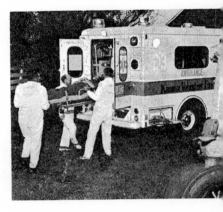

North Central Regional Center for Rural Development

Rural Policy
Research Alternatives

Iowa State University Press / **Ames** / 1978

Volume Editors: David L. Rogers and Larry R. Whiting

© 1978   The Iowa State University Press
Ames, Iowa   50010. All rights reserved

Composed and printed by
The Iowa State University Press

First edition, 1978

Library of Congress Cataloging in Publication Data
Main entry under title:

Rural policy research alternatives.

    Papers of a conference held Apr. 22–23, 1975 at Iowa State University.
    Includes index.
    1.   Rural development—United States—Congresses.
2.   Policy sciences—Congresses.   I.   Rogers, David L.
II.   Whiting, Larry R.   III.   North Central Regional
Center for Rural Development.
HN90.C6R83   309.2′63′0973   77–25082
ISBN 0–8138–1875–3

CONTENTS

PREFACE

EVERY DAY community leaders are faced with decisions that affect the quality and quantity of community services such as health, welfare, education, law enforcement, parks and recreation, sewer and water, and streets. Wise decisions in every instance depend in part on *relevant information* being available *when needed* at the various stages of the issue development and resolution. Community decisions may not correlate very well with the solution suggested by objective analysis. The decision may represent a "power decision" that is supported by objective analysis from the viewpoint of the power actor, but not when the total set of people impacted by the outcome is considered. Policy decisions, after all, are decisions about *what ought to be done*. As such, the decisions must be recognized as the product of values in interaction with objective knowledge and the preferences of those who are in a position to control the resources critical to the issue to be resolved. Nonetheless, information should play a critical role in the process.

Social scientists have speculated on the reasons why their research has not been widely used in reaching policy decisions. Several theories have been offered to explain the low utilization. One theory relates to the constraints operating on the policymakers themselves. Decision makers often need precise information and within a short period of time. Combined with these constraints is the limited number of variables over which the policymaker may have control. Often social scientists measure variables that are not subject to manipulation (e.g., age, sex of the individual, formation and choice among values, and size of community).

A second theory offered in explanation of low utilization of social science research is referred to as the "two communities" theory. Essentially, it is argued, the social scientist and the policymaker operate in separate worlds with different objectives, different languages, different values, and the like. Put differently, they do not understand or particularly trust each other.

A third point of view is that social scientists rely too much on quantitative methods and impose theoretical and methodological restrictions to the point that they refuse to come to grips with the problems posed by the community.

A fourth is that social scientists do not have a single theory; therefore, as one position is put forward they also must say "but on the other hand."

Finally, policymakers are viewed as resisting theory. In effect, they say, "We are not interested in your theory, but only in our own, because each decision whether value based or not is based on someone's theory."

Whether any of these explanations is adequate, it seems clear that there is a gap between the information and data needs of decision makers at all levels and the kind of information and data that social scientists are providing or are willing to provide.

The community developer who assumes a neutral role, the advocacy planner, the power actor, or the average citizen accepts the value of and need for information in decision making. The required information may be of the technical assistance type which specifies such coefficients as cost per foot, expected longevity of materials, or soil characteristics. The information may also be descriptive in nature, that is, describing population change, employment trends, and the like. The information required may also be predictive and thus attempt to forecast outcomes based on past trends, relationships, and assumptions.

In rural community development there is a continuous need for information. Change agents working directly with community leaders are continuously asked for all kinds of information—particularly social and economic data. The community development process itself—which is after all an application of decision making—begins with the assumption that information is available for specifying the problem as well as for evaluating alternative solutions. In addition to questions requiring information that does not yet exist, questions arise about what the situation is or what will happen in a particular situation. The information (facts) about how a community service (such as a demand bus service) worked elsewhere must be overwhelmingly clear and persuasive before most community leaders will be willing to apply the information to their own situation without additional study, that is, without more information. In their defense it should be noted that the typical study involving social and economic analysis rarely explains more than 25 to 35 percent of the variance in the situation being studied.

Partly because of the above situation, social scientists are cautious about generalizing, cautious about speculating, and at times overzealous in maintaining rigor in data gathering and analysis techniques as well as interpretation. Much of this *scientific ethos* is incongruent with the information needs of community leaders. When community leaders ask for help it is not unusual to hear the social scientists respond with something like "Give me $50,000 and two years and I'll try to find out." Such practice may be good science, but it is often an unsatisfactory solution to the provision of needed information. In general too much emphasis has been placed on an essentially "postdictive" approach, where data are collected from a cross section of some population and massaged by the computer looking for the maximum R^2, and then backing into an explanation of the statistical relationships.

Little research is formulated around a policy format where it is critical to sort out the target goals, the policy instrument variables (i.e., those variables that can be changed by the policymaker such as unemployment benefits and tax incentives), and the noncontrollable variables such as chronological age and sex. From the traditional research framework it makes little difference, but for policymaking analysis it is crucial to differentiate between these types of variables in the design of the study as well as the analysis. Knowing that chronological age is a major correlate with the social economic well-being of the elderly is not enough. The policymaker cannot change age. Policy variables that can be manipulated, such as income, must be emphasized in the analysis.

Social scientists need to give more attention to secondary data sources that are collected frequently and from local levels. Five- and ten-year census data should also be used, but obviously these data have intercensus period limitations. Communities are not always able to wait for a study that will generate primary data and take at least two years to initiate and complete. Moreover, great amounts of data are already collected through local government units and/or agency programs. These data are currently underutilized as a source of information for community decision making. The quality of these data, the preciseness of variables, and the limitation on meeting the criteria of statistical sampling are all bothersome to the social scientist. Such deficiencies are likely overplayed because even the most carefully planned and executed survey nearly always has limitations, not the least of which is the failure to have asked the crucial question or having asked it in the wrong way.

Social scientists also need to alter the way research projects are developed when focusing on policy problems. Consideration should be given to the involvement of the potential user of the research in the formulation of the problem. Without such involvement, which is admittedly untidy, the research may miss the questions of crucial interest to the consumer of the research. Such attention to the consumer's needs are common in contract research. Likewise, we see scientists expending enormous energies to satisfy Office of Management and Budget requirements. We do not see as much concern for the needs of the community decision maker.

These aspects of social science research, which come to the forefront in rural development, gave rise to the conference (Alternative Methods for Public Policy Research in Rural America, April 22–23, 1975, Iowa State University) at which the papers in this volume were delivered. The objective of the conference was to improve research design and methods for the study of public policy issues in rural development. Only a beginning was made in this conference to achieve that objective. Much work remains to be done. Nonetheless, the material in this volume does relate to several aspects of the general problem outlined above. The first part of the book focuses on the information needs of decision makers at different levels and suggests broad implications for initiating and carrying out policy-oriented research. A second part focuses on the ways in which different groups of researchers have gone about designing policy research for selected problem areas. A third section centers on five different kinds of research techniques and their uses. A final chapter, an overview and summary, focuses on what is, what ought to be, and where we should go from here.

It is our hope that this book will be helpful by encouraging researchers and research administrators to review and perhaps modify their thinking about the need for and the ways of doing policy research so that it will be relevant to the issues of rural development.

Ronald C. Powers, Director
North Central Regional Center
for Rural Development

Rural Policy Research Alternatives

CHAPTER ONE

FEDERAL RESEARCH AND INFORMATION NEEDS

LYNN M. DAFT

A CARDINAL RULE of effective policy analysis is to question the question being asked, to probe for the reason it is being asked, and to determine what difference, if any, an answer will make. This chapter begins, therefore, not with a review of information needs but with a general probing of the question itself, first by exploring some dimensions of the rural development issue from a national policy perspective, then by examining the policymaking process itself—its composition, its information requirements, and its principal information sources. With this as background, some research and information needs are described.

RURAL DEVELOPMENT AS A POLICY ISSUE. Rural development has never been defined to the satisfaction of anything approaching even a respectable minority of those registering interest in the topic. This is not to say that each of us might not carry around in our heads our own personal concepts, or even that some smaller groups within the larger population might not have arrived at an agreed upon view. But no concensus has been reached. The absence of an overall framework has been suggested as one reason we have so much difficulty developing relevant and useful information on the topic [4].

Why do we lack such a framework? Surely it is not for want of capable, imaginative minds. Although our intellectual investment in the topic has not been on a par with that, say, of agricultural production economics, it has been quite respectable. Neither would it seem to be because the issue is of only passing interest. It has been with us

LYNN M. DAFT was a Senior Economist with the Office of Management and Budget in Washington, D.C., when this chapter was written. Views are those of the author and are not intended to represent the policy of the Office of Management and Budget. Daft is now Associate Director of the Domestic Policy Staff in the White House.

in one form or another for over a half century. Furthermore, there is no evidence of the issue fading into oblivion, at least not in the immediate future. One could also argue that it is lack of resource support or even the intricacy of the issue itself that is the problem. But while we may have more sympathy for these explanations, they are not sufficient.

Another, more fundamental reason ties in directly to the topic of this chapter. We can probably understand its origin better by retracing the evolution of the rural development issue. In doing so, one finds that rural development becomes an accumulation of problems for which the private market did not or could not provide satisfactory solutions: the absence of credit for home mortgages; small communities unable to afford central water and sewer systems; workers displaced from jobs in agriculture, timber, and mining; the unwillingness of utilities to provide electrical and telephone systems of uneconomic scale, and so forth. By the very nature of the problems, market solutions were not feasible. This being the case, the organized interests among the population most affected turned to the political system for satisfaction. Rural development then became a political response to that many-faceted appeal. Copp has written:

> Rural development is not a research problem, it is not a theoretical concept; rather it is a policy goal . . . the term rural development itself will always remain unanalyzable in a sociological (and economic) sense and remain apart from any theoretical system. It is a rubric or code word used by opinion leaders in everyday discourse to refer to a desired goal. It is not, and cannot be, a scientific term [6, pp. 518–19].

Back concluded, after reviewing rural development policy since 1955,

> that political criteria have been a major basis for policy proposals and actions in rural development, especially in events associated with the Rural Development Act of 1972 . . . (and while) there is no alternative to a political process in policy making . . . as experience reveals, a political process alone is not sufficient to assure success [1, p. 1129].

Under some circumstances, a political definition can be helpful. In this case, however, the definition has been a major source of confusion. It has had the effect of extending a very broad umbrella across a wide range of problems for the sake of political convenience. It was also responsible for giving the definition a unique institutional twist by placing it within the agricultural establishment. For purposes of defining and organizing an informational system that feeds into policymaking, we badly need to break free from the constraints associated with the political definition of rural development—not to the extent of disregarding political forces, but to the extent required for correcting the present imbalance in influence.

The design of a framework for viewing rural development is clearly beyond the scope of this chapter. But until such a framework is developed and becomes a part of our common working language, it will continue to be necessary to spell out the informal models each of us carries around in his head. The one used here is rather simple, but it serves as a crude illustration of the sort of framework intended and makes explicit some assumptions that might otherwise go unstated. Let us begin with a list of presumptions:

1. Our ultimate concern is with the well-being of people. This seems obvious, but it is easily lost sight of. Means *do* become ends.

2. Human needs are hierarchical. Some classes of need are of higher priority than others. Maslow's ordering is as plausible as any.

3. For its many imperfections, the private market economy does a reasonably good job of allocating economic resources. Recent U.S. experience with economic controls, as well as the evidence of problems encountered in the planned economies, points up some of the drawbacks of attempting to correct for market failure through the exercise of central control.

4. Rural/urban distinctions generally confuse more than they clarify. As a social dimension, rurality is more useful in identifying the cause of problems than in devising policy solutions or engendering political support.

5. The key to economic and social adjustment is through investment in the human resource. When adequately prepared for the task, people can and do adjust in a manner that comes closer to maximizing their well-being than if the adjustment decisions are imposed upon them. In short, people can be counted upon to make intelligent decisions, given their perception of prevailing conditions.

6. The cost of intervention in the location of economic activity on a scale of the order required to have significant impact is in excess of the amount society is willing to pay, on the basis of present knowledge.

7. American culture is founded on dual principles of democracy and excellence. In combination, these principles lay the basis for a societal guarantee of the opportunity to pursue excellence. They offer no guarantee of its achievement, however. The distinction between equity and equality derives from the same source.

Taken together these presumptions offer a basis for viewing the issue of rural development and for identifying policy directions. They suggest, for example, that the essential problem is one of human resource adjustment to changing economic and social conditions and that the most effective means for coping with this problem is to invest directly in the people themselves. They also suggest that the problem does not conform to jurisdictional boundaries, particularly boundaries established arbitrarily on the basis of population or political divisions; that restricting policy solutions to that part of the problem manifested in "rural" areas is impractical not only from the standpoint of manipulating causal variables but from the standpoint of mustering political support as well; and that half-hearted attempts to deal with the problem through such forms of economic intervention as industrial development subsidies will likely have little more than symbolic value.

Programmatically, this might suggest emphasis on:

1. Human resource investments, in the form of guaranteed minimum levels of educational opportunity, health care, and income, coupled with access to manpower development and training and mobility assistance.

2. Governmental modernization at the local level, with particular attention to improvements in structure, administration, fiscal management, and citizen involvement.

3. Improved information, designed with two specific purposes in mind: (a) to improve the competitive performance of the private market and (b) to expand our knowledge of nonmarket costs and benefits associated with the development of sparsely populated areas.

This view of rural development is not original with the author. It conforms in many important respects with what others have been saying in recent years [1, 6, 20].

INFORMATION AND THE POLICYMAKING PROCESS. To understand the research and information needs of the federal policymaker, one must first understand something of the policymaking process itself. Above all, the process is complex. Lindblom has termed it "the science of muddling through," adding that it is "an extremely complex analytical and political process to which there is no beginning or end and the boundaries of which are most uncertain" [13]. At the federal level, there are many participants in the process. Some are more proximate to final decisions than others, although those most closely identified with decisions are not always most instrumental in the process. There is a great deal of both functional and subject matter specialization among federal policymakers. Their decisions are often serial and incremental. Major policy decisions almost always involve far-ranging trade-offs, thereby making it impossible to consider any one program decision in exclusion of others. A constellation of economic and political "opportunity costs" surround every major decision. Consequently, a mass transit appropriation might be realized at the expense of water and sewer grants, or a civil rights bill might "cost" a housing bill [19].

Information Users. Where does information enter this system? Who are the users of information within the policymaking process? First, we must remind ourselves that the federal government is an accumulation of highly specialized, highly segmented departments, agencies, offices, bureaus, commissions, committees, and courts. Though in theory the chief policymaking responsibility of each of the three major branches is lodged at the top of their respective organizations, in practice, policies are made at numerous points throughout each of the organizations. This is, of course, particularly true of the executive branch, given the size and breadth of its responsibility. President Kennedy was said to have remarked that his greatest surprise on coming to the presidency was to find out how many situations he could not do anything about [16]. This is so not because the situations are beyond control of the federal government but because so much of the federal government is beyond effective control of its chief executive.

Much of the information instrumental to a given policy decision never reaches the "proximate policymaker," at least not in its original form. Thus the demand for information in support of policymaking is not limited to just the policymakers. Intermediate sources of demand are equally important. For our purposes, users are grouped into five classes: (1) research/scientific, (2) program administration, (3) policy planning/evaluation, (4) regulatory, and (5) judicial.

RESEARCH/SCIENTIFIC. This is the community within the federal policymaking system whose members speak the same "language" as the university researcher or information specialist. They come with the same or similar educational backgrounds, read and write for the same professional journals, and attend the same professional meetings. If it were not for the fact that most of them have a greater tolerance for life in and around Washington, D.C., and put a slightly lower value on hunting, fishing, and golfing, they would be hard to distinguish from their university colleagues. The members of this user class are predominately found in the executive branch, though with the strengthening of the Congressional Research Service and the General Accounting Office and with the formation of the Office of Technology Assessment, the Congress is attempting to correct this long-standing handicap. Prominent examples within the executive branch include the National Science Foundation (NSF), the National Institute of Education, the Council of Economic Advisers (CEA), and the Economic Research Service.

The research/scientific information users tend to be the furthest removed from the ultimate policymaking decision of the five classes. Yet their proximity varies greatly. The CEA, for example, is near the center of high-level policymaking while NSF occupies a position near the outer boundary. The needs of this user class are, of course, the most technical of all. For these and other reasons, the demand represented by the research/scientific user comes closest to approximating the type information supplied by the university.

PROGRAM ADMINISTRATION. If the university researchers' relationship to the first category of federal user were to be described as incestuous, their relationship with this user class might be termed extraneous. For program administrators talk an altogether different language and come from an altogether different background than researchers. The administrator's perspective of policymaking is necessarily constrained by the programmatic limits of his responsibility. Despite these limits, many important policy decisions are made by program administrators, perhaps more than are commonly perceived. It is not unusual for legislators and policymakers further up in the organization to defer to the judgment of those "on the firing line." As a general rule, we are substantially underinvesting in the level and quality of information used for support of this function.

POLICY PLANNING AND EVALUATION. In this class the more conventional policymakers are included, principally, the cabinet and subcabinet, the Congress and its committees, and the executive office of the president. In contrast to program administration, which often involves decentralized policy decisions, this decision process is highly centralized. In comparison with other users, these decisions are more global in scope, almost always dealing with issues that involve major trade-offs among programs, interests, and objectives.

REGULATORY. Though not usually singled out, the regulatory functions of the federal government are sufficiently unique and important to merit separate treatment. They are not customarily viewed as policymaking bodies, but their actions have the same effect. Their independent status sets them apart from other federal administrative bodies. Their opportunity for influence over key economic and social parameters is enormous, given their oversight responsibilities in such fields as communications, finance, transportation, commercial trade, power, and the like. Their demand for information varies greatly from one body to the next. In that the adjudication of grievances and differences of opinion is a principal role of these agencies, the law has played a dominant role in their organization, staffing, and operation. The social sciences have played a very limited role, though it should be an expanding one in the future.

JUDICIAL. This too is a less prominent part of the federal policymaking landscape, but "judges too make policy" [13]. And while the influence of the scientist has not been great, the potential is there. Justice Oliver Wendell Holmes once wrote, "I have in mind an ultimate dependence upon science because it is finally for science to determine, so far as it can, the relative worth of our different social ends. . . ." [13, p. 79]. Though this potential remains largely unrealized, there has been some movement in this direction of late. The use of psychological and sociological data in the case of *Brown* vs. *Board of Education* is perhaps the most prominent case in recent years in which scientific information has played an important part. Of course the responsibility for mobilizing scientific evidence still rests with the litigants and their lawyers. Nonetheless, the opportunity for the use of such information to influence important court decisions is likely to grow in time. And since many of these decisions will involve distributional questions, many will have important human resource and community implications. Recent decisions concerning limits on environmental pollution and equal educational opportunity are indicative. Given the courts' emphasis on matters of distributive justice and individual rights, they might, in fact, represent a more significant market for sociological knowledge than for economic knowledge.

The reader might be wondering what this particular list of information users has to do with rural development. It certainly takes one far beyond the U.S. Department of Agriculture, its constituent agencies, and the agricultural committees of the Congress. But it does so for good reason, because it is beyond these institutional bounds that most of the key federal policy decisions that affect the well-being of rural people in direct and tangible ways have been and will continue to be made. If we restrict our attention to those policies and programs labeled "rural development," we will have missed the largest part of the relevant information market.

Conditions. Having identified some key points through which information enters the policymaking process, let us consider some requirements of information entry. A great deal of information never "gets through." Why? Obviously, the requirements vary greatly among and within user classes. The research/scientific user, for example, requires information of a far more technical nature than that required by program administrators. Likewise, information used in either the judicial process or in the regulatory field must be couched within a framework consistent with procedures of the respective groups. The Federal Trade Commission, for example, might require its information within the framework of a competitive model, perhaps using a market structure/behavior/performance approach. For a court case, the information would have to meet certain rules of admissability. Despite these variations, one can usefully generalize.

To be of maximum value in guiding federal policymaking, informational inputs must meet certain tests or conditions. For professionals specializing in communication and the extension of knowledge, nothing is new or revolutionary about this list. The same conditions have been stated many times before. Their simplicity, however, does not diminish their importance.

RELEVANCE. To be influential, information must have relevance to the issue at hand. More to the point, it must be perceived by the policymaker to have relevance. No matter how intellectually stimulating or ingeniously contrived or vitally important in other contexts, if the information is irrelevant to the issue at hand, forget it! To the policymaker it is not contextually informative and therefore is not information. Worse than that, if irrelevant information is introduced into the decision making, diverting thought and attention without contributing to the solution, it is viewed as having negative value. The question also arises as to *who* is defining relevancy, for there are often disagreements over what constitutes relevancy. But this determination is not independent of the other conditions.

TIMELINESS. In a policymaking context, time is all-important. The policymaking agenda changes rapidly and covers a broad spectrum. This is particularly true of macrodecision making. One might liken the policymaking process to a constantly moving conveyor belt, its ends obscured in darkness and a spotlight focused on but one small area. Issues falling within the lighted circle are on the agenda and under scrutiny, albeit briefly. The view beyond this immediate agenda, forward or backward, is hazy at best. Thus if the information is not available or is not introduced during the brief period for which the issue is on the agenda and receiving attention, its policymaking value is greatly diminished. The fact that policymaking tends to be incremental, offering "next chances" helps avoid a complete loss of value.

CREDIBILITY. To be of value in policymaking, information must be credible—credible in the sense that it represents what it is purported to. This is not the same as being objective or unbiased. Most accomplished policymakers presume that none of their informational inputs are entirely objective and free of distortion. As a result, they concentrate on securing information whose biases they feel they know and understand and hence can adjust for. Thus information from a trade association has credibility if it represents the principal interests of the membership of that association, as purported. It need not be free of self-interested bias. In fact, the absence of such bias would be cause for concern.

CLARITY. Clarity is another of those obvious requirements for effective communication. Yet it is all the more critical in this situation—a situation in which highly specialized technical experts produce information to be used by a small and ever-shifting assembly of generalists. Add to this the tendency of scientists to talk and write in their own unique forms of shorthand about such things as elasticities and paradigms and social marginalization, and the obstacles to effective communication become even greater.

CONCISENESS. Although related to clarity, this condition is different. Being concise makes the achievement of clarity all the more difficult, for it precludes the use of lengthy exposition. This is troublesome for the scientific mind for yet another reason. The scientist who knows his subject matter well knows that most issues do not lend themselves to simplification. Few issues are either black or white; most are some shade of gray. Results of scientific study, by the very nature of the scientific method, are never final and seldom are advanced without qualification. To most policymakers, this is sheer balderdash. Most of the qualifications that are important to the scientist are quite unimportant to the policymaker. He is looking for a best judgment given the present state of knowledge . . . period. And he wants it in a form that gets to the heart of the matter as quickly as possible.

Not surprisingly, being concise places a rather serious handicap on the use of technical information in support of policymaking. In the case of nontechnical information, the policymaker generally has confidence in his own ability to evaluate its reliability and its meaning. In the case of technical information, he must usually rely upon others. And no matter how high the degree of trust between policymaker and staff, some element of discounting must enter this transaction.

COVERAGE. Most federal policies have regional if not national implications. Most policy issues also involve a confluence of interests. Policymakers are therefore looking for information that consolidates and aggregates. In economic terms, they seek to maximize the efficiency of information acquisition. Results from a sample of Iowa households might prove useful for a given decision, but if the issue has national ramifications, one cannot stop with information from that state alone. And beyond the problem of differences in the subpopulation itself, there are the imponderables of attempting to collate results based on surveys using different sampling techniques, collected at different times, using different questions, and analyzed using different statistical techniques. The same problem applies to crossing discipline or subject matter lines. For example, the biological effects alone of a given environmental action seldom provide sufficient basis for an informed decision.

Information of an economic, legal, social, and political nature is also needed. Faced with limited capacity for integrating disparate items of information, the policymaker, therefore, places a premium on information that has already been integrated.

ACCESSIBILITY. Finally, there must be a connecting bridge between the policymaking process and those who produce the knowledge. In the absence of this two-way linkage, knowledge producers act without knowledge of an important market while policymakers make decisions unmindful of important informational inputs.

Each of the seven conditions listed above is a necessary but not all-sufficient condition. Though it is possible for information to be useful in policymaking without meeting all these conditions, its effectiveness is greatly diminished. These conditions are somewhat demanding. As a result, they are seldom fully satisfied. But where, one might ask, do policymakers find information sources that even come close to giving a completely effective guide?

Sources of Policymaking Information. Organized *interest groups* are a major source of policymaking information. They probably come closer to meeting the conditions described above than any other single source. If an issue impacts directly and importantly on its interests, an interest group will normally initiate the introduction of information partial to its cause. Since most interest groups recognize the importance of such information in policymaking, most are organized to provide it. The larger the number of interests and individuals represented by the group, the more valued the source. The National Chamber of Commerce, for example, not only represents a large and influential membership but is also vitally interested in a broad range of issues and is equipped to mobilize information concerning any one of them quickly and effectively. The same could be said of the National Association of Counties, as well as others. These larger interest groups have the added advantage of being able to provide a synthesis of information and, in some situations, a resolution of conflict within their respective memberships.

Another important source of information for the policymaker is the *mass media*. Again, the more prominent sources among the mass media measure up reasonably well on the conditions noted above. The fact that the media oversimplify complex issues and misconstrue others is counterbalanced by their timely attention to present-day issues and their formalized structure for receiving feedback, correction, and elaboration.

Of course much of the information for policymaking comes from *internal sources*. Some federal agencies have their own internal mechanisms for collecting and analyzing information. The Department of Agriculture is better prepared in this regard than probably any other agency in Washington. This is particularly true for social science research. However, information from internal staff has its own peculiar limitations. Though it is an important and usually reliable source of information on program detail, it is less so for matters concerning major policy issues and trade-offs among programs. Much of this information travels through formal, highly institutionalized channels. The distortions and "uncertainty absorption" that can result as information travels this course have been described by others [8, 15]. Yet a great deal of information travels outside the formal channels. It is these informal sources that often prove to be the more effective.

The federal government also uses *special study groups* to collect and synthesize information relevant to policy issues. Presidents Johnson and Nixon made particularly heavy use of this device. In 1967, for example, around fifty separate federal task forces were operating in various domestic policy fields. Many of these were "inside" groups, comprised mostly of staff from executive branch agencies. By way of contrast, the Nixon administration in its early months formed about twenty task forces, with most of the members being drawn from outside the federal government.

Finally, federal policymakers turn to *outside specialists* for consultation and information. In the main, such information reaches the policymaking process only indirectly. Lacking institutional knowledge, outside sources generally require a greater investment in time than the policymaker can afford. Thus it is either the research/scientific user or the policymaker's staff who turns to external sources for information that can be injected into the policymaking process at a later time.

None of the sources mentioned here are mutually independent. Organized interest groups, for example, are becoming increasingly adept at tapping outside specialists, including universities, for the information they employ. Special study groups, too, are generally dependent on other sources for the information they organize and interpret.

IMPLICATIONS FOR RURAL DEVELOPMENT RESEARCH.
Up to this point, we have concentrated on description—description of rural development as it appears from the author's vantagepoint and description of how and under what conditions information influences policy formulation on this and other topics. What are the implications of this for rural development research?

First, the federal market for rural development research mostly lies beyond the agricultural institutions and the research/scientific users we are most accustomed to dealing with. This is particularly true if one accepts the premise that much of the federal policy solution rests with human resource investments, coupled with efforts to improve the operational effectiveness of local government. Tapping this market will necessarily require the forging of new institutional ties and new professional relationships. Within the federal government, this means getting to know and be known by such agencies as the Health Services Administration, the Manpower Administration, the National Institute for Education, the Advisory Commission on Intergovernmental Relations, the Office of Revenue Sharing, the Social and Rehabilitation Service, and a multitude of others. At the national level these are the effective submarkets for information affecting the well-being of people, including rural people. If our information is to be influential, if our policies are to benefit from our knowledge, it is within these arenas that the two must come together. We have achieved some success in establishing linkages, but our successes are too few compared with the opportunities foregone.

Beyond the general uncertainties involved, the task is made still more difficult by the need for basic investments in learning about the problems, their institutional settings, and related literature and sources of knowledge. As a result, both the host institution and the researcher must be prepared to invest some "risk capital" (monetary as well as intellectual, and perhaps political) before expecting much of a payoff. For most of us this poses a dilemma. As professionals we are tied to an institutional construct that is not closely linked to the functions and clientele described here. As Gardner stated, "We become caught in a web of fixed relationships" [10]. First and foremost is our membership in the agricultural establishment. Though one can argue that these worlds overlap and are inherently complementary, there are built-in contradictions, too. Institutions can change. Failing that, individuals can change their institutional affiliations.

Though large organizations sometimes give the appearance of

being static and totally resistant to change, few really are. Most are in a constant state of evolutionary change. They move, albeit incrementally, first in one direction and then in another. They do so in response to forces from both within and without. Changes in leadership, changes in clientele, changes in the larger economic, social, and political setting all establish their own set of forces acting on the institution. Some of these attempts at institutional change succeed; many fail. Again, our agricultural institutions offer some clear examples of both. Successful spin-offs from the Department of Agriculture include the Food and Drug Administration, the Weather Bureau, and the Bureau of Public Roads. In these cases, success was achieved by the creation of new institutions. In other cases, for example, the Bureau of Agricultural Economics, the Food and Nutrition Service, and the Farm Security Administration, the larger institution was itself altered to accommodate new functions and clientele.

Rural development, within the context of the agricultural establishment, is engaged in a classic test of the institutional system, and has been so for at least twenty years. The system has yielded some, but not very much.

Second, at least two basic incongruities in the policymaking and information-generating systems must be dealt with in achieving a linkage of the two. One has to do with the nature of our inquiry systems, in theory and in practice. Figure 1.1 portrays an inquiry system. The four benchmarks—reality, conceptual model, scientific model, and solution—are joined by four processes and two cross-checks. In combination, they represent a way of looking at and thinking about a system of inquiry. In theory, an inquiry systematically moves through each phase in its turn, beginning with the reduction of a problem situation to conceptual form and ending with the application of a solution to the original problem. Only when the system has completely cycled and met all the tests along the way can we say the inquiry has been completed. Until then it is partial, incomplete, inconclusive.

Unfortunately, much of our research on this and other topics is confined to certain parts of the system, at the expense of other parts. More specifically, we dwell on modeling and model solving while shortchanging the conceptualization and application phases. And even this might not be so dangerous if it were not for the fact, as Kenneth Boulding says, that we seem to believe the results of these models [11].

Another crucial point of difference that serves as a barrier to effecting a linkage between the systems is that policymaking in a democratic state is in a continuing search for consensus. It is through consensual action that a government of laws is made possible. Scientific inquiry, on the other hand, is governed by many different

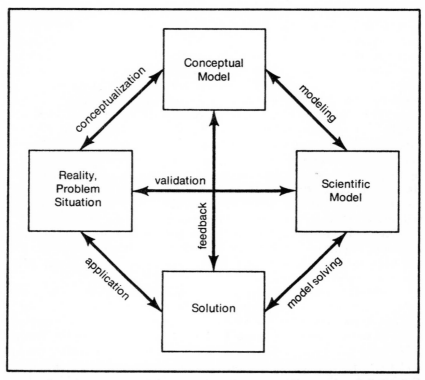

Fig. 1.1. An inquiry system. (Source: Mitroff and Pondy [17])

theories or world views that necessarily result in conflicting findings. Sometimes conflict is even built into the inquiry as a means of exposing hidden assumptions and sharpening differences. Though each method serves the purposes of its respective system well, where the two systems come together there must be an accommodation of sorts. Inquiry must be prepared to help select among alternative solutions; policies must be designed with sufficient flexibility that they can adapt to a changing state of knowledge.

   Third, the most effective policy research is that which focuses on specific program or policy decisions. Most issues of public policy, and particularly those of a social nature, involve extremely subtle and complex objectives and values. Though one can hypothesize a global issue and undertake an analysis of it in the abstract, somehow the results nearly always come off oversimplified and impractical. It seems, Schultze has noted, that "we discover our objectives and the intensity that we assign to them only in the process of considering particular programs or policies" [19, p. 38]. Not only is this where one finds the effective demand for information to be greatest and where it is accorded the greatest opportunity for impact, but also where the information comes closest to being knowledge.

Fourth, university research can make a valuable contribution to policymaking IF it accentuates its comparative advantages while correcting some notable deficiencies. The principal advantages are: (1) an environment that is conducive to study and reflection; (2) greater freedom to evaluate federal programs; (3) the opportunity to tap alternative disciplines and knowledge bases; and (4) organizational flexibility, at least in some cases. The deficiencies of university research as a source of information for policymaking are: (1) its episodic, small-scale nature; (2) the general insensitivity of university researchers to policy constraints; and (3) a system of professional incentives that rewards originality and sophistication of technique above synthesis, application, and conceptualization. These are problems that can be overcome, as exemplified by the University of Wisconsin's Poverty Institute, for example. In fact, we might do well to take a hard look at a few of these examples, including failures, and benefit from their experience.

The successes are characterized by:

1. A program (versus project) orientation.

2. An institutional commitment to a specific set of policy issues.

3. An initial investment in institutional knowledge of the particular policymaking process.

4. At least some semblance of an interdisciplinary approach.

5. A "continuing" program—something between one-shot and forever, so to speak.

6. A tie-in to policymaking at the policy planning/programming level that involves professional peers at both the sending and receiving points.

Fifth, publicly supported research has a special responsibility in the interests it represents. As our discussion of the sources of information for public policymaking would imply, some interests are far more effectively served than others. In particular, those interests that are well organized and well supported have little problem assessing the decision-making process. Furthermore, this information too has utility. After all, in a capitalistic democracy one presumes that economic power has both the incentive and capability of advancing its own best, though narrow, case.

But this also means that publicly supportive research has a particular responsibility to: (1) assist the public policymaking process in the evaluation of information supplied by other special interests and (2) provide information representing the interests of the unorganized, less influential segments of our society. Informational "benefits ought to be available in a useable form at the bottom of society as well as at the top, to the obstructionist as well as to the reformer, to the idealogue, as well as to the technocrat, to those who are investigated as well as those who commission the investigation" [12, p. 24].

There are pitfalls associated with these roles, it should be noted. One is that they can be contradictory. They have the appearance, and can have the effect, of combining judge and jury, especially if the researcher becomes an advocate of one side or the other. This is not to argue against the need for and value of advocates, especially for the disenfranchised. But until something akin to the forensic style described in a later chapter by Peter Brown is more widely adopted, advocacy is a luxury the policy analyst can ill afford.

Finally, policymakers and researchers alike must better appreciate the limits of knowledge. Sometimes as scientists we take ourselves and our research findings too seriously. We lose sight of the fact that

> scientific description is not value-free because one always has had to pre-suppose some normative model of the world in the first place in order that one can collect observations in the second place. The very act of scientific observation expresses a normative commitment, i.e., the meta-physical belief that the world is basically orderly enough so that observation of the world is possible [17, p. 472].

The limits of our knowledge are often, therefore, more tightly circumscribed than we seem to recognize.

Policymakers, on the other hand, intuitively sense the limits of knowledge. Without the aid of the scientist, though, they are helpless to place them in perspective. It is a situation that would seem to call for a greater element of tolerance: for information users, a tolerance growing out of recognition that absolute certainty does not exist; for those who generate knowledge, a tolerance born of humility in perceiving, as Bronowski has put it, that our "every statement should be taken as a question, not an answer" [3].

MAKING THE SYSTEM WORK. From the standpoint of applying knowledge to the formation of national rural development policy, the past record is not good. Some of the reasons for this have been identified. Now let us turn to the question of what we, as researchers and information specialists, can do to correct some of these short-comings.

It is tempting at this stage to turn to a listing of specific un-answered or unsatisfactorily answered policy questions. However, several of our professional colleagues have written on the topic over the past two or three years and have already identified an abundance of important and researchable issues [1, 2, 6, 7, 20]. The North Central Regional Center on Rural Development has itself sponsored an entire conference on the question of research priorities, including those important to federal policymaking [18]. Though a slightly different list might be developed, it would not add much to the existing literature. Furthermore, one can not really come to grips with the central policy questions when dealing with them in the abstract.

There is no substitute for active involvement in the context of a specific decision or set of decisions to give form and substance to those questions. Our base problems are procedural and organizational. And until we tend to them, all other efforts to identify and undertake relevant policy research will be to little avail.[1] Thus the remainder of this chapter is devoted to outlining two needs that seem to be particularly pressing.

Moving toward a Concept. The importance of a conceptual framework cannot be overstated. From a research point of view, it is fundamental. What do we mean by a "conceptual framework"? Briefly put, it is a simplification of reality around which knowledge can be organized and brought to bear in problem solving. Its development requires the identification of strategic variables and interrelationships among those variables. If well conceived, such a concept eventually leads to the specification of objectives that are politically and socially acceptable, administratively feasible, and economically viable. We must recognize from the outset that the formulation of such a concept might lead us in altogether new directions than those followed to date. (Perhaps we should pray that it does.) We should not initially be constrained by the limits of existing programs and institutions, for to do so implicitly assumes they are satisfying these criteria —a doubtful proposition indeed. Such "realities" can be faced later, after we have the concepts more firmly in mind. Who knows, perhaps the existence of a concept would itself provide the impetus for change in these realities. Neither should we be looking for a single concept around which all can be expected to rally. It is doubtful that it will be that easy. Rather, we should expect a good deal of fumbling, false starts, and blind alleys. We might even have to settle for several alternative concepts. Also, we should not expect too much of a concept.

1. J. Patrick Madden persuasively argues that the limiting factor in rural development research is the present administrative structure. He contends that "even with adequate funding, our efforts will prove to be futile unless we (1) avoid scattering our research resources too thinly, (2) learn to organize ourselves into effective research efforts with a well-developed research paradigm, and (3) remain in rapport with the local community and the rural development practitioner" [14].

It is to serve as an organizing point, a frame of reference. Its utility in solving specific policy questions will be minimal. Clearly, there will be substantial gaps of knowledge (empty boxes) in any concept. And, if the concept is to have any lasting value, it must be as dynamic as the reality it is meant to represent.

A tall order? Yes. Unattainable? No, so long as our expectations are kept within reasonable bounds. Castle, for one, has made a useful beginning [4]. He argues that a successful educational or research program in rural development must satisfy certain conditions: (1) reflect a macroorientation; (2) reflect a local orientation; (3) recognize and address value conflicts affecting the rural community; and (4) be concerned with both market and nonmarket phenomena and their interrelation. Though it is just a start, that exposition at least begins the process of identifying key variables and relationships and placing them in a framework. It provides a foundation upon which to begin construction in earnest.

Information Processing. Information processing is nothing more than a system that gets the right information to the right place at the right time. It is closely related to the conceptual requirement just described. A successful information-processing system will require a conceptual foundation to guide its functioning. Unfortunately, there is a fundamental incongruity between the process within which information is generated and that within which it is applied by the policymaker. "Research is usually conducted utilizing a particular theoretical construct. The knowledge gained is usually partial and fragmented. The policymaker, on the other hand, must integrate and synthesize information" [5]. By their nature, the two processes do not lend themselves to a smooth and continuous transfer of information from producer to user.

To put the issue in economic terms, it is as though we are dealing with two production processes, with the product of one (research) being a factor of production for the other (policymaking). Yet the factor market that joins the two processes has never fully developed. As a result, the production of knowledge has become somewhat self-sustaining, creating its own internal demand, while policymakers have found that decision making can proceed with or without research input. Though an exaggeration, this is closer to fact than not. Unlike markets in the private sector, this market has no automatic feedback mechanism to signal its needs and limitations. An effective substitute is urgently needed. If there is any one failure in the application of knowledge to public policymaking, it is the lack of an institutionalized means for collecting, holding, and synthesizing the informational input.

There are no easy solutions to this problem, as our past inability to come to grips with it would suggest. Perhaps the first step is simply to recognize that it is an important problem and one in which both the scientific and the policymaking communities have an important stake. A unilaterally determined solution will not do. So far, there is little evidence that the problem is widely perceived within either community.

Beyond this is need for institutional adaptation and innovation. What form should this take? Should it conform to a single model? Several prototypes, such as the University of Wisconsin's Poverty Institute, can be considered. The Agricultural Policy Institute at North Carolina State and the Center for Rural Manpower and Public Affairs at Michigan State are also university-based operations. In addition, the National Rural Center is about to get under way, with headquarters in Washington, D.C., and a branch unit at the University of Texas. Other approaches are represented by the National Institutes of Health, the National Institute for Education, the Urban Institute, and the Brookings Institution. Still another institutional possibility is suggested by the North Central Regional Center for Rural Development.

The question now is: What is the comparative effectiveness of these alternative approaches? Where have they succeeded? Where have they failed? What do these lessons suggest for where we go from here?

Another element of the solution centers on the individual and his professional training. When all is said and done, it is the behavior of individual scientists and individual policymakers that will bridge the gap—or fail to do so. Their behavior, in turn, will be largely influenced by their depth of understanding of the two processes and with the field of motivational incentives that are at play. Perhaps this suggests, as Dunn has written, "that we develop a new breed of politically oriented scientists and scientifically oriented politicians" [9]. But failing this, we must at least prepare an increasing number of our young professionals for the role of intermediary.

These needs—the need for a conceptual framework(s) and the need for a system within which to process information—are not the stuff of which conventional research is made. But it is also important to recognize the wisdom in Kenneth Boulding's remark that "the crucial element in social systems is not information but knowledge" [11]. It is time we devoted more professional attention to the conversion of the former into the latter.

REFERENCES

1. Back, W. B. 1974. Balanced population and economic growth: Policy and Research. *Am. J. Agric. Econ.* 56 (5).

2. Barkley, Paul W. 1974. Public goods in rural areas: Problems, policies, and population. *Am. J. Agric. Econ.* 56 (5).
3. Bronowski, Jacob. 1975. The Ascent of Man. PBS–TV series.
4. Castle, Emery N. 1973, A framework for rural development. *J. Northeast. Agric. Econ. Counc.* 2 (2).
5. ———. 1975. The role of the university in rural poverty programs and issues. Presented at Symp. on Poverty Dimension of Rural Underdevelopment in America: New Perspectives, University of Florida, Gainesville.
6. Copp, James H. 1972. Rural sociology and rural development. *Rural Sociol.* 37 (4).
7. Council for Agricultural Science and Technology. 1974. Rural Dev., Rep. 35. (Mimeo.)
8. Downs, Anthony. 1967. *Inside Bureaucracy.* Boston: Little, Brown.
9. Dunn, Edgar S., Jr. 1971. *Economic and Social Development: A Process of Social Learning.* Baltimore: Johns Hopkins Press.
10. Gardner, John W. 1963. *Self-Renewal.* New York: Harper & Row.
11. Glasgow, Robert W. 1973. Aristocrats have always been sons of bitches. *Psychol. Today* (Jan.).
12. Green, Philip. 1971. The obligations of American social scientists. *Annals* 394 (March).
13. Lindblom, Charles E. 1968. *The Policy-Making Process.* Englewood Cliffs, N.J.: Prentice-Hall.
14. Madden, J. Patrick. 1974. Evolution of rural development programs: Toward a paradigm to guide the implementation and evolution of rural development programs. Presented at Workshop on Title V (research sponsored by the Northeast Regional Rural Development Center), Ithaca, N.Y.
15. March, James G., and Herbert A. Simon. 1958. *Organization.* New York: John Wiley & Sons.
16. Miller, Paul A. 1971. Federalism and domestic development. In George M. Beal, Ronald C. Powers, and E. Walter Coward, Jr., eds., *Sociological Perspectives of Domestic Development.* Ames: Iowa State Univ. Press.
17. Mitroff, Ian I., and Louis R. Pondy. 1974. On the organization of inquiry: A comparison of some radically different approaches to policy analysis. *Public Adm. Rev.* 34 (5).
18. North Central Regional Center for Rural Development. 1973. *Rural Development: Research Priorities.* Ames: Iowa State Univ. Press.
19. Schultze, Charles L. 1968. *The Politics and Economics of Public Spending.* Washington, D.C.: Brookings Institution.
20. Tweeten, Luther. 1973. Emerging issues for sparsely populated areas and regions under a national growth policy. *Am. J. Agric. Econ.* 55 (5).

CHAPTER TWO

LOCAL RESEARCH AND INFORMATION NEEDS

JOHN M. HUIE

THREE ISSUES are critical in the development of research and information for local public policymakers: (1) audience, (2) functions of information, and (2) characteristics of information. This chapter concentrates on these issues and draws some implications for research and the organization of research efforts.

AUDIENCE. Starting with the assumption that research and information are designed to influence local decisions, it must therefore be useful to persons who have the greatest influence on these decisions. This does not, however, exclude its usefulness to others.

For any community problem that arises there exist different local audiences with different roles to play and therefore with different information needs. For the information to be most useful, these must be taken into account in the development of that information.

Figure 2.1 provides a simplified version of four major groups in the community and the primary roles they play in the community's decision-making process. Each group plays a key role in this process, but because each role is unique, the type of information and the degree of specificity required are different. For community policymakers[1] to establish overall goals and to set general policy for a community requires analysis at a relatively macro level. For elected officials to develop a program for streets and highways requires a more detailed analysis of alternatives. For program directors to carry out the priorities established by a program requires a different set of information and skills. Likewise, for the public to evaluate the per-

JOHN M. HUIE is Extension Economist and Associate Professor, Department of Agricultural Economics, Purdue University.

1. The term "policymaker" is used here to indicate those individuals sometimes referred to as influentials or, as a group, as the power structure. The term is not meant to imply that all policies are made by this group.

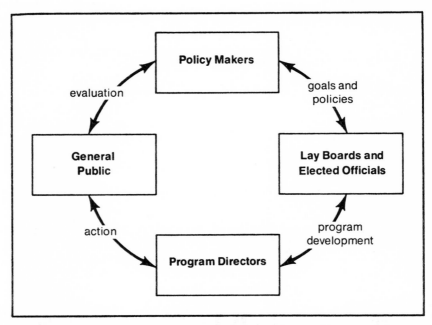

Fig. 2.1.   Simplified community decision-making model.

formance of the service provided requires yet a different type of information. The researcher must know the audience well enough to be able to provide the specific, needed information.

FUNCTIONS OF INFORMATION

Problem Identification and Clarification. One of the important roles that research and information can perform within a community is to help identify or clarify problems earlier than they would otherwise be recognized by local people. Local residents can be so close to their community that they do not recognize problems or opportunities as readily as someone who can look at the community from a more objective viewpoint. Because the researcher is an outsider and is trained to evaluate communities in a more systematic approach, he is in a position to develop information that may uncover problems completely outside the phenomenal field of local residents.

Information can also help clarify the issues or problems being discussed. In working on solid waste issues with communities, a typical opening comment from local citizens might be, "Our problem is that we need a sanitary landfill." That is, of course, a solution—not a problem. By asking a few questions one may discover that the citizens are really concerned about roadside dumping and littering along their streets and highways. Somehow they have become convinced that a sanitary landfill is going to solve their problem. A little discussion soon brings them to realize that providing a sanitary landfill will improve their method of disposal but is not likely to have much impact on roadside dumping or littering. What the community needs is a change in citizen attitude and a more convenient way to dispose of community waste. This suggests an educational program and a better collection system. Information obtained from other communities becomes useful in clarifying the problem and developing some alternatives.

Developing Community Consensus. A second reason for information relates to the process of decision making. All important local public decision making involves the development within the community of a consensus on the direction the community should go in order to solve a particular problem. Although the process of community consensus building is not generally well understood, we all recognize the difficulty of making significant changes when that consensus does not exist. It is not uncommon for local policymakers to spend considerable time discussing a particular issue, come to a decision in their own minds as to what the logical solution to the problem may be, but fail to act. They may think that the public needs to better understand the alternatives and their consequences. Or, they may feel that a significant division of honest opinions due to differences in values still exists. Research to help community leaders understand the process of community decision making and consensus building can undoubtedly contribute significantly to more effective local decisions. One aspect of this is the building of more effective communication linkages among different groups within the community.

As we understand this process better we can provide to local institutions useful alternatives for improving the consensus-building process. In many states the Cooperative Extension Service has taken the lead in organizing community development committees. In some cases these committees have become viable new institutions within the county and have made a significant contribution to the public decision-making process. We need to develop new and innovative institutional arrangements for improving the ability of a community to identify problems, evaluate alternatives, and to reach consensus on issues.

Problem Analysis. This major function of research and information relates directly to the development of major consequences of alternative solutions to specific problems. Information that helps local policymakers decide among types and levels of educational services for their young people, how to provide health services, or how to solve an air pollution problem is critical. Research that helps a community decide what the local policy should be with respect to land use or economic development, or any one of a long list of other specific issues, is in very short supply.

In economics we have devoted most of our research effort to understanding the private sector, with token effort given to state and national policies, and even less effort directed to the local community. Much the same could be said of most other disciplines.

Information is needed that puts what is already known about alternatives and their impacts into a framework that makes decision making easier.

Our experience in working with local decision makers suggests they are most receptive to a framework that does three things:

1. Clarifies the problem. The information should state the problem in a clear and concise statement. For example: How ought Tippecanoe County provide for trash and garbage collection?

2. A list of the major alternatives. Often this involves alternative technical methods, organization or management alternatives, and alternative financial arrangements.

3. Analyzes the major consequences of each. Be careful about pro and con statements. They invariably involve value judgments, which must be provided by local citizens, not the researcher.

Furthermore, research is needed that expands the alternatives available to communities and provides useful information for local policymakers to compare the new alternatives with the old. There is a critical need for innovative solutions to common community problems. Research has done a better job of explaining why certain solutions are not working well than it has in suggesting what changes to make.

To summarize, there are basically three functions of research designed to assist local policymakers: (1) information that helps to identify or clarify problems, (2) information that helps the community improve its process of consensus building, and (3) research on the consequences of alternatives to specific problems or opportunities.

CHARACTERISTICS OF INFORMATION. Given the above functions of research, what can be said about the characteristics of the information needed? With regard to the latter two functions, information is needed that focuses on alternatives. Too often research concentrates on one solution with very few or no comparisons made between that solution and other alternatives. Thus the community development professional and the local policymaker are forced into a situation in which they have much better information concerning one or at best a few of the many alternatives that may be open to the community. When several alternatives are considered, the analysis generally looks at a narrow range of consequences determined primarily by the disciplinary training and interest of the researcher. The economist develops the economic consequences but is seldom concerned with the social, political, or environmental consequences of a particular action. The same can be said about the social scientist, the political scientist, the engineer, or the environmentalist. The community policymaker must consider all aspects in his decision. He must consider the major consequences of each of these alternatives from the social, political, economical, legal, physical, and technical viewpoints.

Questions are going to be raised with regard to who shares in the political, economical, and social costs and benefits. It is indeed rare to find research that has looked at a problem area in this broad perspective. A decision to encourage economic growth in a community will invariably mean that some benefit more than others. It will mean changes in the relative influence of some individuals and groups in the community. Economic development may bring in "outsiders" with somewhat different value systems. Some who do not benefit directly will be asked to help pay for added public services. Research and information that also recognize this breadth will greatly enhance the usefulness of such a decision. And the final decision will reflect local values that may be quite different from the researcher's values.

The responsibility of the individual who must provide the information (in some cases, this is the researcher) is broad. He must know the local situation either from direct contact or indirectly through knowledgeable people. He must understand the local issues that are being asked and be aware of the consequences that are most important in that particular case. The information must be provided in a concise form and it must relate directly to the most critical issues being asked. While several communities may be facing the same general problem, each case is somewhat unique and therefore requires adjustments in the information provided. The critical issue will change from community to community, and the relative importance of various aspects will not be the same in all communities. Let me provide an example.

A couple of years ago I was invited to a community in which the local and area cooperative extension agents had been sufficiently involved in the local solid waste discussions that they were able to convey to me the key issues being discussed. I was able to tailor the information I presented very closely to their needs. At the point I became involved, the county was considering the development of several sanitary landfills in the county, but had not given serious thought to alternatives. They had recognized the importance of having a convenient way of disposing of their waste. Without it, roadside dumping and littering would continue to be a problem. Since I had been working on this problem with a number of other counties, it was relatively easy to compare some of the consequences of three major alternatives: (1) several landfills in the county, (2) one county landfill, with a countywide collection system that would put a storage bin within a mile of each rural resident, or (3) a countywide collection system and a landfill operated jointly with an adjoining county. As a result of that night's discussion, and others that followed, the two counties now have a joint landfill and each has a countywide rural collection system.

An example of the other extreme is provided by a recent trip to a county to discuss solid waste with county and city officials. I had limited prior knowledge of the local details involved. Given my limited understanding of the situation, I put together some information I thought would be useful to a joint session of the county and city council. Several other interested persons including the news media were brought into the session. I presented information with regard to alternative methods of disposing of solid waste and developed some fairly detailed estimates of the cost of operating a sanitary landfill in their county. It became clear in the discussion that followed that the two critical issues in this case were: (1) where the new landfill should be located and (2) how the cost should be divided between city and county. Not having recognized these as the critical issues prior to my presentation, I was not as helpful as I should have been.

An important characteristic of information is timing. Inadequate but useful information at the time the decision is being made is far more valuable than the best research and information a week after the decision is made. Unfortunately, given our present method of generating research, particularly within the university, it is more typical for us to be a year or two late.

IMPLICATION FOR RESEARCH. The above discussion seems to have several implications as it relates to research and information needs. First, we must improve the lines of communication between researchers and the local public policymakers. We need to make it easier for local people to articulate their needs more directly to those involved in developing the research and information. In the university setting, joint research and extension appointments help. As the issues are better communicated, it then becomes possible for the researcher to make his response much more applicable to the questions being asked. Thus it helps him to set his research priorities so that the issues with which he deals are significant from the local decision makers' viewpoint.

The importance of timing suggests that our research procedures and organizational framework within the university must be changed to speed up our ability to respond more rapidly to specific questions. Under the normal operating procedures of most universities, a minimum of a year, and more typically two or three years, is required from the time a staff member decides on a particular research need to the completion of a graduate student dissertation addressing that need.

Community information needs require research that is issue oriented, not discipline oriented. Most community issues have an economic aspect. However, none are restricted to an economist's answer. They invariably include social, political, legal, technical, physical, and psychological aspects as well. Since most university research is a product of graduate training, the output tends to be discipline oriented and restricted to problems that fit "appropriate thesis topics." One extension specialist recently commented after reading a Ph.D. dissertation, "Well, that gives me about enough information for a fifteen-minute extension program." The need is to improve the flow of available information on existing alternatives and develop new alternatives so that the scope of choices considered by the community is broadened and hopefully the choice made is more often the right choice for that community.

If we expect our research to be used in public decision making, we must improve our dissemination techniques. It is currently most rewarding to the researcher if he disseminates research findings to other scholars and researchers. Within the land grant university, it has become the primary responsibility of extension educators to disseminate findings to local decision makers, a probably necessary division of responsibilities, but the lines of communication between the researcher and extension person must be improved. Too often extension persons have had little chance to influence the research output. What would be the impact if we required each researcher to document how his research had been used to solve a community problem? Invariably, a section at the end of most dissertations draws implications for public policy. Too often that is about as far as it ever gets.

IMPLICATIONS FOR RESEARCH ORGANIZATIONS. Good researchers are driven by an unquenchable thirst for answers to questions that intrigue them. Therefore, one of the most effective ways to channel a researcher's effort is to provide a climate that develops interests in local issues. If it is impossible for them to be given direct contact with local decision makers, then the more contact they have with personnel who must work with local policymakers the better. Every researcher who is expected to provide major input into local public policy decisions must be given some responsibility to see that his research is used. This will undoubtedly influence the nature of the research.

Second, an increasing proportion of our research effort must be directed toward the application of existing knowledge from several disciplines to the analysis of current issues being faced by local policymakers. Our inability to foresee new issues far enough in advance will not permit complete reliance on graduate student research for our information. Of course, graduate student research needs to be continued. The training of researchers is important and much of the research output has been extremely useful. Also, research that expands our ability to do a better job of researching current issues is necessary.

One option open to every university is to decide against being involved in the short-run type research necessary in the public policy decision arena—rather, to concentrate on longer-run issues and improvement of theoretical and analytical techniques. But universities cannot divorce themselves from both responsibilities. The question then becomes, what mix?

Third, if we are to provide the necessary climate indicated above and the necessary support and encouragement to provide the type of research suggested, changes must be made in the current reward system. We must increase the relative rewards for research output that communicates directly to the policymaker. Also, we must provide incentives for persons to become involved in joint multidisciplinary research efforts.

Fourth, in any university where a substantial effort is being devoted to teaching, research, and extension, with a major focus on local public issues, some mechanism must be developed for constant interaction among those involved. Three major options are informal or formal faculties or committees, interdepartmental institutes, or a new department. These actually are listed in reverse order of their effectiveness. Many departments within the university are multidisciplinary faculties with a problem focus rather than being single-discipline faculties, but a major commitment must be made to the area before a departmental organization can be justified.

Even when a new department is justified, there is still a place within existing departmental boundaries for discipline-oriented research that can be fed into the knowledge stream of those whose primary focus is community development.

Local policymakers are eager for help in solving local public issues. Although they are not going to accept someone else's solution, they are most appreciative of assistance in thinking through the consequences of alternatives. Colleges and universities, especially land grant institutions that already have a delivery system, have an opportunity to provide research and information that can be extremely helpful to local people in problem identification and clarification, in improving the decision-making process, and in analyzing specific problems faced by local communities. It is time we made the commitment and began to make the internal changes necessary to get the job done.

CHAPTER THREE

FACTS AND VALUES IN RESEARCH: SHOULD WE KEEP THEM APART?

PETER G. BROWN

MANY OF THOSE presently engaged in policy-relevant research are trained in the natural or social sciences. As scientists they pride themselves, quite naturally and justifiably, on upholding the canons of their discipline. Science, for a modern individual, is understood to be concerned with matters of fact and matters of deduction, as in mathematics and logic. Statements about facts are true when there is a correspondence between the statement and the empirical conditions or when attempts to prove that a statement is false continually fail. Statements in deductive systems are true by definition. Science deals with factual and deductive matters.

But moral and ethical statements seem to fit neither of these classes. How do we then justify our moral judgments? One answer proposed during the 1920s seems to have obtained nearly the status of unreflective dogma among professional policy scientists: that moral judgments cannot be justified. On the contrary, the scientist would argue that moral and ethical statements are precisely the kind of statement for which evidence should not be expected. Factual statements and theoretical explanations of certain factual conditions are the kinds of statements that may be meaningfully made, along with statements that are true by definition, for example, "All bachelors are unmarried." When we utter a sentence such as, "Murder is bad," we seem to fall into neither of these two camps. We are left then with the question of how value judgments (or moral judgments) are ever justified. The prevailing answer among social and policy scientists is that they are not justifiable; or, in a weaker and somewhat

PETER G. BROWN is Director of the Center for Philosophy and Public Policy at the University of Maryland.

different version, at least if they are justifiable, it happens in a manner beyond the domain of science. Matters of ethics and values are best left to resolution in the political process.

An interpretation of the stronger version of this view was expressed by A. J. Ayer during the 1930s:

> We shall . . . show that insofar as statements of value are significant, they are ordinary "scientific" statements; and that insofar as they are not scientific, they are not in the literal sense significant, but are simply expressions of *emotion* which can be neither true nor false [1, pp. 102–3].

A few pages later, Ayer writes that when he says " 'stealing money is wrong' I produce a sentence which has no factual meaning—that is, expresses no proposition which can be either true or false" [1, p. 107]. He essentially consigns ethical statements to a realm totally lacking in scientific validity. They are expressions of how we feel about something at the moment, but have no signficance beyond the reporting of that emotion.

Enter the researcher. True to the scientific canons of his training, he wants to concern himself with objective facts, not reports concerning the vagaries of subjective emotions. He will focus on what is subject to experimental verification or falsification. He wishes nothing to do with propositions that can be neither true nor false. Like Jack Webb, he wants the facts and nothing but the facts.

But here is where a dilemma begins to emerge for the researcher. Insofar as he is a *scientist,* he is charged with doing research within the constraints just described. But insofar as he is a *policy* scientist, he is charged with developing findings relevant to a process for accommodating conflicting assessments of what should be done. This process is often obliquely referred to as the political process.[1]

The root question is, How can a person who prides himself on sticking to the rigorous canons of empirical analysis in the domain of science develop tools that will be relevant to a process laden with values and designed to be expressive of them? The canons of science —at least as presently understood—conflict with the needs of policy, not only in causing an imperfect fit between research and the process into which it is supposed to flow, but also because this view of values and the related view of the scientific method make for poorly constructed research. The research will be poorly constructed because, if

1. The term "political process" is not without its dangers. As presently used it frequently covers (over) very different types of institutions, with varying degrees of responsiveness to different clientele. Research designed for regulatory agencies—because of the nature of those agencies—will often be fed into a system removed from normal accountability procedures, unless accountability to the groups allegedly regulated is to matter.

its parts are not justified, the research itself can be dismissed as arbitrarily structured—in a way analogous to being wary of a house built on sand.

Policy-relevant research is necessarily value laden itself. Indeed, to be relevant and nonarbitrary, it must be *value permeated* for two reasons. First, the overall choice of a problem worthy of research invokes, at least implicity, a norm by which certain forms of behavior or a set of conditions are judged as being inadequate or falling short. Second, an appropriately elaborated research effort will necessarily contain a detailed moral structure. Thus the problems of defining and defending a norm occur at two levels: choosing the overall problem and elaborating its structure. Consider these in turn.

When we talk about malnutrition, we have in the back of our minds a healthy human being, fed in such a way that he is able to carry on a normal set of activities. These issues quickly lead into problems of defining health and determining an appropriate level of activity for individuals whose nutrition is in question. It is a short but necessary step from these questions to those about the appropriate objectives of human life (i.e., defining the good life), to consider what sorts of energy level a person *should* be able to expend.

Or, consider land use problems. Land use patterns are thought to be problematical because present allocations fail to fit some norm(s) or standard(s) thought to be preferable. Some think of land as a commodity to be turned to its highest monetary return, some as a scenic resource, others as a link in the chain of life. Assessment of land use practices will necessarily occur against the backdrop of standards such as these.

Second, not only is there some norm that causes us to examine the problem to begin with, but appropriately conducted (i.e., relevant and nonarbitrary) social research will, of necessity, be fine textured in that it will involve a number of subsidiary questions which will themselves be value laden within the overall statement of the problem. When we talk about malnutrition, do we mean protein malnutrition, vitamin malnutrition, bulk malnutrition, maternal malnutrition, child malnutrition, agricultural worker malnutrition, and so forth?

Each of these categories will lead us to consider not only the definition of the needs in question, *but insofar as the aim is policymaking, who is entitled to the satisfaction of their needs, and who ought to provide the resources to meet them? Clearly, these are normative questions central to the resolution of an issue from a policy perspective.*

In the land use area, we are soon pushed to consider who should pay for scenic resources and preserving ecological systems. What

limits can there be on property rights? Who can promulgate and en-
force them? What reasons for limitations can be offered? What constraints on locational decisions are and should be legal?

Each category for data generation and analysis itself implies some
norm by which this data is understood as relevant to the issue. But
under the present model, the scientist does not take it to be part of
his task to analyze these norms, to come up with as accurate and com-
pelling a formulation of them as possible. On the contrary, he regards
it as his task to eschew such interest as belonging to the vagaries of
ethics and not to the domain of the true and false. Resolution of
these matters, he will argue, can be left to the political process.

Under the prevailing model of policy research, the researcher can
regard himself as having completed his task when he has supplied
information that can be inserted in conditional sentences. He is to
supply the policymaker with information about what will, or is likely
to, happen "if" such and such a course of action is pursued. The researcher is to supply the theoretical or factual basis for the necessary
predictions; the policymaker provides the values or goals. In an ideal
world this model might work. But under present conditions it is
misleading for two reasons.

First, because of his understanding of the nature of science, the
researcher will concentrate on development of the factual and theoretical aspects of the issue. This will often lead him to fail to make a
complete fit between the categories of his research and the moral issues actually involved in policy. Trained to work with data, he will
put his energies there. In some areas that have been researched for
a long time, a complex elaboration of the moral categories may have
occurred, though by trial and error. Including ethical reasoning as
part of the research would greatly expedite this process.

Second, this "conditional model" of policy research implicitly
rests on a division of labor between the researcher and the policymaker. The policymaker is to say which option is to be preferred.
But where will the policymaker receive *argument* about what *ought*
to be preferred? One place would obviously be to include such argu-
mentation in the research itself.

Failure to abandon or modify the conditional model can only
contribute to the irrelevancy of research to the political process and
to undermine the internal validity of the research itself. Because so
very many norms can be selected, many with some plausibility, the
research itself is haphazard unless such norms are carefully selected,
formulated, and justified. Cleaving to the factual, at the expense of
the normative, leads to failure to develop appropriate normative/
conceptual frameworks. In areas as diverse as land use, national
urban growth policy, and children's rights, almost no attention is

paid to developing a conceptual framework prior to *or even in conjunction with* the expenditure of vast resources on empirical analysis.

This line of argument may provide at least a partial answer to some of the issues raised by Lynn Daft in Chapter 1, where he states that we frequently shortchange the conceptualization phase of research. Since conceptual analysis in policy research necessarily involves a concern with normative categories, eschewing the normative will often lead to a neglect of the conceptual framework of the policy issue.

MORAL REASONING AND POLICY RESEARCH. In this section some ways moral reasoning can be conducted in the context of policy research are sketched. The question of the ultimate basis of moral judgments—a topic far beyond our present purpose—is not addressed, but some intermediate level methods that can be used are examined.

In policy research, we are almost always confronted with a situation which in one way or another we wish to change. We want to reduce unemployment, curtail inflation, retard rural-urban migration, reduce drug use by teenagers and others, improve nutrition, rationalize land use, and so forth. The research aims at bringing into existence, or at least bringing to the attention of relevant policymakers, the appropriate instruments for restoring conditions to some norm, or at least moving them toward it. The issue here is how we decide what the norms should be and how we decide what means are morally permissable to reach them. We are confronted, in short, with discovering the goal to be achieved and the rightness of the means for approximating it.

Three ways of getting at this kind of question are: (1) appeals to general moral rules, (2) working with examples, and (3) examining the presuppositions of accepted views.

Let us turn to the first. We can identify some widely accepted and defensible moral rule under which this goal or norm falls. Such a norm might be as widely accepted as, "Teenagers should have respect for their parents," or as abstract as, "One individual's freedom should be consistent with a similar freedom for others." The method involved here is the application of an existing moral rule to the problematical situation under discussion. This involves clearly formulating the rule, showing what circumstances in question fall under it, and analyzing the means to the objectives. Analogy serves as an important methodological instrument here. For instance, in the area of juvenile rights, one of the most pressing issues is a clear formulation of what "adult rights" are and then deciding to what extent, if any, children should fall under them. In formulating land use policies, we must come up with a clear idea of what it means to "own something" and then decide to what degree land fits under that definition.

A second manner for formulating the goal and analyzing the appropriateness of the means to it is to work with a series of examples that seem to have the same structure as the goal we are trying to formulate. By this method one begins with an intuitively clear example, that is, a description of a set of circumstances in which the norm one seeks seems self-evident, or nearly so. For instance, one might begin by considering the example of an active child seemingly in possession of all the characteristics of well-being. Then by examining this child, or the characteristics of such a child, at least conceptually, one would begin to formulate an idea of the goal one had in mind and the means for achieving it. If one wanted to decide on the question of fairness of municipal tax burden and benefits from public services, he might begin by examining the federal tax system to the degree it could be taken as fair *prima facie* and then see to what extent the same principles should or should not govern the local situation. Or beginning on a microlevel, one might examine what would appear to be fair in terms of the allocation of burdens and benefits among individuals and then examine whether the same relationships should hold at the community level. The basis of this method is to seek some fixed point in moral judgments and to use this point as a place to stand in assessing what objectives one should be following. As in the first method, analogy plays a key role.

The third method begins with accepting the view of another individual, that is, a citizen, a protagonist in debate, or a person of another school of thought. Here one takes the stated objectives as given and then examines what they must presuppose morally.

For instance, suppose it is argued that the allocation of individuals between rural and urban areas should reflect free market forces, unconstrained by government intervention. Thus one might argue that the depopulation of rural areas was not a problem toward which federal, state, or other public resources should be expended. Rather, on this view, one should let the creation of jobs, location of transportation facilities, and distribution of population across the landscape occur as the interplay of multiple private decisions. This view would be defended by arguing that this will result in the most efficient use of resources. The outcome will reflect individuals expressing their true preferences and trade-offs among various options. Individuals will maximize their welfare, subject to the constraints in which they find themselves. This position appeals to us on the basis of its efficiency as an allocative mechanism and on the grounds that it builds on and maximizes individual freedom of choice without the intervention of inefficient and constraining collective action.

But what does this view presuppose? Does it not presuppose that individuals will have a system of communities among which to exercise choice? It also implies that individuals have the wherewithal, in terms of resources, to make and act on their choices—the health, education, and information to formulate and implement their choices. These questions direct our attention to the human resources which function as the preconditions of choice.

This in turn forces us to consider who should be in position to guarantee these preconditions of choice. Should education, health, and income be the responsibility of families? Where and under what circumstances should the state step in as a grantor of these things?

The purpose of this method is to isolate the moral and other presuppositions involved in a policy and, having isolated them, argue that insofar as the position is justified to begin with, the policy must take its presuppositions into account as well. As the above example illustrates, preserving a free market in location decisions may require certain investments in at least the present generation of rural inhabitants. Hence, examing the presuppositions of a seemingly straightforward set of policies may lead to recommendations that seem contrary to it when it is first examined.

This is the method used by Hobbs in *The Leviathan,* arguing that basic safety must be guaranteed for any life other than one that is nasty, brutish, and short to be possible [3]. Since such a life is thought nearly universally to be unacceptable if alternatives are available, Hobbs urges that the state be invested with coercive powers to insure minimal social stability. Hobbs believes the powerful state is necessary if a life of frequent and unpredictable violence is to be avoided.

AN ALTERNATIVE MODEL? As an alternative to the model normally used for assessing social research, some issues are sketched in evaluating a model which, if it governed the funding, conduct, and use of social science research, might substantially improve the mesh between policy research and the political process in these three areas. A preliminary outline for initial examination and evaluation of this alternative model is proposed. On its face this model seems intriguing and stimulating, though much investigation is needed before recommending its adoption or approximation.

This alternative to the more traditional approaches is referred to as forensic science. As a preliminary definition, a "forensic" model may be construed as a model that incorporates the feature of a rule-governed adversarial relationship between contending viewpoints, a characteristic of the Anglo-American legal system. (It should bring to mind the image of two lawyers: one dedicated to achieving a guilty verdict, the other actively seeking acquittal.) A systematic examination of such an alternative model will serve as an occasion to identify somewhat more closely certain problems inherent in present procedures and institutions; and it may well serve as a framework for generating solutions to these problems.[2] By way of introduction, two such problems are discussed below.

Forensic Science and the Problems of Objectivity. If one is dissatisfied with the attempts to develop objective policy sciences or a science that remains value free for the sorts of reasons discussed above, then the issue can be clarified by systematically focusing on a suggestion made by Rivlin in her review of Christopher Jenck's *Inequality*. Dr. Rivlin suggests that this book is:

> part of what may be emerging as a new tradition of forensic social science in which scholars or teams of scholars take on the task of writing briefs for or against particular policy positions. They state what the position is and bring together all the evidence that supports their side of the argument, leaving to the brief writers of the other side the job of picking apart the case that has been presented and detailing the counter evidence [4].

This suggests that we should think of social science, as it pertains to public policy formulation, as a process that (1) to some extent works in ways analogous to the legal process and (2) perhaps should do so more explicitly. On this view the claim to objectivity would not involve asserting that any given researcher or team had eschewed value judgments. Objectivity would be found when all relevant perspectives had been identified and fully argued, even though value judgments were promulgated on both sides.

Forensic Science and the Problem of Unequal Resources. Frequently, a rather marked inequality exists in terms of financial and informational resources available to individuals and groups on either side of a particular policy issue. The evaluation exercise often is dominated by those with large stakes and *their* criteria for assessing policy options as well.

In the case of technologies or proposed environmental changes that are financed primarily by private monies, there is a market incentive for the individual or corporation in question to be highly organized and to actively promote the cause. Those who may question

2. These issues are discussed in more detail in [2].

the desirability of the technology or environmental change are often relatively unorganized and have significantly fewer financial and informational resources at their disposal.

In the case of technological or environmental change sponsored primarily by the public sector, the imbalance is frequently more acute. New policy alternatives may be resisted by the operating agencies, who wish to justify their own activities by showing how readily they can improve social conditions. Their studies and justifications of these programs may be unconstrained, due to the relatively large resources available to public agencies.

What these points suggest is that in some cases the policy assessment process presently proceeds according to an adversary-advocacy model, but that contending viewpoints are not effectively represented. In terms of the legal analog, this would be similar to a criminal trial in which the defendant was not represented by counsel. The formulation of a forensic model might well serve to suggest appropriate changes in the rules governing funding, conduct, and use of research and appraisal efforts.

Class action suits may be construed as a partial step toward providing a vehicle to deal with the problem of unequal resources. But this means of handling the problem may have passed its zenith already, due to some retrenching on the part of the courts. And, indeed, further extensions of this method may be undesirable because in matters of considerable technical complexity, they draw the courts into areas in which they are ill equipped. One attractive feature of forensic science is that it could retain many of the strengths of the legal system while using them to design a system more suited to the sorts of issues associated with policy formation.

Moreover, a well-articulated forensic model could supply a rigorous and structured way to handle many of the concerns behind the citizen participation movement. This movement has floundered at least in part because there are no rigorous rules governing what sorts of considerations may be introduced and how certain concerns are to be treated, once they have surfaced. Further, the legal notion of a jury of one's peers as a decision-making mechanism might give a more adequate expression to some of the concerns underlying citizen participation than do procedures for public hearings and the like, though, of course, exactly what the analogy with a jury entails would have to be examined and evaluated.

Evaluating Forensic Science. Deciding on the virtues (or lack of them) in a forensic model is a complex task and not to be undertaken lightly. However, it is not necessary to come to a conclusion about the desirability of this model to begin incremental alterations in the "conditional" approach. This can be accomplished by the research community directly facing the issue of which policies are desirable and why.

REFERENCES

1. Ayer, A. J. 1953. *Language, Truth, and Logic.* New York: Dover.
2. Bermant, Gordon, and Peter G. Brown. 1975. *Approaches to Problem-Solving Number Five: Evaluating Forensic Social Sciences.* Columbus, Ohio: Academy for Contemporary Problems.
3. Hobbes, Thomas. 1958. *The Leviathan,* parts 1 and 2. Indianapolis: Bobbs-Merrill.
4. Rivlin, Alice M. 1973. Forensic social science. Perspectives on inequality. *Harvard Educ. Rev.* Repr. Ser. 8, pp. 25–39.

CHAPTER FOUR

PRINCIPLES IN DESIGN AND MANAGEMENT OF POLICY RESEARCH

PAUL R. EBERTS and SERGIO SISMONDO

THE DESIGN and management of policy research requires a clear intellectual posture regarding central issues of definition, classification, methodology, and communications. The first such issue deals with the distinction between various kinds of policy research and their respective roles in the decision-making process. A second distinguishes policy research in the social sciences from other types of social research. A third guides social scientists through the major dimensions and implications of a proposed scheme for policy research. And a fourth spells out the meaning and usefulness of such policy research to the policymakers to whom it is communicated. Covering this quartet of interrelated issues is a decision brought about by the realization that such matters are often not obvious either to researchers or to policymakers—expectedly so, since, as we practice and think about policy research through the years, we find the subject not wanting of complexities. Let us tackle these issues one by one, recognizing that there will be considerable overlap among them and that various aspects of the general problem will not be covered.[1]

CLASSES OF RESEARCH IN POLICY ENVIRONMENTS. Five broad classes of social science research are conducted in association with policymaking institutions. We label these: descriptive research, public opinion research, evaluation research, basic research, and pro-

PAUL R. EBERTS is Associate Professor, Department of Rural Sociology, Cornell University.

SERGIO SISMONDO is Senior Policy Analyst, Policy Research and Long Range Planning, Department of Health and Welfare, Government of Canada, Ottawa.

1. This chapter expresses the professional judgment of the authors. Points of view or opinions do not necessarily represent official policy of the institutions with which they are connected.

active research. Naturally, not all of these are dealt with in the same depth in this chapter.

Descriptive Research. Descriptive research derives largely from the needs of policymakers to quantify situations and problems so that the magnitude of proposed programs and budgets may be estimated. Answers to policy issues are sought largely through surveys, analysis of secondary data, and analysis of administrative data. Its general format is to seek particular answers to questions of the type: How many people live under specific conditions? For instance, How many people are in poverty? How many children do they have? How many are eligible for a program being considered? How many for an alternative program? And what do these figures tell us about the projected cost of the program under consideration?

To document such questions has been the "stock in trade" of social scientists and social science departments since they were founded. The rationale is: "Before anything else is done, we must assure we have the evidence." The unfortunate part of this history is that often surveys have been the only part of the research completed. Moreover, remarkably little information is given in the research literature on what should be done after the surveys are completed.

Up to now, no systematic techniques have been developed for disposition of such research or for its transformation into effective policies, programs, or budgets. Social scientists have had a marginal role in the decision-making process. In turn, the marginality of their role has its roots in the fact that many policymakers have felt that social scientists often abuse budgets and research grants when doing detailed analyses to explicate the obvious. Moreover, policymakers never quite trust the findings, largely because of such problems as the sampling techniques that may be involved. Thus when a survey in a rural New York county showed 34 percent of the people in the sample were below the poverty line by USDA standards, a local legislator immediately commissioned the county planner "to obtain the truth." The county planner reported two weeks later that the U.S. Census showed that 34.7 percent were in poverty according to USDA standards [8]. The fact is that surveys by themselves are incomplete and are sometimes misleading as well as potentially controversial. And because they seldom get to root causes of issues, they often raise as many problems as they solve. In this regard they are often not perceived as cost-effective.

A final criticism of descriptive research is that within bureaucracies the same kind of quantification of problems and problem areas is performed continually. Census and other data banks are manipulated to produce table after table of cross classification of target populations. As censuses and computer technology increase in sophistication, more and more of this work is done "in-house," negating to a large extent the utility of traditional sociological area surveys. The relevance of expensive and time-consuming survey research is severely constrained by such development, not because all the information sought is available elsewhere, but rather because the pace and expectations of bureaucracies make marginally superior information appear less important and less cost-effective than before.

Public Opinion Research. Public opinion research answers variants of the type of question: What do people really want or need? This may be done at various levels of sophistication—everything from a public hearing, reading and analyzing "letters to the editor," and "talking to a lot of people from different walks of life," to systematic surveys and polls. The data may not only seek answers in terms of documenting the key frustrations of people, but also may explore preferences for various alternative means of alleviating these frustrations.

Generally speaking, many procedures utilized in this kind of research may not be properly termed scientific, as is readily admitted by a majority of practitioners, who in the larger part are not social scientists. We note only that much interesting use can be made of these data beyond their collection. Feeding tabulated responses to each household after a survey of community needs, for instance, proves to be an effective way to move community leaders to action corresponding to community priorities—communalities established between households precipitate unified political representation and/or open debate of issues.

In the final analysis, the best pollster is the politician. Surveys on values and preferences of the constituency can aid and guide his task, and the interpretative role of social scientists can be of great value to him. Methodological traps aside, the problems of social scientists interested or involved in public opinion research reduce to the problems of political action. A paradigm of policy in the social system discussed later in this chapter may further clarify this issue.

Evaluative Research. In evaluative research social scientists are cast in the roles of evaluators of programs usually instituted on a pilot basis. An extensive literature has grown in the tradition of evaluation which specifies the necessary steps to be taken in order to assure results will be scientifically reliable [7, 19, 33]. In essence, this literature is concerned with making evaluation research meet the rigorous requirements of any social science research—a before-after experimental design, an adequate sample size to accommodate several simultaneous control groups, reliably and validly tested instruments, elaborate techniques for controlling all other extraneous variables, and so forth.

It should be noted that most often evaluative research is completed after the program evaluated has been terminated. Consequently most research reports based on it are of little use to people who are engaged in the project while the program is still under way. Indeed, often social scientists are brought into the research process only after the program is launched, thus nullifying much of the potential for using important aspects of experimental design in it.

In addition, a common lament among evaluation researchers is that most of their reports are filed away in obscure places, unread by policymakers or by key advisors to future programs. Such a routine truncates both the accumulation of scientific knowledge and the accumulation of policy knowledge, thus breaking away from an important characteristic of science itself. Without a tradition for accumulation, each new program tends to reinvent the proverbial wheel, adding little to effectiveness in policy.

In fairness to policymakers, evaluation reports tend toward the turgid and rarely avoid long excursions into academic issues judged peripheral by the client. A particular drawback to social scientists' reports, in the main, is their preoccupation with objectivity which often prevents making full use of their understanding in the presentation of conclusions and recommendations.

In the final analysis, the fundamental problem of evaluation is that it deals with the past and is constrained by the requirement to focus on that past. This is a true impasse for social scientists. If they concentrate uniquely on the programs being evaluated, they will be accused of blindness and lack of imagination; but if they examine true alternatives, they will be accused of not abiding by their terms of reference. The real world, on the other hand, changes sufficiently rapidly to render particular findings of the past insufficient; social, fiscal, institutional parameters change, and so do attitudes, expectations, and behaviors of people, giving no assurance that dissections of historical events are particularly valuable to designs for the future. The social system is simply not recursive; it is iterative, but in a most complex manner. It is for all these reasons that evaluative research has come to be known as reactive research; it deals with whether we should have "more or less of the same," as opposed to what we should have to modify or replace in "the same old things" under new and changing circumstances.

Basic Research. A fourth category of research conducted within policymaking environments is basic research. It is in essence no different

from basic research conducted in academic environments. Traditionally it has focused on methodological questions uniquely important
to large-scale government, such as the methodology of the census, the
collection of economic data within minimal time lags, the estimation
of errors and biases in such data, or the software required for its appropriate storage and retrieval. In recent years, however, governments have increased their interest and capability in traditionally
academic concerns, particularly in theory development. This trend
is of such significance as to merit underscoring. Social Indicators and
Technology Assessment are two recently developed fields within
which government researchers have had opportunities to make substantial theoretical contributions.

A likely continuation of such a trend would relegate further to
the periphery of policy concerns the efforts of those social scientists
and research institutions which for one reason or another are undis-
posed to enter the public research arena.

Proactive Research. The fifth category of policy research attempts to
correct some of the weaknesses of descriptive and reactive research. It
is based on the concept of simulation—we call it proactive. It attempts to foresee problems policymakers will face and forewarn them.
It is an emerging form generalized largely from the work of economists and systems theorists, especially Tinbergen [14, 20, 28, 30]. In
proactive policy research, social scientists assist in the design of proposed programs and policy strategies for dealing with actual or potential social issues needing resolution. The most widely known
model for proactive policy research is implicit in the activities of the
Council of Economic Advisors. These social scientists monitor the
economy on key dimensions (or variables) of economic life, compare
them to the abstract theories and models of their intellectual disciplines, project or simulate the future progress of the economy under
varying conditions, and, on the basis of observations linked to their
theories, make recommendations to policymakers on what adjustments in policies might be made to better achieve the goals established in the policy. Essentially, then, on the basis of both their theories and closely monitored data, they suggest more effective means
by which policy objectives can be attained.[2] We believe other social

2. Apparently, part of the present problems of the Council of Economic Advisors is arising because the models and theories it is using are not sufficiently
sophisticated to deal with some emerging issues in our society, such as oligopolies
and monopolies of both supply and demand factors in certain key industries, and
effects of a more thorough merging of the U.S. political economy into the world
political economy where money shifts rapidly across national borders and across
industrial sectors. In other words, some of the problems faced by the council are
those for which social scientists other than economists have a great deal of sup-
plementary expertise.

scientists can and do have similarly useful theories and models with which to understand the same and other issues and they can provide comparable assistance to policymakers in various jurisdictional areas (e.g., federal, state, local). An examination of such a general model is discussed in the remainder of this chapter.

We will explicate, elaborate, and extend the type of model of which the Council of Economic Advisors is but one example. On the basis of our collected experiences, we have found the proposed model to be viable, to correct the most glaring weaknesses of the reactive model, and to be beneficial both to social scientists and policymakers. Indeed, our concerns are primarily to deconcentrate development and take it where the human needs are greatest and where the available expertise to produce required resources is least [13, 16]. A broader conception of method and organization, viable at levels of analysis more disaggregated than the nation, is necessary to focus both research and policy issues.

As such, we feel that basically enough has been said about descriptive and evaluative forms of policy research and that the proactive form incorporates the other two and yet opens new horizons, both for the multiple roles of social scientists and for a democratic society to respond to its emerging problems with more efficacy and viability for its people.

Our final word on this general introduction to conceptualizing proactive policy research regards a major strength in such a proposed method, for it focuses on symptoms and causes of people's needs as well as on the needs themselves. It seeks to uncover the multiple and circular causation patterns of such needs, enabling policymakers to better understand them and to adjust their policies in such ways as to counteract root causes and deficiencies most effectively. Descriptive research makes no pretense of such understanding, and evaluative research is mostly focused on a single issue—whether a given program is effective—rather than on the multiple causes of conditions in the real world. Proactive policy research focuses on broader and contrasting perspectives, because only as causes are identified and become well known can policies and programs be expected to be effective in ameliorating conditions and resolving the needs of citizens.

What we are proposing is not esoteric. It is an extension of what many groups concerned with social issues in their localities do all the time, albeit less systematically and self-consciously. But what we are endeavoring to do here is to make this set of research procedures self-conscious so that future mistakes can be avoided where possible and so that information, if not wisdom, can be accumulated in the various problem areas. In this regard, the proactive policy research paradigm presented below will be quite informative, not only to social scientists and policymakers in various levels of government, but also to concerned citizens involved in specific issues in their home localities.

RELATIONSHIPS OF SOCIAL RESEARCH TO POLICY RESEARCH. Policy research should stand in the tradition of the best social research. It uses the same methodologies, both theoretical and empirical, the same types of instruments, and works to the same end— a more complete, systematic, and empirically documented understanding (theory) of the relationships between events taking place in the social world.

The major difference between policy research and other social research is in the delimitations of its boundaries. Policy research delimits itself according to the goals and means specified by the policymakers for whom the research is being executed, whereas general social researchers feel no such constraints. Since most policymakers have multiple goals, and since they permit a variety of means through which to achieve those goals, social scientists in policy research roles should not necessarily feel great constraints. Furthermore, whatever limitations are imposed on the research by the reality and immediacy of the problem being studied are more than compensated for by the awareness of the work's potential social significance.

Some social scientists are cynical about their usefulness to decision making and about the sincerity of policymakers themselves in terms of their commitment to resolving the most pressing needs of their constituencies. In part, at least, such cynicism is justified. But insofar as cynicism interferes with commitments to the quality and quantity of badly needed policy research, then it is only the society that will suffer.

In general terms, then, policy research is related to social research in that it uses the same (best) methods. The major difference is in the choice of variables for theories and models, with most variables being chosen in policy research endeavors on the basis of their direct or indirect causal relatedness to people's needs and to policy instruments. The goal is the attainment of empirically well-documented sets of interrelated theoretical propositions, which is what is meant by theory. As is asserted in an adaptation of an old adage, "There is nothing so practical for a policymaker as a good theory about how things work." Once he understands the theory, the probability of his finding a viable resolution to a problem is considerably enhanced.

Sometimes policy research is more demanding than its counterpart in academia. Concrete circumstances impose upon a researcher both the location and population to be studied and a set of parameters with which to contend. Such conditions often mean researchers must use devices for controlling extraneous variables that are not standard and likely not optimum. Policy research may actually require more rigor than general social research. Its process is not restricted to the examination of relations between two variables; it is rather the prediction of sets of outcomes from manipulations of sets of policy variables. When executed seriously its conclusions and recommendations may also be used seriously. Mistakes at this level can be costly, both in terms of money and in terms of the damage that may be wreaked on a social system by misguided choices.

Some of our colleagues are actually quite reluctant to engage in the policy research process on the basis that "We do not yet know enough to do an adequate job of it." We concur that we do not know enough. But, our position is that by becoming involved we will learn more and faster than in any other way. If we continue to do research separately from policy problems, where the stakes are not high and where results are not subjected to the dynamic test of implementation, then it is unlikely that we, as a collectivity, will ever "know enough" to engage effectively in policy problems.

An example of policy research either not done or not well done is revealed in Hansen's chapter in *Rural Industrialization: Problems and Potentials* [18]. Fourteen thousand industrial development organizations have been produced in the United States to compete for 500 to 750 new plant locations per year. Actually, then, over a twenty-five-year period the probability of obtaining a new plant is not insignificant. But the cost of maintaining such organizations for twenty-five years may be astronomical. The policy research questions to be asked before such national ventures are implemented are of the type: How might the same public funds be spent more effectively for a similarly protracted rural development scheme? Would, in the long run, industry behave similarly without the program? And so forth.

Missed opportunities for pursuing other types of activities can also be costly both in the short run and in the long run. Jobs are more scarce and income less than it might have been had other public investment policies been followed. People may have migrated from their communities who might not otherwise have had to. General morale, therefore, might now be lower than it might otherwise have been. Strategically, changes now must face the failure of previous plans and policies. And, if we are correct regarding the deterimental effects on the most rural areas of economic and political concentration trends, then failure to address these issues in policymaking and policy research can be detrimental to rural development.

In any case, stock answers by social scientists or their consultant equivalents to the effect that rural development happens through industrial development organizations, or that the job of industrial development organizations is to attract new plants must be carefully examined by policy researchers. Good policy researchers must foresee the shortsightedness of such arguments and do so not simply in terms of folklore (which requires a large number of cases before it is established) but in terms of their analytic tools (particularly through their theories and empirical evidence). It is to add to those tools, in order to avoid costly mistakes, that becomes the goal of knowledge accumulation in policy research.

To reiterate, policy research, when correctly executed, is at least as rigorous and often more rigorous than other social science research because of the seriousness of its consequences. It is unfortunate that most university social scientists have not engaged in policy research. The major outcomes of such attitudes have been that many communities have wasted resources obtaining "stock" answers from "consulting firms," while social science disciplines have missed many excellent opportunities for cumulative research. Part of the reason many social scientists have not engaged in policy research is that they have not had the opportunity to understand it more fully. It is to this fuller understanding that we now turn our primary attention.

PARADIGMS FOR PROACTIVE POLICY RESEARCH. Because policy research builds upon techniques and findings of general social research, before examining the paradigm appropriate for proactive policy research, some attention must be given to processes in general social research.

Paradigms of General Social Research. A basic premise in all social research is that its most important part is the research design itself. If the design is good, the research will be easier to implement, more conclusive, and easier to manage. If the design is poor, much time will be lost in wasted motion and even its best managers will be courting disaster. Furthermore, if the design is clear, specific techniques can be very useful. If it is not clear, then the most sophisticated techniques will be wasted. Primary efforts in poorly designed research are usually toward "salvage operations," often taking the form of testing a new technique rather than testing a theory or producing alternatives for policymakers.

The key to good general social research design is clarity in the theory underlying it. Despite the fact that much social research appears to be in terms of data collection and analysis techniques, the process centers around theory. As we have noted above, the very purpose of social research is to test and otherwise develop theory.

Theory reduces the virtually infinite set of interrelations between concepts and variables to a parsimonious set which is causally interrelated [4]. We need theory, as we begin by theory, because theory is not an a posteriori ordering of data; it is a producer of hypotheses and a guide to data collection. Theories are invented, not inferred from data [21].

AN ELEMENTARY PARADIGM OF SCIENTIFIC PROCESSES. The various aspects of social research are put in perspective in a diagrammatic way in the work of Wallace [32]. Figure 4.1 presents a modified version of his basic scheme [32, p. 18]. The diagram reminds us that there are four basic steps in social research and a series of subprocesses in each step.

1. Theories are formed.
2. From them, hypotheses for testing are derived.
3. From the tests, empirical generalizations or significant findings are induced.
4. These findings are incorporated to modify existing theories, or at least certain propositions in them.

For policy research, the first step is creating a plausible theory

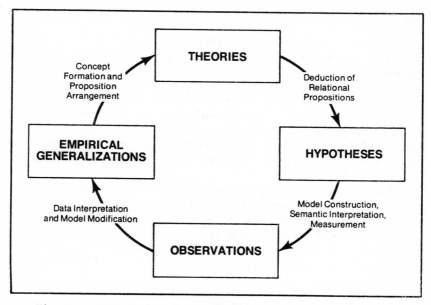

Fig. 4.1. Principal informational components, methodological controls, and information transformations of the scientific process. (Source: Adapted from Wallace [32])

to be tested. Hence the process begins with a review of research literature on issues related to those set by the policymakers (or by their chief assistants). Although most people engaged in policy research do not believe they are testing theories as they accumulate their evidence, we contend that they would produce better research, theory, and policy if they would begin to perceive themselves in a theory-testing perspective. It is probable that often theories being tested are less abstract and less general than those of "basic" social theorists, but that they are theories cannot be disputed. The goal of policy research is to discover what course of action should be implemented to alleviate certain given conditions and/or to facilitate the production of other conditions.

Policy research, like general social research, must deal with concepts and attempt to discover whether a change in the level of one conceptual variable will change the level of another conceptual variable (written abstractly as: $\Delta X_1 \rightarrow \Delta X_2$). Such relationships, technically called propositions or hypotheses, are the basic material derived from theory and upon which more comprehensive theory is produced. A theory, then, is the elaboration of a set of interrelated propositions in verbal or mathematical form [4, 6]. It does not need to be general, although a theory that is more abstract and general (if empirically supported) is more useful for explaining a greater range of observations.

Rigorous thinking requires that diagrammatic schemes be produced to incorporate all of the most important variables and their hypothesized causal effects on each other [4]. This scheme is like the flow chart, familiar to people who work with computer programs and evaluation systems. But key elements in the flow chart are not seen as simply real phenomena but potentially as *variables,* whose value attained can be influenced by policies. Thus a flow chart (or, as it is often called, a path diagram) schematically presents the probability of changes of one variable occurring as a result of changes in a previous variable.

For instance, in our previous example of the relation of industrial development organizations to rural development, it is probable that most policymakers approving of the industrial development organizations did not view them as variables in a theory. They probably could not distinguish forms of such organizations, nor could they legislate particular forms that are more successful in their operations than others.

Social science variables, and especially their abstract causal interrelations, are the most difficult set of ideas to communicate to nonsocial scientists. Most people find it difficult to conceptualize alternative intervention strategies in terms of the structures they bring about and the alternative outcomes or effects due to those structures. Indeed, the concept of time-lagged relations between abstract variables in the social realm is beyond common understanding, highly problematic within the political framework as we know it, and subject to much skepticism by nonsocial scientists. Insofar as most policymakers are not trained in such matters, they are not only skeptical of social theories but label them jargon and harbor a predisposition to dismiss them out of hand. Thus they often will receive communications only through many oversimplifying concrete examples. But until they understand the nature of variables and of their interrelations, examples will be misleading to some degree.

A major dilemma (whether to abstract or not) and a problem of education (along with its attendant frustrations) confront social scientific policy researchers, therefore, from the start. Both researchers and policymakers must realize that due to their positions they are mutually dependent and must remain so for a considerable period of time if their mutuality will be of benefit to the people they serve.[3]

Since the concept of variables is essential to the formulation of theory, let us consider two additional aspects of the nature of variables. The first specifies some formal characteristics of variables and theory to meet the requirements of general social theory and research; the second provides some distinctions between different theoretical forms.

Social theory requires that its variables meet four basic criteria, and the requirements of policy-oriented theory add a fifth criterion [14]. They are:

1. Conceptual variables used in a theory will be handily operational. Indicators for the conceptual variables will be readily apparent and experientially meaningful to those associated with the development exercise.

2. The theory will be dynamic. It will express relations between variables in sequential chains as opposed to static relations in order to establish the time-lagged consequences of policies on other variables.

3. The theory will be deterministic. It will demonstrate that time-lagged relations between changing variables hold, even when controlling for other relevant variables.

3. Let us not underestimate the personal problems faced by scientists willing to pursue this line of work: doors are not always open, time to discuss freely is seldom available, and rewards are scarce and far between. A fundamental problem of decision-making environments is their profound dedication to dogma for purposes of justification. Threatening statements (and particularly threatening theories) are not well received and less well entertained. This, among others, is a cause of major frustrations in the academic-political marriage being discussed here.

4. The theory will satisfy a condition of relative closure. All principal variables in the social unit under analysis will be included in the theory and will be shown to be interdependent with other variables, at least in the long run.

5. The theory will include some variables that are manipulable by public policies. Variables initially viewed as exogenous may be such that public decisions can directly and predictably affect their value, reading, standing, or range.

The five criteria themselves are not unusual. They are desirable for both general and policy social science research. In essence, these criteria require that our variables are clear, that their effects are efficacious in time-based analyses, that the variables explain a large amount of variance found in each other, and that they be controllable at least to some degree through public policies. These are obviously ideal conditions for policy research. Most such research will not meet all these conditions. If the fifth is not met, however, it is not policy research. Following the outlines of the paradigms below should aid researchers to meet the desired five criteria.

INTERFACE OF SCIENCE AND REALITY. Figure 4.2 presents the basic distinctions, and yet interrelatedness, between concepts, variables, propositions, paradigms, models, indicators, and the empirical reality of events, objects, and attributes. Paradigms specify the major concepts with which theory must deal but do so in a definitional and intuitive manner. The major types of relationships at the paradigmatic level are those caught in Venn diagrams, that is, in an effort to include or exclude or otherwise distinguish one concept or idea from another. Theory states causal relationships of concepts (under the five formal conditions for variables stated above) and other formal desiderata too technical to be of significance here. The model level specifies the nature of acceptable and valid indicators of the variables under the conditions set forth in the theory. Finally, "reality" tests the accuracy of the model as specified through systematically collected observations or data.

From the theory, certain hypotheses are chosen for testing through the systematic observation of events, objects, and attributes of reality. These observations become the data (subject to mathematical and statistical manipulations) utilized to discover to what extent the model (and therefore presumably also the theory and paradigm) conforms to the real world. The results of these tests (the empirical generalizations) are then examined for their implications for the model as stated, and hence for the theory. But when these points are reached, then the policy researcher is, in effect, reviewing knowledge, which is where we began this excursus into general sci-

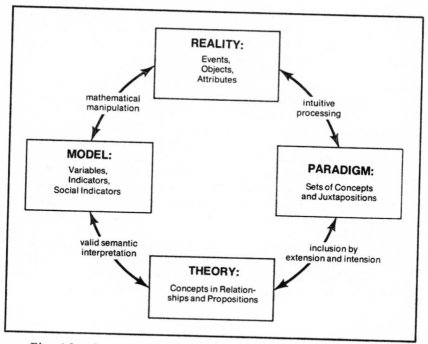

Fig. 4.2. Systematic relationship of paradigm, theory, model, and reality. (Source: Adapted from Sismondo [28])

ence. The process of general science, then, iterates through these procedures indefinitely in an accumulating effort to make its theories match the real world with refined detail.

These first two paradigms offer the foundations of proactive policy research. On the basis of intellectual constructs, social scientists take initiatives in designing proposed programs and policy strategies for dealing with actual or potential social issues needing resolution. These conditions are not an invitation to irresponsible pronouncements on behalf of untested theories and unproven hypotheses. They stand in the best scientific tradition of developing as complete a theory for implementation as possible, based on the most valid and reliable findings known; of collecting (or monitoring) data on the theory at every point of its implementation, suggesting adjustments in the implementation where necessary, feeding this information to policymakers where appropriate; and of adjusting the theory on the basis of the rigorous analysis of the data and models, again feeding this information back to policymakers.

Paradigms of Policy Research. One of the more convenient techniques for focusing reasoning in proactive theories is the basic feedback scheme adapted from the General Systems Theory, with additional details presented in Figure 4.3 [also 5, 9, 10, 12, 17, 30].

GENERAL SYSTEM PARADIGM. The paradigm in Figure 4.3 indicates that policy changes (as inputs) are possible in any given system and that they can be formulated in such a way as to bring about change of structures (as throughputs), determining in turn specific outputs. Structures and outputs are themselves interrelated by deterministic or causal chains. On the basis of new circumstances produced by such outputs, policy options can again be assessed, negotiated, and modified (after considerable refocusing of issues among population segments) in order to keep the system capable of sustaining a high quality of life for its members. The nature of feedback is in the political process implied by such reassessment.

The major advantages of a general paradigm as in Figure 4.3 are that it reminds us of the categories of variables and relationships which must later be substantively specified for particular analyses, and it shows that these variables are directly or indirectly related in

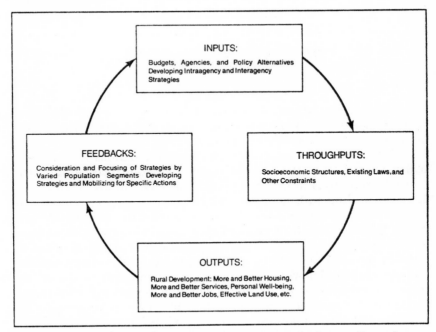

Fig. 4.3. Policy-oriented paradigm for relating policy alternatives to rural development. (Source: Adapted from Eberts [15])

a circular feedback system. It does not provide the specific nature of the substantive variables nor the closeness of their causal links. But it does give us their taxonomy and a mental set for their general characteristics. The nature of the theory and model to be derived from such a paradigm will depend on the nature of the output parameters emphasized by the policymakers to whom the research is addressed.

Thus for General Systems Policy Analysis it is important to be able to translate the concepts of Figure 4.3 into more concrete terms. The next paradigm is an intermediate step between the general concepts and more specific theories.

GENERAL PARADIGM OF POLICY IN THE SOCIAL SYSTEM. Figure 4.4 incorporates several features not seen in Figure 4.3. First, it divides inputs into its two primary components: policies and agencies (with their programs and budgets). Second, the throughputs are specified as the sets of public and private institutionalized socioeconomic structures. The sets of throughput variables implied in this sector are the structures connected to various institutions found in every macrounit, be it society, state, region, or locality. Naturally, they include the economic institutions (with their multiple industries), the political (parties and government), the educational, the legal, the media, the protective, the religious, and so forth. These institutional structures are normally considered the major causal variables that produce the many different types of material and nonmaterial resources available in our society, such as income, education, and so forth. Obviously, the bland label of socioeconomic structures in the box of the figure masks the complexities of the variables and their interrelations. Throughput variables are conceived of as structural— that is, the patterns of relations between organizations included within the system under consideration.

Output variables are aggregate variables, or the aggregated resources available from and/or to each individual in the system. The distribution of these resources to individuals, in turn, affects their well-being and subjective values. These values are equivalent to what economists call utilities and are translated into political processes by lobby, pressure, interest groups, and political parties. The political process itself is identified as the feedback part of the system.

In fact, the figure is divided into two overlapping sections [28]: the Domain of Democratic Action and the Domain of Policy Research. They overlap because people and their values, as well as political policies and agencies, are and should be directly part of the political process; they are also subjects policy researchers must monitor, to discover whether policies are having their intended and hypothesized effects and which policies could be more effective. In the

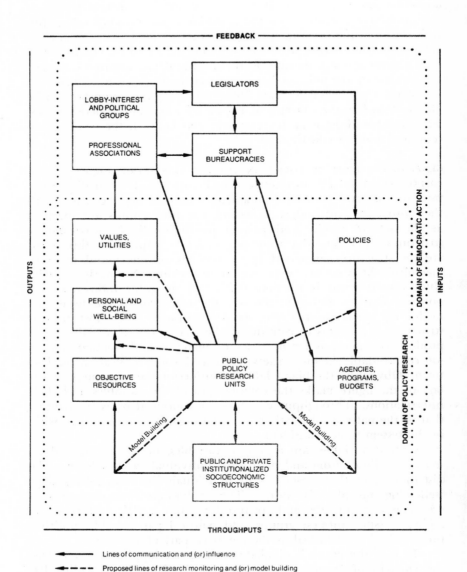

Fig. 4.4. *General flows of major influence and information in development processes: The general paradigm of policy in the social system.*

view presented in Figure 4.4, policy researchers do not otherwise interfere in the political process. Their function is to transmit to policymakers information accumulated on the basis of data monitoring and model building. Our conception of policy research includes the concept of multiple accountability, involving accountability to the democratic process that creates and supports institutions within which policy research can be conducted. The replacement of this process by a technocratic vision, short-circuiting election-appointment-decision-election routines, is inimical to our vision of viable open, competitive, and participatory government and an institution of policy research compatible with it.

The most distinctive feature of Figure 4.4 is the inclusion of the policy research unit. Its presence or absence, as well as the types of activities in which it engages, must also be considered a variable in the analysis of policies. Most of these research units are in some way connected to support bureaucracies. Virtually every federal department has some type of research unit, as do many state level departments. If these units exist at all at the local level, they are most often found in local planning offices. Naturally, as we noted earlier, at least some research at each level of jurisdiction is performed by consulting firms. Land grant universities also perform research functions for policy purposes. In addition, functions served by these research units are often performed on an informal basis by interest groups. Figure 4.4 renders explicit their scientific and informational roles.

Such roles include monitoring key agencies, structures, resources, and values in any potential issue area, as well as building statistical models of the relations between the variables represented by various elements in the system. From the diagram it is easy to see that proposed new policies for ameliorating a given condition in any issue area can affect a great many different variables and propositions about which it may be necessary to obtain additional information through various research techniques. It is important that policy analysts not only interact with existing institutions and publics in the conduct of their research, but also think of them in terms of variables describing their existence and characteristics. Major research tasks are to investigate the causes and effects of changes of levels attained along the ranges possible in such variables. To produce analyses of such variables and their causal interconnectedness is the subject of theoretical research. Effective policies will be produced when causal networks are rendered explicit and are empirically well documented.

Three steps, therefore, are to be undertaken by a proactive policy research unit. First, it must make the variables explicit. Second, on the basis of previous information, it must produce a theory of how these variables might hypothetically interrelate to each other and to proposed policy alternatives. And, third, it must collect data on its own system at least (and perhaps on other systems which are comparable to its own) in order to discover whether the sets of variables are interrelating in the hypothesized directions.

It may be sensible to begin policy analysis by defining desired outcomes. The next step is to consider the various types of activities by which variables either at the resource or structure levels could change in order to achieve the established target goals. Likewise, efforts should be made to discover the determining relations between these variables, and so forth, until the policy research unit can work back to a set of statements such as: "If policy P would be changed, then agency A would have more capability to perform a certain role, so that institutional structure S would be more likely to produce resource output R, which will in turn permit population segment L to have more access to the resource output and thus have a higher reading on value V. Hopefully, there will be several alternative policies (P_1, P_2, etc.), which will affect several agencies (A_1, A_2, etc.), and so forth through a deterministic and precise model. The systems analysis approach is compatible with path analysis, where both direct and indirect effects of variables on each other can be assessed (although systems analysis is not uniquely wedded to such a form of statistical manipulation). Thus these relations are capable of being translated into at least one set of regression equations [4]:

$$\Delta V_2 = \alpha + \beta_1 \, \Delta V_1{}^c + e_1 \tag{1}$$
$$\Delta V_1 = \alpha + \beta_1 \, \Delta R_1{}^c + \beta_2 \, \Delta R_2{}^c + e_2 \tag{2}$$

Such a model indicates how the causal variables influence the effect variable in terms of direction and size of impact [31]. Furthermore, such a statistical system underlies the methodology of most input-output and simulation systems, rendering them compatible and complementary to what is presented here.

Policy analysts commonly produce facsimiles of path analyses, especially at the federal level, although less well at local levels.[4] Such analyses most often are informal and verbal rather than formal and mathematical. In fact, although many such analyses are far more

4. In decision theory the cost of obtaining information is taken into account. Decisions involving lesser amounts of funds may often require a lesser degree of sophistication in the analytical preparation. At the federal level virtually all service budgets are very large. Intuitively we can argue that complete analysis to the limits of our technical abilities is justified. At the local level the cost of equivalent research may be too high to be warranted. On the other hand, we are arguing here that with accumulated expertise and local data banks, the cost of research is reduced over time. The payoffs of initial research investments, in other words, may be spread into the future.

complex than the example constructed here, they are only partially elaborated in terms of their implications and poorly documented empirically for their ability to predict outcomes, because the formal and mathematical conditions are not met. In contrast, formal and complete analyses such as suggested by path diagrams can assist considerably in clarifying alternate plans of action.

Multivariate models permit the presentation of alternatives and their consequences in terms of comparable estimations. Policymaking involves the selection of choices, and the more unified the presentation of each choice's consequences, the more likely choices will be made on solid grounds. Researchers must avoid presenting the outcomes of two competing alternatives in terms different from each other. Comprehensive models avoid this pitfall—one more reason for following the methodology suggested here. At the federal level, such policy alternatives can be simulated and projected on the basis of giant data banks comprising the universe of communities, households, or individuals in the nation. At the local level, research of this quality requires data access not commonly available. For instance, issues relating to pollution control, its costs and consequences, require the study of communities with comparable experiences. Because such data are uncommon, yet increasingly sought, it is necessary that land grant universities, among other institutions, establish general policy research units utilizing localities as their units of analysis in order to perform routinely such studies of action alternatives for neighboring communities (see footnote 4).

As more experience is developed in proactive policy research, it would be expected that information and wisdom would accumulate. Key variables and their interrelationships would be specified, so that units in one location could share with those in other locations. Indeed, it would seem necessary at least for some research institutions to develop extensive monitoring and model-building systems, as suggested in Figure 4.4, to serve as repositories. Since short-run analyses are often shown to be inadequate in the long run, considerable in-depth science may be necessary to sort and update the relevant variables and relationships in any given sector. New laws are constantly being passed that fundamentally alter relationships, new technologies discovered that have equivalent effects, and new structures developed to meet certain kinds of needs and also to affect distributions of resources. The policy research task, then, appears to be never ending; it is symbiotic—and perhaps a survival issue. More and better professionals will be needed to work on such problems.

LEVELS OF JURISDICTION WITHIN THE POLICY PARADIGM. Figure 4.5 presents additional complexities of the model. It shows that the para-

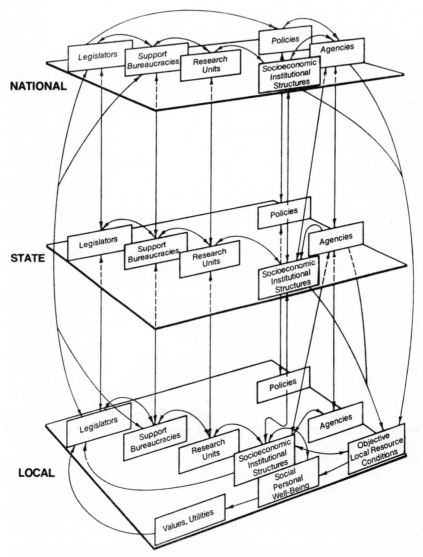

Fig. 4.5. Levels of jurisdiction within the policy paradigm: General flows of influence and information in development processes interrelating federal, state, and local levels.

digm of policy is applicable not simply to one level of public jurisdiction, but to each level—federal, state, and local (and perhaps several more—regional, county, metropolitan).

As any particular issue area is faced, it is important to understand the laws and rules in the various jurisdictions that affect the
issue. Thus in most states land use zoning laws are left to local jurisdiction, while social service laws are made at the state level. Policies made at the federal level affect state policies, which in turn affect
local policies. Likewise, institutional structures, both public and
private (e.g., government agencies or giant corporations), affect conditions at the national level through their influence on agencies, legislators, and policies; at the state level through their influence on
state agencies, legislators, policies, and other corporations; and at
the local level by their establishment in communities, their participation in community affairs, and their influence on other local agencies, structures, resources, personal and social well-being, legislators,
and policies.

As mentioned above, major problem areas in rural development
originate from nonlocal units of government. Data and information
needed to document cases for policy changes may be quite extensive.
For instance, in New York State the case for implementing agricultural districts in counties was made to the state legislature because
it had to delegate jurisdiction to counties so they could establish the
districts. Until this state law was passed, no county could pass its
own laws to establish special zones for agricultural districts.

Once the state level agricultural district law was passed and
signed by the governor, then the issue turned to local implementation.
This in itself often creates problems. Agricultural districts by and
large favor farmers, but certainly not all farmers. Moreover, agricultural districts, with their special taxation and zoning restrictions, are
most often opposed by local realtors and developers. Thus political
issues in land use for any given locality may be considerably more
complex than might at first be recognized.

PARADIGM FOR POLICY IMPACT ANALYSIS. Further suggestions are possible for professionals engaged in research using this policy paradigm.
In keeping with a system's perspective, because of the complexity of
all possible interrelationships between variables and so that they
might be understood in a more orderly fashion, a logical extension
of the paradigm would be to conceive of the variables' interrelationships in terms of a matrix. A suggested matrix is presented in Figure
4.6. Because it is designed to analyze the impacts of various policies,
it is called a policy impact matrix. The variables on the horizontal
(causal) axis have indicators both for "point" (in time) and "change"

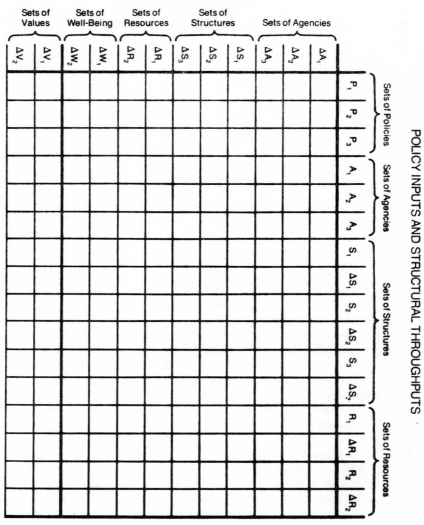

Fig. 4.6.   Matrix of variable relations for policy impact analysis.

(over time), because both the level of a variable and its changes have been found in various studies to be significant in causal analysis. Since the primary interest of decision makers is to change things for the better, variables on the vertical (effect) axis are in terms of change indicators.

The body of the matrix could contain at least five different statistical symbols: the sign of the relation between the variables; the size of the b (or slope) (i.e. the relation of a unit change in one variable as affecting the unit change in the other variable); the standardized beta; a statistical significance test such as the F ratio; and the contribution to R square (the amount of variance in the effect variable explained by the causal variable).

It is possible that each variable in the figure can be interpreted as both a determinant from the horizontal axis and an effect on the vertical axis—each can be considered as an output and as having an impact. Thus although certain of the cells will be filled with zeroes (so that certain relations show no influences from certain variables), both direct and indirect effects of policies, agencies, and structures can be calculated from such a matrix following the rules of path analysis [3].

Several additional things must be noted about the matrix. First, a different matrix must be built for different jurisdictions (i.e., different units of analysis). Although we expect the signs in each cell would be similar from one unit of analysis to another, we also expect that the magnitude of relations is likely to be quite different, due to "aggregation effects" [2, 11]. In this regard, although there may be structural isomorphism between the relations of variables in one level of jurisdiction and another, the isomorphism is not complete.

Second, since we expect a similar phenomenon from one time period to another, different matrices must be built for different time periods. Although the signs of the coefficients should normally remain the same, the size of the expected relations may differ considerably. Ultimately these trends might become predictable (that the transformation of the matrices from one unit to another and from one time period to another follows some theoretical regularity). Still, we do not foresee that in our lifetime social science will have detailed success in such an endeavor. This is why proactive analyses must be for the relatively immediate short run. Given our present understanding, the long run is too unstable to withstand quantitative prediction.

Since the long run is unstable, however, it is imperative that the variables and trends be continually monitored. Without such monitoring and consequent model building, people—but especially the least advantaged or most deprived—will have lower probabilities of controlling the most important variables, which are keeping them in their present conditions.

Third, monitoring and model building make it necessary for policy researchers to collect, store, retrieve, and process a considerable amount of data on the social units that represent the jurisdictions of their concern. In fact, several layers of such data are necessary—those of the larger units of policy influence, the data from their own system in some detail, and, as we mentioned previously, the variables from other systems most similar to their own.

If proactive projections and simulations are going to have some degree of accuracy, then the steps of research presented in Figure 4.6 must be generated. This type of matrix is generally considered the first step in building a more accurate simulation model [10, Chap. 5]. If the signs in the matrix are stable, and the coefficients demonstrate that significant impacts are being produced, then some policy research unit should be performing the necessary data banking on some jurisdictional units in reasonable detail in order to document the nature of the influences. As various functional sectors in the real world become ever more interrelated, then monitoring and model building on their relationships becomes more imperative. Probably all of us have observed the calamities affecting some communities as they suffered the consequences of unseen or even foreseen trends. On a larger scale, the multiple effects of the oil crisis have not yet worked themselves out on the most rural localities. As often noted, the days of the early 1960s (when the wealth of resources could be wasted) are gone from our lifetime and probably for considerably longer. Today is not a day to squander resources. Just how many of these resources should be devoted to monitoring social scientific variables, however, is a very difficult question. Consideration of this question underlies the final section of the chapter.

USEFULNESS OF THE POLICY RESEARCH PARADIGM TO POLICYMAKERS. Usefulness is relative. To most policymakers, usefulness is defined in terms of cost-benefit or cost-effectiveness. Virtually anything is useful if it costs nothing. But usefulness can also refer to whether a conceptual scheme is adequate for use by a variety of actors, in this case actors under the jurisdiction of public policymakers.

Use in Decision Making on Local Policy Issues. A first way in which the proactive policy paradigm is useful to policymakers is simply in the general conceptual input-throughput-output-feedback system's perspective itself. As we noted earlier, our perception is that most policymakers tend not to think in terms of multiple and circular causation between variables. Yet their policies often have wide-ranging implications and seldom directly affect only the target variable. If we would assume that policymakers want to bring about "the good life" for as many of their constituents as possible, then the complexities of definition and interaction of "things good" become awe-inspiring.

The paradigm points towards specific ways of thinking about the causal chains of variables. Again, most policymakers, especially at the local level, probably think only tangentially in terms of policy manipulable variables, nor are they likely to distinguish between variables directly manipulable and those only indirectly manipulable. Moreover, probably only a few of them think in terms of "structural" variables as opposed to "aggregate" variables. Nor, without excellent documentation, would they accept that in most cases structural variables are causal of each other and of aggregate variables. Even though most social scientists understand such principles, most policymakers still believe in the efficacy of individuals, whether structured in any particular way or not. "People are the causes of things, not structures," is their dominant mode of thinking. We agree; but people are also affected, constrained, and manipulated by structures, as nearly any piece of social science research demonstrates. This principle is incorporated into the proactive policy paradigm. The policy research paradigm, therefore, summarizes and organizes key conceptual categories necessary for effective decision making by top policymakers in a jurisdiction.

Use of Policy Research in Cost Analysis. The proactive policy research paradigm also directs the way for making cost-benefit analyses. When detailed models of the relations of policies through structures to resources and other outcomes are built, then policy researchers and their policymaking sponsors can better assess where the weakest links are in the causal chain and, in so doing, begin the process of creating a concrete framework for cost-benefit analysis. Just as economists perform feasibility studies on possible new operations for businessmen, so feasibility studies can be done on the cost-benefit of which research to undertake. From the causal chains, which include alternative routes from policies to outcome ends, a number of hypotheses will undoubtedly need more research than others in order to establish the sign, size, and consistency of relationships.

In addition, alternative research techniques can be presented for estimating relations between the variables. It is possible to think of a ladder of evidence in social research, each step giving a range of certainty regarding the estimation. Each step would in general also cost more to implement than the previous step.

The lowest step on the ladder is probably the *informed guess of a keen observer* of the general social system. Anything lower than this would probably not be permissible as evidence, and even this initial step might be classified hearsay by lawyers. A second step would be the *informed guess of a trained researcher* who is a specialist in the area at issue. Both these people will make errors. But their guesses would probably be more accurate than simply random ones or than those of people less well trained. In any case, such guesses may become the base hypotheses from which further research might be undertaken. Such guesses, by the way, can usually be found by reviewing relevant research in the journals and books of a variety of social scientists.

A third step in the ladder of evidence might be the *estimation found in the research literature* for cases more or less similar to the one under question. A fourth step might be what politicians describe as *hearings,* where several specialists come to testify under questioning by other experts. Only a small step away from this one is the one called *key informant interviewing.* The difference in the latter is that the key informant might be chosen carefully and with a definite purpose in mind. Beyond the key informant step is the one which would *survey a wider sample of people* in appropriate positions, who might all be key informants, in an effort to seek congruence. A next step might be to *use such surveys* along with sophisticated computer analyses to estimate relations between variables.

The set of top steps would be the *congregation of various levels of data* from systematic and random sample surveys, as analyzed by the most knowledgeable and sophisticated social research analysts, perhaps using a variety of different types of surveys, over time, along with data obtained from a variety of other sources, and processing them together in complex simulations under varying conditions.

Table 4.1 presents a set of suggestions for some categories of variables and for general alternative procedures in measuring them within the general policy research paradigm, using economic development as the background. The procedures themselves are not mutually exclusive. Although it is impossible to set definitive costs and cost comparisons on each step, it is rather obvious that the higher steps depend on data from lower steps and cost more to implement than the lower steps. The higher steps should also give more definitive estimates of the relations between key variables in the paradigm.

The point is that various steps in the ladder have varying costs as well as varying levels of accuracy. The cost-benefit question is: How important is it to obtain precise information on any given hypothesis?

When asking such a question on each of the major hypotheses in the causal chains, an overall estimate of accuracy and cost can be

Table 4.1. Suggested variables from each component of the policy paradigm relating to economic development

Preputs Mobilization, planning, simulation	Inputs Policies, agencies, budgets	Throughputs Structures	Outputs Resources
Variables	*Variables*	*Variables*	*Variables*
1. Organizing an effective interest group	1. Specifying the various laws that could affect economic development, e.g., federal or state support for: water and sewer facilities, "comprehensive planning agencies," zoning, manpower programs, urban renewal or rehabilitation, roads, highways and transportation, tax (write-off) incentives, etc.	1. Effects of alternate programs on existing political economic structures, e.g.: retailers, wholesalers, banks, transportation, manufacturers, farmers, political parties, etc.	1. Jobs, number of and type
2. Mobilizing population segments			2. Level and distribution of income
3. Planning an overall strategy		2. Effects on local government agencies, e.g.: social services (welfare), police, highway department, utilities (water and sewer, especially), health, hospitals, educational institutions, housing and urban renewal, land use	3. Same as above regarding education
4. Generating accurate and sympathetic publicity or communications with: other local groups, local-public, nonlocal groups, each other	2. Same as above regarding programs: local and state, governmental and private		4. Same as above regarding service
5. Raising money to support activity	3. Same as above regarding budgets	3. Geographic location of each activity	5. Same as above regarding social and personal well-being
	4. A new law (program and budget) for a new, more effective approach	4. Interrelation of one activity to another	6. Effect of resources on morale, values, utilities

Table 4.1. (continued)

Preputs Mobilization, planning, simulation	Inputs Policies, agencies, budgets	Throughputs Structures	Outputs Resources
Techniques 1. Reviewing literature 2. Collecting data comparing locality to other localities (secondary data) 3. Conducting key informant interviews with local economic officials 4. Contacting various other groups for their information; disseminating own findings (also, participant observation) 5. Surveying attitudes (regarding economic development by various population segments) 6. Surveying various government programs that might support economic development activities 7. Assessing appropriateness of various strategies and hypotheses 8. Simulating various models by different techniques	*Techniques* 1–8. (see Preputs) 9. Drafting laws to affect budgets, agencies, programs	*Techniques* 1–8. (see Preputs) 9. Guttman Scales of organizational specializations	*Techniques* 1–8. (see Preputs)

*Techniques should be tied to variables through "decision theory" criteria, especially the one asking, "How important is it to be absolutely accurate, both in terms of valid and reliable indicators and of estimating relations between variables?"

made for any given piece (or even all the pieces) of the policy research. Much will depend upon the resources of the research units, as well as their purposes. But to make an analysis of which social research techniques to use requires that as many links as possible in the causal chain of variables be conceived prior to considering their individual cost and benefit questions. The normal procedure would be to examine the causal chain, rank the various hypotheses needing further research in order of their importance as "weakest causal links" or "critical paths," estimate probabilities of making more accurate estimation of the variable relations for given amounts of money available in the research budget for each proposition, and then, under all these conditions, come to a decision whether or not to research given propositions. Such procedures are developed to a very high level of systematization in operations research and decision theory [1]. Again, the *sine qua non* is a hypothesized causal chain between potential policy manipulable variables, as their effects are simulated through the other sets in Figures 4.4 and 4.5 up to the desired outcomes. In fact, the quality of the final decisions will probably be a direct result of the quality of the causal chain created. Nothing is so embarrassing and disturbing as to discover key missing links in in the chain after cost-benefit decisions are made and the research process is irrevocably in gear.

For instance, when making a local housing plan, most people immediately want to know: What is the present occupancy rate? or How many houses could be remodeled? or dozens of other such questions. Thus groups concerned with such plans often engage in expensive and time-consuming housing surveys, with their potential for getting bogged down at many points and always being open to all the methodological considerations raised by policymakers and professionals about the survey reliability and validity. Although for certain types of government funds a housing survey is a prerequisite, by paying attention to the model as presented in the general policy paradigm of Figure 4.4, such groups may find that expending as much effort in discovering which governmental programs (policies, agencies, or budgets) are appropriate for which types of situations would be more time- and cost-effective than conducting a survey. Then if even one appropriate situation exists in the locality, efforts to inform those responsible might be the critical path that should receive particular attention for policy changes. Thus under some conditions, efforts on a housing survey might be redirected into other efforts more cost-beneficial to conditions of people in a locality. The specification of a model of relations between key variables, therefore, may become an indispensable stage in directing both the general activities of groups in any given program area as well as in their research efforts.

Specific research techniques would depend upon the accuracy of the theoretical model in any given content area.

The potential variables in each of the four major areas in Table 4.1 can be easily dissected further into subvariables. Relationships between variables could also be specified, but these are issues each research unit must face for itself. Moreover, it would take another long chapter to justify a complete set of hypotheses [22, 24, 26, 27, 29].

In addition, the more common research techniques specified for assessing various propositions implied by the variables listed in the table are not exhaustive; other appropriate research techniques are available. For example, case studies and participant observation are implied but not specifically included. Choice of appropriate techniques depends upon financial, research, political, or administrative constraints.

A key for cost reduction in research, of course, is to use data collected by others for other purposes. Many agencies collect specialized data which are largely unanalyzed but which can provide considerable insights regarding structures and trends. For instance, planners often have maps showing population trends in different localities. Likewise, boards of election have election data showing registration and voting rates. County clerk offices have documentation on building permits and a variety of other matters. The major caution in using such data is that researchers must recognize and compensate for the possible biases agencies introduce in the collection and storage of their data. Such consideration must be part of the weighting process in the cost-benefit analyses.

In any case, the organization of hypotheses in the framework of the general policy paradigms can be useful to decision makers in policy research by clarifying the relations of the various important hypotheses to each other, by facilitating assessments of the weakest hypotheses and thus of most needed research, and by permitting cost comparisons of the various types of research for obtaining the needed information.

Use of Research Decision in Local Policy Analysis. The general policy paradigms of Figures 4.4 and 4.5 also facilitate substantive decisions regarding crucial concepts and variables to be used in policy research analyses. Table 4.1 presents some concrete examples in relation to economic development. The first column (preputs) sets out general modes of activities of which researchers in policy research units must be aware in managing the relations of a research unit to other organizations in a locality.

The second column (inputs) specifies some of the policies, laws, and agencies that might be considered. Current policies must be well known and their effects in the local setting (as well as in other settings similar to the particular locality under consideration) must be documented.

A third column (throughputs) calls attention to certain key structures and their dynamics. Patterns of relations between structural variables in society are complex and require much analysis. "Differentiation" as indicated by Guttman Scales is one mode. The level of fluidity of information and resource flows between structures (whether competitive or concentrated, open and accountable, or secret, rigid, and dominating) is another mode. Interlocking relationships between various levels of private and public structures falling between the open and the secret often exist in rural localities. The relationships of local industries to banks, and of banks to mortgages in local housing markets, are problems to review when considering local economic development. Particularly in rural localities, these socioeconomic institutional structures have well-articulated working relationships, which may assist or resist the introduction of potentially competing operations. Many local elites find it very comfortable to stay where they are under current levels of well-being and find the risks of introducing certain types of economic development into their localities greater than they wish to take, at least in initial observations. Thus a new shopping center outside the present central city may pose a threat to local merchants and would only be possible with the support of banks or other businesses at a regional or state level. Or the introduction of new plants and facilities in a local area that will affect the current labor markets may well be opposed, perhaps surreptitiously, by existing businesses in a given locality.

Column four (outputs) presents some major expected outcomes of the system. In the case of economic development, more jobs and income represent primary expected outputs. Because of them, more education and services and greater well-being with higher morale among the people in the locality should also be expected to follow. Naturally, some of these hypothesized relations should be given serious research attention, while others are already very well established.

Some of the variables, of course, are significantly related to other rural development issues, such as resource management and other forms of local quality of life. The policy research paradigm would organize such variables in ways comparable to the one presented here on economic development. A test of the impact of these variables on each other may very well be analyzed through a matrix such as suggested in Figure 4.6. Continued updating of the indicators and data and continued experimentation to discover new sources of data and

new significant concepts would of course be important for the cumu-
lation of more adequate models on which policy decisions might be
based. The policy research paradigm can assist in such endeavors.

USE AS AN INSTRUMENT IN GUIDING CONCERTED ACTION PROGRAMS TO IN-
CREASE LOCAL LIFE QUALITY. The proactive policy paradigm was self-
consciously developed and implemented in one action research program, New Brunswick NewStart, in eastern Canada. This program
is the only one of which we are aware that attempted to implement
a relatively complete version of the paradigm in an economically
lagging rural locality. Thus this project provides the best evidence
for the paradigm's viability at the local level. Although space does not
permit detailed documentation of the program, it should be noted
that great effort was expended to implement all the suggestions identified in Figure 4.4. The efforts were financially supported by the federal government of Canada in cooperation with the governments of
the province of New Brunswick and the county of Kent at the rate of
nearly $1 million per year for five years. Half this sum was spent on
research and the other half on action programs. These efforts are
thoroughly documented in the 155 publications of New Brunswick
NewStart [22, 23, 25, 28].

Ten general conclusions were drawn from this experience [25]:

1. Proactive policy research and action programs based on the
research, formed in cooperation with policymakers from the multiple
levels, are both feasible and viable. They can be implemented and
can be cost-effective. In addition, a pluralistic research program aim-
ing to serve multiple needs of people in various population segments
can be implemented, effectively performed, and made to produce results satisfying to significant numbers of people in these segments.

2. Information dissemination to a wide variety of population
segments can also be meaningfully accomplished with the format of
the proactive policy research paradigm. The future orientation of
the research assists people in localities to think ahead not only in a
community sense but also for their personal lives.

3. Paraprofessionals playing a variety of roles can become meaningfully and knowledgeably involved in the social science proactive
policy research process with benefit both to the process and to themselves as individuals.

4. A locality about the size of a county is a viable unit for analysis by a proactive policy research unit. It presents a wide variety of
opportunities in agriculture and other industries and has multiple
rural communities upon which to base comparative research analysis.
Since at least some problems in rural development are focusing and
disseminating wide varieties of information, a proactive research unit
conforms well to a causal model for rural development.

5. A board for a proactive research unit—representing a good cross section of local people, a variety of specialists (perhaps from outside the locality or university) and low-income people who may be concerned and wish to participate in such activities for their own benefit—can be helpful in focusing issues for the research and also in disseminating information. Such a large board may be imperative if the research unit is government backed, but under any conditions it will be helpful (even if it is time consuming) to establish initial communication processes.

6. Macroeconomic and macrosociological techniques used for regional, multiplex, and growth center analyses are also useful for the analyses of small rural villages and their systems. Concepts such as multipliers (which approximate input-output and Guttman Scale tables for very small villages and very small populations) can also be meaningfully and insightfully introduced in such research units and populations.

7. A division of the efforts of a proactive research unit can with profit be spent (a) evaluating its own activities and (b) researching issues for others in the area. Such a procedure is particularly important if the research unit works with only some people and organizations in a locality rather than with many and is publicly rather than privately supported.

8. Citizen participation is necessary, feasible, and essential. In fact, the research project itself can coordinate community organizations and create community organizations where they do not exist. The research unit can become an effective countywide social planning council or make major contributions to such a planning council if one already exists.

9. Assistance to planning and implementation processes in a locality by the research unit will have more impact the more clearly and intimately the people involved in these three activities (research, planning, implementation) can communicate with one another. In a complex social world, the three activities are complementary rather than idiosyncratic.

10. Staffing a proactive research unit outside a university setting is very difficult; the more rural the locality, the more difficult it is to staff it, because a large base of expertise is usually not available there. It is extremely desirable that someone in the unit have, in effect, professional social science research status and that his involvement in the project be as high as possible. The most desirable staff contains people with considerable experience both in research and in development activities. The broader the theoretical orientation in the group the more likely that political, community, bureaucratic, and research obstacles can be overcome.

In summary, we strongly suggest that future policy research forsake the traditional reactive evaluative model in favor of the pro-active model. As we see it, the major issues of policy and society are much less to discover where we have gone right or wrong in the past than to try to assist policymakers to do better in the future. The struggle to achieve this status is not easy. Policymakers, as we have indicated previously, are not social scientists, and most of them show at least some resistance to social science. The model perspective among them is of the lawyer who thinks not of variables but of real, even if abstract, entities. But it is our contention that until such policy-makers begin to become self-conscious about the theoretical and vari-able nature of the entities they are manipulating, they will neither accurately recognize the phenomena they are manipulating nor pro-duce effective entities affecting these phenomena. We set forth the proactive paradigm, then, so that people who live in our respective societies and communities can take the steps to become more aware of and so be able to control the events which at present, often without their knowledge or consent, control them.

REFERENCES

1. Ackoff, Russell L., and Patrick Rivett. 1963. *A Manager's Guide to Operations Research.* New York: John Wiley & Sons.
2. Blalock, Hubert M. 1964. *Causal Inferences in Nonexperimental Research.* Chapel Hill: Univ. of North Carolina Press.
3. ———. 1971. *Causal Models in the Social Sciences.* Chicago: Aldine-Atherton.
4. ———. 1969. *Theory Construction.* Englewood Cliffs, N.J.: Prentice-Hall.
5. Buckley, William, ed. 1968. *Modern Systems Research for the Behavioral Scientist.* Chicago: Aldine.
6. Bunge, Mario. 1967. *Scientific Research. Studies in the Foundations, Methodology, and Philosophy of Science.* New York: Springer-Verlag.
7. Carter, Novia, and Brian Wharf. 1973. Evaluating social development programs. Canadian Council on Social Development, Ottawa.
8. Clippinger, Judi. 1975. Chenango development project: An evaluation of theory and program. Unpublished M.S. thesis, Cornell University.
9. Coleman, James S. 1971. *Resources for Social Change.* New York: Wiley Interscience.
10. DeGreene, Kenyon B. 1973. *Sociotechnical Systems.* Englewood Cliffs, N.J.: Prentice-Hall.
11. Duncan, Otis Dudley, Ray P. Cuzzort, and Beverly Duncan. 1961. *Statistical Geography: Problems in Analyzing Areal Data.* New York: Free Press.
12. Easton, David. 1968. A systems analysis of political life. In Walter Buck-ley, ed., *Modern Systems Research for the Behavioral Scientist.* Chicago: Aldine.
13. Eberts, Paul R. 1975. A brief assessment of U.S. rural development programs. Hearings of the Rural Development Subcommittee on Agri-culture and Forestry. U.S. Senate, March 6.

14. ——. 1972. Consequences of changing social organization in the Northeast. In Olaf F. Larson, ed., *Proceedings of the Workshop on Current Regional Development Research*. Ithaca, N.Y. Northeast Regional Center for Rural Development.

15. ——. 1971. A theoretical perspective toward an action-oriented model of community change and development. New Brunswick NewStart Rep. R–41–52. (DREE, Ottawa, Microfiche NB–66).

16. ——. 1974. Trends in equality in the northeast: Major empirical dimensions. Cornell University, Ithaca, N.Y.

17. Fox, Karl A. 1974. *Social Indicators and Social Theory*. New York: Wiley Interscience.

18. Hansen, Niles M. 1974. Factors determining the location of industrial activity. In *Rural Industrialization: Problems and Potentials*. Ames: Iowa State Univ. Press.

19. Madden, James P. 1974. Evaluation of rural development programs: Toward a paradigm to guide implementation and evaluation of rural development programs. Presented at Conf. on Rural Dev. Act Activities, Ithaca, N.Y.

20. ——. 1972. Social indicators research and policy research—A synthesis. Presented at Meet. of World Rural Sociol. Soc., Baton Rouge, La.

21. Popper, Karl R. 1963. *Conjectures and Refutations: The Growth of Scientific Knowledge*. New York: Basic Books.

22. Sismondo, Sergio. 1973. Applications of structural indicators for the measurement of development: Selected findings for rural communities in Kent County. New Brunswick NewStart Rep. R–73–120.

23. ——. 1975. A Bibliography of New Brunswick NewStart. Moncton, N.B.: New Brunswick NewStart.

24. ——. 1974. A concept, not a proxy: The meaning and measurement of differentiation. New Brunswick NewStart Rep. R–74–133.

25. ——. 1973. New Brunswick NewStart: An experimental action research program in community and regional development and monitored social change. Presented to Semin. of Policy and Evaluation Branch, Can. Int. Dev. Agency, Ottawa.

26. ——. 1972. Notes toward a psychology for regional development and planning. New Brunswick NewStart. (DREE, Ottawa, Microfiche: NB–97)

27. ——. 1971. Rural development: Policy implications derived from the New Brunswick NewStart research framework. New Brunswick NewStart Rep. R 71–53. (DREE, Ottawa, Microfiche NB–87)

28. ——. 1973. Social indicators for policy research and democratic action: A paradigm and some examples. New Brunswick NewStart Rep. R–73–119. (DREE, Ottawa, Microfiche NB–105)

29. Sismondo, Sergio, and Thomas A. Beaver. 1974. Equality in theory and practice of regional and rural development. New Brunswick NewStart Rep. R–74–136.

30. Tinbergen, J. 1964. *Central Planning*. New Haven, Conn.: Yale Univ. Press.

31. Tuft, E. R. 1974. *Data Analysis for Politics and Policy*. Englewood Cliffs, N.J.: Prentice-Hall.

32. Wallace, Walter L. 1971. *The Logic of Science and Sociology*. Chicago: Aldine-Atherton.

33. Weiss, Carol. 1973. *Evaluation Research*. Englewood Cliffs, N.J.: Prentice-Hall.

CHAPTER FIVE

COMMUNICATING RESEARCH RESULTS FOR POLICY PURPOSES

EDWARD O. MOE

AN EXAMINATION of the issues in communicating research results for policy purposes could be approached in a number of different ways. This chapter attempts to:

1. Explore briefly the concern about communicating results and the demands for communication that are internal to land grant research institutions and those that are external to them.

2. Examine the institutional framework within which we work and identify some of the forces either facilitating or impeding communication.

3. Analyze some of the emerging patterns for linking researchers and users of policy information that seem most promising in creating a policy research constituency.

4. Propose some institutional innovations within the station framework that will more effectively link users of policy research and researchers.

It is not the intent of this chapter to show what experiment station social science or rural development research has contributed or where it has failed to contribute. Larson, in 1965, reviewed and illustrated some significant contributions of agriculturally related social science research, both to policymakers and to the welfare of rural people [4]. Hightower identified what he called "the failure of the land grant college complex," provided another view of land grant research, and suggested some reasons for the inadequacy of research policy within the land grant system [3]. Here is an analysis of some of the issues within both a national and an institutional context and some of the emerging opportunities. We need to understand our own system better than we do.

EDWARD O. MOE is with the Cooperative State Research Service, U.S. Department of Agriculture, Washington, D.C.

RESEARCH FOR POLICY PURPOSES. To help assure communication of the perspective of the chapter, some clarification of the concept of research for policy purposes is needed. This term is defined to include:

1. Making basic systemic analyses of development issues and problems in their institutional settings, including causes, effects, and consequences.

2. Analyzing, devising, and testing strategic alternatives to attain selected policy or program goals, including evaluation of inputs and outputs or costs and effectiveness.

3. Devising, assessing, and testing specific institutional and technological innovations, including new sets of rules that influence what is to be done, how, by whom, and at what levels or standards with respect to public goods and services.

4. Devising and testing information and evaluation and monitoring systems that make it possible to assess the extent to which programs achieve their objectives and determine their overall impact, intended and unintended, on the conditions they were to improve.

5. Analyzing and evaluating program agencies as social systems and as part of the larger system through which policies and programs are implemented—their goals, their organization, their place in the field or the community, and their relationships to other organizations serving the same area.

The ultimate and discriminating product of policy research is a policy, program, or action modified by research results. While such research may be a contribution to existing knowledge and may in whole or part be published in the favored journals, this is not what distinguishes it. Important characteristics of disciplinary research, such as parsimony and elegance, are overshadowed by the correctness of predictions. As Coleman points out, "The policy research problem enters from outside any academic discipline and must be carefully translated from the real world of policy or the conceptual world of a client without loss of meaning" [2]. It is increasingly recognized that most applied research and much so-called policy research are not policy research at all. It is not because the research is not done in a policy context nor that the findings are not adequate to modify a social or development policy or program at any level from the local to the federal. The questions of various types of research—policy, disciplinary, basic, applied, and developmental—will be addressed in the final section of the chapter.

CONCERN ABOUT COMMUNICATING RESULTS AND DEMANDS FOR COMMUNICATION. The growing concern about research for policy purposes and the communication of results may be seen as a constellation of forces. Some are internal in our system of higher education and specific to the land grant university and its research traditions. Others are external to higher education and rooted within the struggles of society to achieve quality in living and to solve some horrendously complicated problems. These sets of forces combine to heighten concern about the uses of research.

Forces Internal to the Land Grant System. A major internal force is the basic design of the land grant university, with its functions grounded in the functions of knowledge itself, that is, acquisition and discovery of knowledge in research, transmission of knowledge in teaching, and application and utilization of knowledge in public service extension. The intricate interrelation among these functions is critical; it is in these interrelations that the functions are tested, as former President James Perkins of Cornell observed:

> Knowledge acquired must be transmitted or it dies. Knowledge acquired and transmitted must be used or it becomes sterile and inert. Even more the chemistry of knowledge is such that the very process of transmission, together with the discipline of application, stimulates and guides those who work at the frontiers of knowledge.
> Knowledge is in many respects a living thing—it grows and changes, and various of its parts are replaced as they become obsolete, but the dynamic nature of knowledge is traceable to this interplay and tension with its acquisition, transmission and application. It is this interaction that creates the needs for new knowledge, that brings inaccurate teaching to account, that shows what could be rather than what is. Taken separately the three aspects of knowledge lead nowhere; together they can and have produced an explosion which has changed the world [5].

The pretensions of this system are more than rhetoric, although there is never any shortage of rhetoric. A deep and continuing concern exists within the system about the interplay among the functions of knowledge. Even when a lack of concern seems to be evident, implicit are both substantial uneasiness and uncertainty about what research is needed and how to put the results to use.

A second major internal factor is that of the value systems of the researchers themselves. Many station researchers seem committed to the idea of doing research that meets the needs of users. The researchers are elated when their results are used by policymakers and program administrators. They are also deeply aware of the inadequacy of much of their research for policy purposes and the lack of an institutional framework which supports policy research.

Another aspect is the growing recognition that the failure of development policies and programs is, in part at least, a failure of academe and its intellectual and research enterprises. While a feeling (widely held) that policymakers—Congress, state legislatures, the "feds," state agencies, county commissioners—always "screw things up" puts the monkey on the backs of others, the lurking fear is that back of their failure may be an intellectual and research failure.

A fourth factor is the recognition of increasing development and policy research competence in the social sciences. Of particular importance are the richer and more adequate bodies of theory from different disciplines, the development of more sophisticated research methodology, and the uses of computers which enable researchers to deal with problems of the complexity and magnitude inherent in policy and program issues. This growing competence has been built in part by the increasing investment in rural development research as indicated in these figures:

	1970	1974
Hatch funds (millions)	$1.6	$ 6.0
State funds (millions)	2.3	7.0
Colleges of 1890 (PL 89–106) funds (millions)	. . .	7.0
Title V (PL 92–419) funds (millions)	. . .	1.5
Grants to regional research centers (PL 89–106) funds (millions)	. . .	0.3
Total (millions)	$3.9	$21.8

Over these years the number of projects has increased from some 350 to 975. A body of information and knowledge is emerging. While it is not as good research nor as relevant for policy purposes as we would like it to be, a base both in knowledge and competence has been established. Maintaining this base and substantially improving its quality are now urgent priorities.

The final point is the emergence of a research constituency in rural development. Included in this constituency are such national and local groups as the Extension Service; executive and legislative branches of national, state and local governments; rural development subcommittees of the House and Senate and the staffs of legislators; Coalition for Rural Development and the Rural Caucus; the Farmers Home Administration, Soil Conservation Service, and Forest Service; national, state, and local planning and development agencies, public and private; citizen planning and development bodies; state and national associations of municipal and county officials; the National Association of Regional Councils; Rural Education Association; Rural Housing Alliance and Housing Assistance Council; American Bankers Association; rural section of the American Medical Association; and the Office of Rural Development in the Department of Health, Education and Welfare. The list is very long, and those listed are only illustrative of the types of groups interested in rural development. The fact that they are increasing in number is reassuring. There is someone out there with whom we need to be in continuing communication.

Forces outside Higher Education and the Land Grant System. A number of insistent external forces are also part of the constellation of influences supporting a new relationship between researchers and policymakers. Among the more important of these forces are:

1. The growing demand that institutions of higher education, generally, and researchers, particularly, respond to national needs and help in the alleviation of human problems. Creation of a program entitled Research Applied to National Needs (the RANN program in the National Science Foundation) is a case in point.

2. The increasing requests from decision makers, citizens, and program and agency administrators for: help in understanding development issues, assessing policy and program alternatives, and evaluating impact of programs.

3. Closely related to point 2 is the increasingly sophisticated oversight function performed by congressional subcommittees, such as the subcommittee on Rural Development of the Senate committee on Agriculture and Forestry chaired by Senator Dick Clark of Iowa. Senator Clark does an excellent job of questioning and probing. He is attempting to get at the equity issues in the allocation of resources and to get some better estimate of the impact of policies and programs. This serves a very useful purpose.

4. The observation of President Frederick P. Thieme of the University of Colorado: "It seems inevitable that for the next twenty or so years the new and major incremental federal support for universities will be to purchase their services in an effort to solve national problems" [6]. The necessity to respond to national needs and the growing emphasis on accountability and what the investment in education and research produces must be taken into account.

Confluence of Forces—A New Opportunity. What we are confronted with, then, is a confluence of internal and external forces, which seems to support a stronger, more vigorous attack on development and policy issues. This is an opportune time. The turnaround in population growth and job creation in nonmetropolitan-rural areas since 1970, identified by Beale [1] and others, seems to usher in a new era. Some old issues persist and new ones are emerging. Stabilization and new growth will likely create a more favorable climate for improving economic opportunities and social services. Less effort will have to be expended to overcome the discouragement of continuing decline. The time is opportune and a basis has been built for a significant new response.

THE INSTITUTIONAL FRAMEWORK—FACTORS FACILITATING AND IMPEDING COMMUNICATION. Communication and the processes by which it is achieved are always embedded in an institutional and relational context. This is as true in communicating research results as in communicating any other kind of subject matter or information. Researchers working on policy and development issues through the agricultural experiment stations are caught up in a powerful institutional complex. It is a magnificent system in design and implementation. Its achievements in the service of scientific agriculture, for which it was designed, are indisputable. At the same time, it has not and does not now serve the social sciences and policy and development research to the same degree it serves agriculture. An understanding of why it does not is basic to the problem of communication.

The Land Grant System: Education, Research, Extension, and Public Service in Agriculture. The system came into being through great legislative acts in 1862, 1887, and 1914. Social and institutional innovations based on these legislative acts raised the farmers' educational levels, provided basic and applied research findings related to their needs for solutions of immediate problems, and put into the field a corps of extension workers who both supplemented researchers' understanding of the problems of farmers and facilitated the flow of information to them. The full impact of this system and its elaboration over time was great, both in prospect and retrospect. Recurring cycles of expanding knowledge, new problems confronted by farmers, further applied research, application of research, alleviation of problems, and emergence of new problems became institutionalized, and a structure to support the functions emerged. Continuing researcher-user contacts were built in, and a basis for establishing and maintaining credibility was built. This system, like every other system, needs renewing on a continuing basis; for the most part it achieves such renewal. It has been kept alive and vigorous through contacts with farmers on their farms, through bringing farmers to research stations and college campuses, and through a lively continuing exchange with general farm and commodity organizations.

Research on the processes of diffusion of agricultural technology by social scientists made a distinguished contribution. It increased understanding of how ideas are disseminated and how new products and recommended practices move from research stations into use. It illuminated the operations of the system. This body of findings is being reexamined for ideas about the diffusion of the results of development research.

A significant point that needs emphasis and reemphasis is that researchers helped create the system and helped establish researcher-user contact. Within the system, and especially when it works best, the researcher makes his contribution and the system itself keeps the researcher involved and facilitates the flow of information to people whose needs it is designed to meet. It is significant also that the researcher knows the farmers-users, farm firms, and agribusiness firms of various types and is directly conversant with their needs.

Another distinguishing feature, and one that is very different when one works on policy and development issues, is that the decision to use research findings is the decision of a farm operator, a farm family or a farm firm, or an agribusiness enterprise of some type. The situation is very different where many decision makers are involved or where the decision is made through political processes, as is generally the case with policy and development issues.

The Case of Social Science and Research on Policy and Rural Development. The present education, research, and public service extension system for social science, policy research, and rural development is in its early and more primitive stages. There is rather solid evidence that the principles inherent in the work with agriculture apply in these areas if two significant conditions are taken into account—the differences in the content and the differences in decisions about use which are made through a political process replete with trade-offs and compromises to generate support and gain acceptability.

Against this backdrop one can identify a number of factors impeding communication:

1. Lack of a system that effectively links users, researchers, and the extension staff in community and resource development.

2. Mutual suspicion and distrust between researchers and users or decision makers on policy and programs.

3. Users not aware of what research is available and not having had a voice in the formulation of the problems researched.

4. Difficulties researchers face in accepting the fact that, from a user point of view, partial information available at the time of action or decision is better than complete information after that time.

5. Lack of appropriate, periodic, research information releases and publications for users.

6. Failure to follow up significant relationships and exchanges that are initiated with users.

7. Research results that tend to be separate, fragmented findings

—not strategical in nature and not combined into policy and program alternatives.

8. Failure to provide technical and educational assistance to users for interpretation of findings and for adapting them for use.

9. Research that has not been made a built-in, continuing part of the development processes.

10. Lack of a broad-based public education program that builds public knowledge about policy issues, policy alternatives, and development.

Factors Facilitating Communication. Essential elements in the communication of research findings are implicit in the preceding discussion. An illustration of successful communication will help highlight these elements.[1] The eastern shore of Virginia is a lagging region with low income, substantial unemployment, and heavy out-migration. To help define alternative courses of action, the Division of Planning and Development of the state of Virginia and the Virginia Planning District asked the Department of Agricultural Economics at Virginia Polytechnic Institute and State University to initiate two studies. One study dealt with the agriculture-agribusiness sector to define development opportunities in agriculture. The other was an interindustry input-output analysis of business and governmental activities to examine income and employment impacts of changes in various sectors of the economy. The studies were done and the results discussed with local citizens and planning and development groups. The researchers and the university were praised for what they had done. Their work was said to be uniquely helpful and in distinct contrast to other occasions when the area had been surveyed and analyzed. An analysis of this case shows these factors to be critical:

1. The researchers involved citizens and local and state officials in the formulation of the problems to be studied, the project design, and the analysis.

2. They dealt with a major problem and one recognized as such by all parties involved.

3. They not only diagnosed the ills, they explored the alternatives and recommended a treatment.

4. They involved a team including senior researchers with complementary skills and graduate students.

5. Findings were reported promptly to local people and local and state officials.

6. The studies opened the door for further analyses, which are continuing.

1. Illustration described in a letter from Dr. Joseph D. Coffey to the author, dated July 17, 1973.

Obviously, this example does not deal with synthesized data, a mass audience, or mass communication media. It may be, and likely is, more typical of the types of exchanges that occur on policy and development issues.

EMERGING PATTERNS FOR LINKING RESEARCHERS AND USERS. It has long been recognized that the linking of research to policy formulation and to decisions about policy and development is hazardous. There may be some tendency to overstress hazards, controversy, and political entanglements. However this may be, a kind of defusing takes place when the emphasis is put on researcher-user relationships and patterns emerging in these relationships.

Having the opportunity as a sociologist on the staff of the Cooperative State Research Service to participate in various kinds of research reviews, to meet with regional technical committees and planning committees, to review both the Hatch and Title V rural development projects, and to work in a variety of ways with the four regional centers gives one a perspective on what is happening. A number of emerging patterns show high promise for the system.

First, a stronger and more consistent emphasis is placed on researcher-user relationships and on the specific identification of actual and potential users of researcher findings. In some cases departments array their publications of all types against users of the publications. All too frequently the only identifiable users are other researchers or students. This has been the pattern, but it seems to be changing. The thrust now is not toward users in a vague, detached way nor the mere listing of groups who might be users, but how to build and maintain relationships with specific users. Development research constituencies are emerging. The constituency is defined as users who meet two conditions: helping define problems to be researched and receiving back results from the research when it is completed.

Another emerging pattern is to involve users in research reviews and to get their evaluation of the research being done. This is useful and appropriate and is done usually with the full recognition that users should be involved not after the fact but in the initial formulation of the research problems.

In some cases users or persons in the channels of communication to users have been made members of technical committees. This was true of NE–58 (An Economic and Sociological Study of Agriculture Labor in the Northeast States) and S–81 (Human Resource Development Potentials of Southern Rural Youth and Their Patterns of Mobility). In the former, representation was from the Department of Labor, and in the latter, from ERIC-CRES (a research information system in rural education based at New Mexico State University) and the Northwest Regional Educational Laboratory (a development organization in rural education based in Portland, Oregon). Both ERIC-CRES and the Northwest Laboratory have helped relate research and the researchers to potential users. NE–58 held a conference at Ohio State University on "Unemployment Insurance for Agricultural Workers" to explore results, issues, and implications with people who were in a position to influence policy. The comments of William H. Kolberg, assistant secretary of Labor for Manpower on the work of NE–58 are revealing: "It is a rare occurrence when the results of research conducted by the academic world bear such a close and timely relationship to legislative proposals of the administration."[2] These are significant developments and they seem to indicate a trend in user-research relationships.

Another factor of note is the creation of the regional centers and the work they are doing to upgrade rural development research. The inventories of research, the rosters of researchers, the clarification of research needs, the establishment of research priorities, the creation of collegial research networks, and some syntheses of findings have helped put rural development in a new, more understandable, and more significant context. The centers may provide a stronger institutional base for the conduct of regional research. A case in point is the social marginalization project in the Western Region. Of more specific relevance in terms of communication among researchers and users is the creation of a Social Services Committee by the Northeast Regional Rural Development Center, which brings users and researchers together to define issues and to formulate critical problems that need to be researched.

Perhaps as important as any of the activities of the centers or any of the developments of recent years is the linking of research and extension through joint programs initiated under Title V. Over the years stations and extension services, responding to their own institutional needs, have become isolated from each other. No one intended it to be so, but it has happened. A variety of new linking mechanisms have emerged to facilitate collaboration, such as joint project groups, joint working teams, and research and extension responsibility vested in a single project leader. These are now being tested. It is likely that recognition of the research-extension estrangement and efforts to overcome it will continue after Title V, whenever it may end.

It is obvious that we cannot move from a loose system (in which

2. Letter from William H. Kolberg, assistant secretary of Labor for Manpower, Department of Labor, to Dr. Bernard L. Ervin, chairman of the Technical Committtee for NE–58, Ohio State University, June 20, 1973.

research problems have been defined by researchers, for the most part outside of a development or policy context) to a system of policy-related research in one drastic move. The important point is: we seem to be moving toward such a system. Another point of some significance is the developing relationships between the centers, the Cooperative State Research Service, and the Office of Rural Development in the Department of Health, Education and Welfare. Such a relationship holds many mutual advantages. To the extent that it becomes possible for center directors and other station researchers, CSRS staff, and appropriately placed people in Health, Education and Welfare to exchange views on the formulation of research problems and needs in the fields of income maintenance, health, education, and social services, another gap in the emerging rural development research system will have been filled.

A final point is that both on the basis of research done to date and the widening network of contacts with users, researchers are now more conversant with and more competent to work on policy issues in development. These emerging patterns as they have been labeled here rest on the significant investment of dollars and scientific manpower reported earlier in this chapter. Running through this range of contacts is a reaching out for help both by researchers and users. The reaching out is supported by pressures on both parties to communicate with the other to help solve pressing problems. So far, little thought has been given to the overall system, including the communication system needed for the conduct of research and delivery of rural development research findings, with all that such a system implies. The last part of this chapter deals with such a system.

SOME INSTITUTIONAL INNOVATIONS WITHIN THE STATION AND THE LAND GRANT FRAMEWORK. On the basis of what is happening now among users and potential users of rural development research, and among scientists engaged in such research, it would seem that we are edging up to an important innovation in the land grant–experiment station–extension system. The genius of the innovation is that it fits within the system and is a logical outgrowth of the user of development research–development researcher relationships. What is needed now is some way of nurturing and supporting this relationship within the present organizational-institutional context.

Two major features may be brought together into such an innovation. The first is a recognition that the classical view of the research-extension relationships is a partial one and does not take into account the significant steps that occur between the discovery of a basic idea or set of ideas and the eventual utilization of these ideas shaped into a new institutional form. A more accurate view of the flow of ideas is from basic research to applied research to developmental research through community resource development extension, to the testing of innovations, to the institutionalization of alternatives into an ongoing system. Any innovation in the "delivery system" for rural development research has to take these functions into account and relate them to each other in such a way that each performs its basic tasks and facilitates the performance of the other functions in the chain. A breakdown at any point weakens the system or destroys its effectiveness altogether.

Development research in this chain of events is interpreted as research that combines ideas into strategical alternatives and assesses their impacts. The first four functions are seen as legitimate functions of universities. The last two are in the domain of public and private agencies and organizations. What we are concerned with then is a chain of events in which university-agency or researcher-user collaboration is needed to make the system work. Recognition of the movement through these steps or phases and the part played by different kinds of research is essential.

A second major feature of the innovation is that it is solidly based on the involvement of users and potential users as a change strategy, which may be and is often viewed also as a communication strategy. When users and researchers are jointly involved in the formulation of problems and appropriate contact is made throughout the research process, interest in findings is increased and the feedback and interpretation of findings becomes more effective. It follows, also, that the utilization of findings is more likely to occur. Given all the demands on researchers, it is impossible for them to do the quality of research needed and at the same time compensate for the deficiencies of the system in building and maintaining contacts. The concept of Title V and some of the activities it has spawned have confronted us with some old issues in a new form and a new setting.

Some Functions That Need to be Strengthened. If the research-extension-user system is to work in accordance with the principles of the classical model, some important functions need to be established and strengthened. Among them are:

1. Building on and strengthening established researcher-user contacts. This would obviously include an analysis of what contacts already exist and what new ones are needed for the institution to carry out its responsibilities in rural development.

2. Interpreting to users and the public the university's development research role and functions.

3. Interpreting the existing body of data as it relates to issues, problems, and alternatives of major interest to users.

4. Helping identify development and policy issues involving researchers, extension workers, and research administrators—from the user point of view.

5. Bringing user groups of all types to the campus to (a) meet with researchers and administrators, (b) help clarify issues that need to be researched, and (c) make possible direct researcher-user exchanges on the meaning and limitation of findings and implications of findings and on the possible/probable impact of alteratives.

6. Helping define user needs for continuing communication and how various media might be used to get findings to users.

7. Helping use and build on the research and extension experience under Title V .

8. Helping utilize the instrumentality of the regional centers as a backup for state programs and a mechanism through which the states of the region can cooperatively attack common problems.

9. Helping arrange new types of liaison between experiment stations-extension and a variety of significant user groups, such as county and municipal officials, planning and development bodies, and state agencies in planning and development. Some consideration might be given to setting up new types of joint university-user advisory and technical groups, and having persons from user groups in a liaison capacity on campus for extended periods.

This is an imposing set of functions and it is certainly not complete. If we are at the opportune time described above—opportune in terms of the psychological moment and the availability of the capacity to do policy research in development—what we will be able to do is contingent on the performance of these functions. Performing them in effect will help bring into being for development research an appropriate modification of what exists in agriculture. One way to help bring this about would be for the experiment stations in consultation with extension to designate a knowledgeable researcher who knows extension and ask him to undertake the job. It should be clear that he is putting pieces together into a new system. Empower him to surround himself with a few research and extension colleagues who understand the problem and who have imagination in building innovation. The activity should be legitimized by the experiment station and extension. The designated researcher would be identified as a member of the experiment station administrative staff. It might be possible in some stations to have a member of the station staff undertake the job.

Some Possible Payoffs. While it is not possible at the beginning of such an effort to know what the payoffs would be, there are some intriguing possibilities. Researchers and users could be linked more effectively. Such research findings as presently exist could be put to use in development programs. Research could come to grips with some of the more basic issues in development, particularly with aspects of the problems important to significant users. It is very likely that a wider support base could be built both in understanding and funds. The experiment station, extension, and total university could gain in that the university might be seen as a more effective partner with communities, counties, the state, and the nation in improving the well-being of people, specifically, rural people, which is the hallmark of what we are about.

Rural development research, despite the continuing frustrations, is coming of age. A framework is emerging which both gives it meaning and increases its effectiveness. Relationships to users and potential users are the keys to a change strategy and a communication strategy. A cautious optimism about the future seems reasonable if we can survive the present.

REFERENCES

1. Beale, Calvin L. 1974. Rural development: Population and settlement prospects. *J. Soil Water Conserv.* 29(1): 23–27.
2. Coleman, James. 1973. Ten principles governing policy research. *Footnotes* (Am. Social. Assoc.) (3): 1.
3. Hightower, James. 1972. *Hard Tomatoes, Hard Times.* Washington, D.C.: Agribusiness Accountability Project.
4. Larson, Olaf F. 1965. Income and welfare of rural people—Agricultural research significant to public policy, public welfare, and community improvement. *Rural Sociol.* 30(4).
5. Perkins, James A. 1966. *The University in Transition.* Princeton, N.J.: Princeton Univ. Press.
6. Thieme, Frederick P. 1972. The university interface with societal problems, consequences, and prospects. In Robert N. Fairman and Maurice E. Oliver, eds., *A Question of Partnership.* Washington, D.C.: National Association of State Universities and Land Grant Colleges, pp. 38–40.

CHAPTER SIX

ECONOMIC DEVELOPMENT: A CHANGING SCENE, SOME CHANGING NEEDS

VIJAY DESHPANDE, GLEN PULVER, and EUGENE WILKENING

HISTORICALLY, advocates of economic development have called forth visions of new factories, more jobs, burgeoning payrolls, expanding tax rolls, greater material well-being, and a general improvement in life quality for everyone. Debate on a national basis centered around issues such as the comparative impact of growth in the manufacturing sector as contrasted to agriculture and the effect of policies of government intervention as contrasted to a stance of relatively free enterprise. On the local level, millions of dollars were invested in industrial parks, promotional materials, tax write-offs, and other enticements aimed at bringing new businesses to town. Through it all economic development was judged to be good and absolutely necessary.

In recent years people have begun with increasing frequency to raise a number of questions about economic development. No longer are the assumptions that growth is good and that an expanding industrial base is the best route to economic development accepted without serious examination. There are growing indications of a broad citizen consciousness about the need to make economic growth more compatible with—and in some cases even subservient to—environmental quality and natural resource limitations.

This change in perspective raises some serious questions about the adequacy of existing research methods dealing with public policies

VIJAY DESHPANDE is Research Specialist, Upper Great Lakes Regional Commission, Washington, D.C.

GLEN PULVER is Professor, Department of Agricultural Economics, University of Wisconsin.

EUGENE WILKENING is Professor, Department of Rural Sociology, University of Wisconsin.

on economic development. Here an attempt is made to identify some of these basic questions on economic development needing additional research and to suggest some of the research techniques that might be useful.

When changing circumstances and conditions require a major shift in the approach to a public policy area such as economic development, three things must occur:

1. A change in people's and decision makers' views of the development problems and the way in which they relate to their value systems.

2. A responsiveness and flexibility on the part of the institutions and procedures needed to implement these policies, including a change in the boundaries of our institutions, to meet the challenges of new problems of wider scope.

3. A positive effort from the public policy research community, in terms of new tools, innovative approaches, and appropriate methods, to support the above two needs.

CHANGING VALUES AND PERSPECTIVES. More and more people are realizing the side effects of growth and are taking increasingly vocal and firm stands against some economic development activities having questionable benefits. There are numerous examples of highway projects being halted, dam constructions being delayed, mining operations being stopped, paper mills being closed, new industrial parks being discouraged, and so on.

The underlying reasons are many. First, people are finding that there is no such thing as a "free lunch!" Associated with most activities of economic growth is a certain level of environmental degradation. It might be in terms of increased air or water pollution or an irreplaceable loss of unique land resources or an alarming depletion rate of finite quantities of resource materials such as minerals. Second in many areas, especially in rural areas, new economic growth introduces tremendous forces of social disruption. New class distinctions, new value systems, and new leadership patterns are suddenly imposed. Residents increasingly feel that their communities are no longer "nice places to raise a family" or "to enjoy life." Further, in many cases the new economic growth results in increased social inequities—either in terms of local residents not getting some of the better-paying new jobs or in terms of local residents bearing an increased cost of providing additional public services and facilities. A third reason is people's increasing concern for the quality or nature of growth. The unpredictable and painful ups and downs experienced by communities and areas with one large industry (or several footloose industries) has convinced many community leaders about the need for a carefully thought out strategy of selective economic growth —a strategy to attract more permanent-type industries, to create a diversified economic base, and generally to build a stable, industrial base, less vulnerable to national business cycles.

Finally, some community leaders are taking a more cautious approach toward the traditional economic growth, particularly growth through manufacturing industries. It is their gradual realization that manufacturing and the resource extraction sectors are becoming relatively less important in the economy. Labeled by some as the "post-industrial" stage of national growth, this situation is typified across the nation by an absolute decline in agriculture and mining employment, a slight increase or stagnation in manufacturing and contract construction, and a rapid growth in the general services sector. Most of these service industries also perform rather well on the increasingly important criteria of environmental impact. The service industries (including the government sector) have different locational requirements and resource needs and they need different kinds of locational incentives.

The above combination of factors has resulted in recent years in a challenging situation for both the policymakers and the researchers dealing with economic development. The next question is: How are they responding to this challenge?

SOME EMERGING RESPONSES. Over the last four to six years, some significant policy responses have emerged at national, state, and local levels. Some are characterized by a "slow growth" or "managed growth" approach (e.g., Florida and Oregon), some are advocating growth moratorium (e.g., Petaluma, California), and at the state and national levels increasingly serious consideration is being given to more rational, systematic planning. As a result of the need for more rational planning, states throughout the country have begun to develop policies on growth and development. They are asking: What do the people want their state to be like twenty-five years from now? What level of population can be expected? How much economic growth is necessary to support population expectations? Where should the population and economic growth occur for the greatest well-being of all without destroying the state's unique and critical natural resources? Many states, with the support of the U.S. Economic Development Administration, are struggling with the concept of "growth centers." This implies a spatial selectivity in economic development efforts and is radically different from the traditional concept of inducing/encouraging growth everywhere.

Some states (e.g., Maine and Hawaii) are attempting to be selective in types of industries. "Desirable" or "suitable" industries are being identified (as in the case of Wisconsin) on the basis of their environmental impact, energy consumption, wage structures, growth potential, and so forth. (The service industries generally rank very high on such desirability scales.)

In specific communities within the United States, many people have begun to express concern about the undesirable effect of population immigration. As populations grow, more people are using limited resources. There are more motor boats on the lakes in the summer. The solitude of winter woodlands is broken by the roar of snowmobiles. The exhaust fumes of automobiles and factories fill the air. Hillsides are interrupted by electric power lines and garish billboards. Economic growth may be contrary to community wishes. Increasingly, many are saying, "You are welcome to visit—but don't stay here for good." Some communities (e.g., Baraboo, Wisconsin) are moving away from the highly vulnerable position of a "single-industry town" to a community with a healthy, diversified economic base.

At the federal level, a longtime suspicion about states' capabilities and concern often resulted in a direct federal-local funding partnership, bypassing the states. Such a situation, though highly desired by the communities, generally precludes any areawide or statewide systematic planning and coordination of economic development efforts. The loan and grant programs of the Economic Development Administration or the Title V commissions (such as the Upper Great Lakes Regional Commission) were typical of such individual community-focused economic development efforts.

The 1974 amendments to the Public Works and Economic Development Act of 1965 seem to correct this situation. These include attempts to (1) encourage the establishment and/or strengthening of state-level comprehensive economic development planning; (2) coordinate the activities of EDA and Title V regional development commissions; (3) require project funding priorities to be consistent with some broader (statewide) framework; and (4) require that the state economic development process be based on close cooperation and coordination among various state agencies, regional bodies, and communities.

Some of the recent changes in our ideas and attitudes about economic development and some of the ways the institutions, at various levels, are responding to these changes have been briefly outlined. In the next section, areas needing new or additional research that will improve the public policymaking process relating to economic development will be identified.

RESEARCH NEEDS. Based on emerging program needs, four broad areas needing major research efforts or new tools and techniques can be identified:

1. Articulation and reconciliation of economic development goals at local/regional/state (and even national/international) levels. tional/international) levels.

2. Trade-offs among functional goals, such as economic growth/ environmental quality.

3. Design of specific development strategies.

4. Internalization of research in public decision-making processes.

Goal Articulation and Reconciliation. Anyone looking at economic development programs, whether at the local, regional, or state level, will be surprised at the lack of clear and specific statements about their operational goals or objectives. At the most, one finds some rhetoric about "economic well-being of the people" or "more and better jobs," etc. With this prevalent level of ambiguity and generality, it is extremely difficult to systematically design appropriate strategies or to meaningfully evaluate their cost-effectiveness. Obviously, very strong political forces exist, resulting in policymakers shying away from such specific goal statements. But an economic development planning process without specific goals is like a rudderless ship. Even a small business operation (e.g., a corner grocery store) sets some tangible goal in terms of, say, net profit or return on investment.

A community considering economic development planning should be able to answer the primary question: What are our economic goals for this community? Two percent annual growth in population? Five hundred new manufacturing jobs over the next five years? Five percent increase in the median family income? The community needs help in identifying some meaningful goals and their priorities. Citizen survey is one possible tool. Nominal group sessions for community leaders is another. Even at the community level, the diverse interest groups and their respective value systems and aspirations pose serious methodological problems in arriving at community goals. How do we ensure a fair representation of all subgroups, such as elected officials, organizational leadership, minorities, labor, the elderly, women, businessmen, etc.? Should there be a weighting system attached to the subgroup goals?

The process becomes increasingly complex as we move on to a higher level of political entity, such as a region, a state, or the nation. At these macrolevels, the problem of reconciliation becomes very real and tough. Are the state economic goals a mere collage of regional goals? Or do we derive those by averaging out all the regional goals?

Given each region's unique resources and problems, there are likely to be economic disparities among them; so, how do we define acceptable levels of disparities? Or, on the other hand, what is the feasible/desirable level of homogenization of regions' economic well-being? At what point does a state goal become an imposition on the region, or a community lose its autonomy or freedom of choice (on economic matters) in reference to the regional objective? There are no easy answers to these questions.

Trade-Offs among Functional Goals. We are increasingly aware that in most public policymaking situations there are no clear-cut decisions—in other words we encounter a situation where the basic question is: How much economic growth do we allow and at what price, in terms of environmental quality? And to be meaningful, this question must be answered in clear, specific terms, indicating some tangible outcomes. Example: 300 new retailing jobs in a new shopping center would result in loss of ten acres of valuable agricultural or wooded area. Certainly, we do not expect planners or economists to make these choices—the people and their decision makers should do so. But planners and economists can help people make better decisions by developing techniques showing the specific trade-offs involved. Two examples of some progress in this direction are the recent work of Walter Isard [2] and the state of Arizona's Trade-Off Model (ATOM) [3]. There is a great need to refine these techniques and to make them easily accessible and understandable to the policymakers.

One of the prerequisites for a trade-off analysis is a set of measures of growth and development, or some type of indices of various aspects of quality of life. The policymakers cannot satisfactorily handle or comprehend hundreds of bits of information on their community or state. They need some composite indicators, some aggregated piece of information in their decision making. (For example, rather than trying to monitor prices of all the necessary goods and services, we try to monitor the cost-of-living index or a consumer price index.) Several attempts have been made to develop such indices (Midwest Research Institute, Denver Research Institute, Wisconsin Rural Development Council, etc); their methods and techniques need to be further refined.

Perhaps the toughest part of the trade-off analysis is to get the policymakers and citizens to use it and participate in it. Several possible techniques include: preference surveys, simulation modeling, and game playing for citizens and community leaders. Carefully designed preference surveys can create scenarios or situations where the respondents are forced to make some real trade-offs—based on their personal values, sense of priorities, and so forth. (Example: the Activity Patterns Survey designed by Professor Stuart Chapin [1].) Gaming achieves similar results, but more through group interactions, feedbacks, peer pressures, and increased personal awareness/education. A computerized simulation model helps a decision maker try out various policy alternatives, each representing a different type of goal trade-off. Refinements are constantly being made to all the above tools. Unfortunately, however, most of these are still being viewed as fun games or educational toys and have not been accepted as decision-making tools. Work needs to be done on making these tools more realistic and less esoteric and also on convincing the policymakers of their value.

Strategy Specification. Traditionally, development strategy theory has been one of the major strengths of economists and other researchers in economic development. Sophisticated tools such as input-output analysis and interindustry linkage have been used in designing economic strategies. Techniques such as cost-benefit analysis and cost-effectiveness analysis further evaluate the strategies. Also, there is a great body of research on location theory, firm location decisions, and so forth.

However, a significant gap remains between the body of theory and its application in policymaking. Although the methodology exists to weigh the costs and benefits of public investment in industrial parks, tax incentives, capital plant, and so forth, seldom are studies actually carried out. Industrial parks are created, tax incentives are passed, and buildings are constructed almost on blind faith that something good will happen. A great deal is known about the relative growth potential and location requirements of specific industries, but how often do communities, regions, or states make highly directed searches? How many have seriously compared the potential for employment growth in the manufacturing, nonmanufacturing, and government sectors? The theory exists, but it needs to be applied in decision making. This may call for the development of simplified tools of development strategy theory application.

A major refinement needed—common to all the above tools—is the incorporation of some noneconomic rationale, criteria, or dimension. Or the research question is: How do we deal with the externalities of economic development? In deciding on suitable or desirable industries or mix of economic activities for an area or region, how can we include evaluation criteria, such as energy consumption, environmental degradation, human resource versus capital intensive, and so forth. In deciding on the location of new economic activities, how do we deal with criteria such as potential impact on the region's ecology/natural beauty, equity among regions or population groups in those regions, and so forth? In evaluating the cost-benefits of an economic policy (e.g., exemption of new industrial property from tax assessment), how do we make sure that the analysis includes the impact of the new policy on different regions or areas and different industry groups. Also, how do we learn who is *really* paying the costs?

Typically, economic policy research tends to suggest an optimum solution based on narrowly defined economic criteria and constraints. Perhaps what is needed (from the point of view of a policymaker) is a "satisficing" solution, which might be less than optimal if only one functional set of criteria is applied. Again, some work (especially in the area of water resources economics) has been done on the design and evaluation of multiobjective, multidimensional development plans and projects. That needs to be refined and expanded to cover some of the above concerns.

Internalization of Research in Public Policymaking. Perhaps the most critical need in economic development is the linkage of research and public policymaking activities. Three principal actors involved in such an effort are: (1) the researcher—who creates, refines, and experiments with new research tools and techniques; (2) the policy analyst—who has some familiarity with the research tools and who has to make policy recommendations to the decision makers; and (3) the decision makers or policymakers (elected chief executives, legislative representatives, agency heads, etc.)—who constantly work under the pressures of time constraints and pressures from interest groups and must come up with pragmatic, acceptable public policies.

It is clearly recognized that not all research needs to be oriented to meet the requirements of policy analysts or the policymakers. Research projects do have a long-term payoff in terms of our better understanding of social-physical-natural phenomena and systemic relationships. At the same time, we simply cannot afford to have a total and complete separation between research and policymaking. Some research efforts should be specifically geared to meet the needs of improving the public policymaking process. With this note of caution, we suggest five specific hypotheses or statements for further consideration.

1. The researcher needs to show more willingness to work with inadequate and less-than-satisfactory data. As we all know, availability of sound data is a universal problem. And yet, look at the alternatives—the policymakers must decide issues whether they have all the data or not.

2. The researcher needs to seriously examine "satisficing" solutions and not constrain himself only to optimum solutions.

3. The researcher must show an increased level of sensitivity, awareness, and recognition of the institutional (implementation) dimension of public policies. Some of the best public policies have resulted in total disasters or frustrations because the institutional element was ignored (e.g., the Model Cities Program).

4. The researcher must recognize the critical element of timing of the research inputs to the policymaking process.

5. Finally, special efforts must be made by both the researchers and the policy analysts to expose the policymakers to some of the new tools, techniques, and innovative approaches to public policymaking. This must be done in a nonthreatening way, and the basic idea should be to increase their awareness and heighten their consciousness about some of the newer criteria for decision making.

SUMMARY. It is apparent that changes have occurred over the past few years in the public perception of the need for economic development. Although severe crises such as the current high level of unemployment generate widespread interest in expanded employment opportunity, citizen groups continue to question the impact of unbridled growth on natural resource utilization and environmental quality. At all political levels people are seeking more involvement and more rational planning. Increasingly, today's problems are being examined within a long-range planning perspective. Policymakers could benefit greatly from articulation and reconciliation of economic development goals at all levels, examination of trade-offs among functional goals, design of specific development strategies, and the internalization of research in public decision–making processes.

REFERENCES

1. Chapin, F. Stuart, Jr. 1975. *Urban Land Use Planning*. Urbana: Univ. of Illinois Press.
2. Isard, Walter. 1972. *Ecologic-Economic Analysis for Regional Development*. New York: Free Press.
3. State of Arizona, Department of Economic Planning and Development. 1973. The Arizona trade-off model. Summary Rep.

CHAPTER SEVEN

ALTERNATIVE METHODS FOR RURAL TRANSPORTATION POLICY RESEARCH

ROBERT O. RICHARDS, KENNETH A. BREWER, and R. L. CARSTENS

IN CHAPTER FOUR Eberts and Sismondo make a number of points about policy-related research that are pertinent to and readily illustrated by the case studies in transportation discussed in this chapter. First, they note the interplay of classes of research; the case studies outlined on the following pages display how and what they define as descriptive, basic, and proactive research interconnect.

Second, they note that sound policy research must meet all criteria established for all other social science; policy research ultimately has the same goals of knowledge as other scientific enterprise and it achieves that goal with the same scientific method. The studies described in this chapter aspire to that scientific method and to that goal of knowledge. Indeed, a significant objective of this chapter is to provide through these case studies pathways to creating sound methodological techniques and information concerning alternative measurement and analysis concepts in pursuing such research.

Third, Eberts and Sismondo state that while the methods and goals of policy research are the same as in all scientific research, policy research may be more demanding, in that it requires ingenuity and

R. O. RICHARDS is Associate Professor of Sociology, Iowa State University.

K. A. BREWER is Professor of Civil Engineering, Iowa State University.

R. L. CARSTENS is Professor of Civil Engineering, Iowa State University.

The authors acknowledge the support provided by the U.S. Department of Transportation Contract Number DOT-OS-30106. Administrative support of the Engineering Research Institute and the Sciences and Humanities Research Institute is also acknowledged. Findings and implications drawn are solely those of the authors and are not meant to convey or imply approval by the U.S. Department of Transportation.

rigor to delineate conceptual relationships within the confines of real world situations. These transportation case studies will exhibit the constraints, the methodological improvisations, and the compromises to which the authors refer, while deriving research that will meet the rigorous standards both of academia and of policy planners.

Finally, Eberts and Sismondo criticize "colleagues . . . quite reluctant to engage in the policy research process on the basis that, we do not yet know enough to do an adequate job of it . . . . Our position is that by becoming involved we will learn more and faster than in any other way." Certainly the authors of this chapter have learned much in the conduct of the research to be described, and others should find the following description of research strategies instructive for their own purposes.

RESEARCH ISSUE I: CHALLENGES IN CONCEPT FORMATION.

Three related but independent research enterprises are described. The first illustrates several characteristics of policy research resulting from the presence of both generality and specificity in the statement of policy goals, which thus demands considerable ability to establish basic assumptions and definitional parameters on the one hand, while dictating certain design constraints and goal properties on the other.

In this case, the research issue in its policy context was: "What is, and what could be, the role of transportation in articulating the relationship between rural communities and their hinterlands in the course of rural regional economic development?" [2]. Obviously, researchers addressing such long-range policy issues must take an equivalently long-range perspective upon the parameters of their research. Certainly the level of generality—and perhaps ambiguity—in this research mandate is not unfamiliar to many readers. In approaching this problem, as engineers we cannot help but view our experience as analogous to surveying and constructing a highway over unknown terrain within a fixed budget of time and money. Hopefully, others will find insight and solace from review of problems the researchers faced along the way.

Problems in concept formation ranged from the macrodevelopmental issue of the role of transportation in rural regional growth to operationalization of measurements. In the case of the first issue, literature and common sense dictated the assumption that transportation would not be considered a "first cause" of regional economic development; it is a necessary but not a sufficient cause of such development. Therefore, the role of transportation has to be conceptualized within the context of given levels of existing economic development and the likelihood of future capital expenditures for industrial development in the regions under study.

Furthermore, it was assumed that trends historically evident in the development and distribution of socioeconomic growth characteristics could, within limits, be projected into the future.

In this sense, the development of transportation is appropriately seen as a reflexive accompaniment to economic growth. Thus the retionship between the growth and distribution of transportation facilities relative to that between the growth and distribution of socioeconomic facilities became the operational conceptualization of the original research issue.

An obvious major conceptual question is: What is a rural region? Economists and sociologists have historically viewed rural areas as social systems (e.g., as market areas in the former case, and as ecological communities in the latter). Certainly such concepts as central place theory posit highly structured, systematic relationships within a hierarchy of population centers and their hinterlands [1]. In contrast, students of political science and public administration are increasingly interested in the idea of regional policies. The problem is that although the spatial boundaries delineated by these various conceptual models of regions overlap, they do not describe the same areas. What definition of "region" is most appropriate for research involving transportation as a regional growth factor? In this case, researchers elected to study regions as designated by state officials within which state long-range planning is to be coordinated.

Delineation of these planning regions represented an amalgam of formal research findings (primarily Functional Economic Area Analysis) [5] and practical political considerations; thus the regions vary widely in degree of conformity to central place theories and other academic approaches to region specification. Nine such rural regions were selected for study (see Fig. 7.1).

Measurement tools must be developed for both transportation and socioeconomic indices encompassing both growth and distribution of these phenomena. Cursory knowledge of major person and commodity movement within the study regions provides an indication of categories of transportation modes that must be inventoried, including the highway system, truck service, rail mileage, rail boarding opportunities, bus boarding opportunities, and airport service.

Identifying Regional Transportation Characteristics. The research question required investigating not only the current role of transportation but also the role of transportation in future development. Thus the object of gathering both capacity and usage information is to achieve an adequate measure of total regional transportation

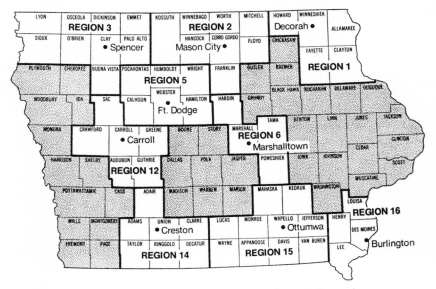

Fig. 7.1. Map of Iowa indicating the nine study regions.

potential; capacity information alone may overestimate potential use because qualitative aspects of opportunity for use cannot be reflected in such measures; however, usage information may underestimate capacity, given changes in socioeconomic factors.

The highway system measure included system investment, traffic volume (use), mesh density of network, and relative capability to carry traffic. Volume can be estimated from existing origin and destination data; highway sufficiency data are obtainable from previous studies, which permitted calculation of structural, service, and safety factors of highway surface relative to road mileage and number of lanes.

Truck service is difficult to assess, given the paucity of reliable and appropriate data. A partial solution is to describe truck service in terms of the number of terminals serving each community within the study regions and the number of trucking companies serving each of those terminals as reported in available directories.

The railroad mileage index should be constructed to account not only for amount of trackage as observable from county maps, but also to reflect the quality of service of rail lines in terms of interstate versus intrastate service and major versus minor route structure in terms of access to mainline or local routes. Rail passenger movement can be estimated by available schedule and passenger volume data to provide a weighted rail boarding opportunity index.

Similarly, a weekly bus boarding opportunities index can be constructed from available schedule information. Airport service can be measured in terms of level of available service and runway, lighting, and navigation aid equipment.

Having compiled the above data by transportation mode, an aggregate transportation index can be calculated to indicate the relative total potential transportation activity of any one region in relation to any other. The formulamatic statement of that aggregate transportation index requires derivation of some criteria for weighting the relative significance of the several modes of person and freight movement. Those criteria were derived largely from data gathered by the researchers through mailed survey instruments to businesses and industries employing twenty or more workers within a cross section of the study regions. Firms were asked to approximate the proportion of total shipping and receiving volume by mode and to indicate person/business travel also by mode. National transportation survey data on the relative use of each mode were also considered. Transportation of persons was weighted equally with transportation of goods and commodities.

Thus development of constituent parts of a socioeconomic measurement tool of the same form as the Aggregated Transportation Index (ATI) involves a methodological triangulation between constraints introduced by problems in concept definition and operationalizing, research design requirements, and limitations in secondary data. Resulting estimations of appropriate model weighting for the ATI were carefully reviewed and revised on the basis of the expertise of members of the research team and an informal sample of others knowledgeable about rural transportation activity.

Identifying Regional Socioeconomic Characteristics. The description of transportation characteristics is incomplete without a parallel description of socioeconomic characteristics. The efficacy and potential of transportation systems is obviously related to the society it is intended to serve. To that end, census data can be used to describe population distribution as well as employment data reflecting commercial, industrial, and professional development. As another indicator of economic development, census data also provide differential income level data by county. Because transportation plays a crucial role in delivery of institutional services—particularly in rural areas—the distribution and level of development of hospitals and high schools must be investigated. Data, such as number of specialized services and hospital beds in the case of hospitals and number of curriculum units in the case of education, can be used to indicate the quality of services available.

Measuring the Relationship between Transportation and Socioeconomic Characteristics. Having achieved indices of both transportation and socioeconomic development, the problem becomes one of demonstrating the relationship between the two. How does one compare apples and oranges; how does one relate route structures to number of hospital beds? An appropriate tool employed in this research is regression analysis, employing the linear model achievable through rank-size analysis. This approach is based upon the "law" of the "K distribution," which states that the plotting of rank by size of given attributes describes a straight line when graphed on a log-log scale [7]. Thus the beta values of equations plotting both transportation and socioeconomic characteristics by region indicate degree of centrality about the designated growth center (if it is the largest community in the region); changes in the alpha intercept value within any region over time reflect overall growth or decline in terms of the measured attribute. Thus both the development and distribution of transportation as measured by the ATI can be quantitatively compared with the growth and distribution of population, employment by occupational category, distribution of institutions, and the like, through examination of the regression equations. This tool should prove useful in a variety of research contexts where subunits within the study unit (e.g., counties within regions, departments within organizations) can be rank ordered on the properties to be measured, but the measured attributes have an unknown interval scale relationship to one another.

Furthermore, on the basis of regression analysis of regional transportation and socioeconomic growth and distribution patterns, regions can be typed by degree of development and centrality (see Fig. 7.2). Thus regions may be identified which have a mature agricultural and industrial economic mix and an equivalent transportation system. Within this category, two subtypes can be discerned: (1) regions with strong centralization of socioeconomic and transportation patterns around the region's designated growth center and (2) "localized" regions, in which the growth center evinces no such relationships with the hinterlands.

Regions that are more rural can also be classified into two subtypes. First are those that offer evidence for actual or potential transition to the mixed agricultural-industrial development type; there may as yet be no one dominant central place or several contending communities for that role. Correspondingly, transportation networks may not display as fine a mesh as in more urban regions and may not focus upon one community. Whether such regions will move toward greater industrialization and greater transportation network maturity or will retain their present character indefinitely will depend upon

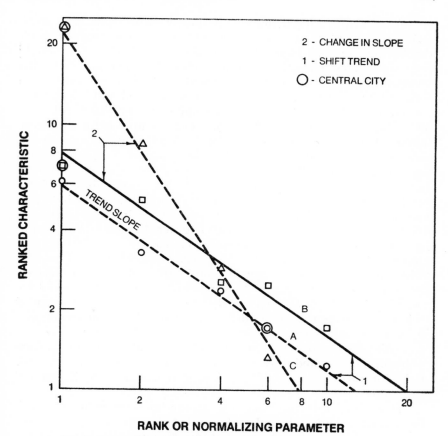

Fig. 7.2.   Rank-size analysis concept.

external socioeconomic trends and the intervention of the planning process. The second subtype of the more rural regions conforms to the stereotype of the "stranded" rural region of rapidly depleting population, marginal agricultural economy, and a low level of transportation service.

Functional Typologies for Regional Planning. These particular four classes of rural regions can be identified in many regions of America and are probably the predominant forms of regionality in the upper Midwest. Through the regression technique, supplemented with other socioeconomic analyses, other types might be isolated or the four types discussed here might be further subdivided. The main point is that once a region can be identified as to type, particular planning alternatives may become applicable.

For example, capital intensive improvements emphasizing large-scale "hardware" priorities are appropriate for fostering economic development through regional industrial growth. Such policies would have the greatest potential in rural transitional regions, which offer "take-off" resources for such development, and in mature centralized regions where industrial growth is to be maintained and advanced.

On the other hand, the hardware approach may have little pay-off in the more rural stranded regions or in the localized agricultural-industrial mixed regions. In the former case transportation investment unaccompanied by industrial growth may result in "roads starting nowhere and ending nowhere." In the latter case, the historical lack of interdependence between central place and hinterland for development may cancel growth benefits from capital intensive transportation development, which posits regionwide interdependence in development. This does not mean that stranded and localized regions require no attention from transportation planners. It does suggest, however, that planners consider the specific needs of such regions; for quite different reasons "software"-emphasizing delivery of services should receive first priority in both types of regions. This should enhance quality of life throughout the region in the case of stranded regions, and make the social advantages of the dominant community in localized regions more accessible to hinterland residents.

This description of conceptualization and operationalization problems incurred and dealt with in the course of one policy research study illustrates a number of responses to points made by Eberts and Sismondo.

First, descriptive and basic research are interdependent; although the research mandate includes an explicit descriptive aspect (assessment of regional socioeconomic and transportation attributes), designation of fundamental research requirements such as reporting categories is dependent upon rigorous theoretical and analytical formulations.

Second, throughout the conceptualization process, important criteria in decisions concerning concept development and operationalizing are the empirical validity and practical utility of those decisions for planners. For example, the definition of "region" employed only approximates academic definitions at best, but it is the only definition meaningful in the administration of planning. Also, it is a definition that assumes the planning process creates regional hegemony.

Third, this conceptualization process illustrates the demands and constraints placed upon research design, and ultimately variable measurement, by policy research. Since the ultimate goal of such research is to relate transportation to the change process of economic development, a longitudinal analysis of transportation in relation to socioeconomic development is required. As a result, although measurement needs could be more precisely met through primary data-gathering instruments in some cases, the resulting data would not be comparable with available historical data. Thus the necessity arises of utilizing secondary data and accepting all the problems attendant upon them. Often, available data are ambiguous, not totally appropriate, or incomplete. Nonetheless, there is no other choice, given the research design derived from the policy goals.

Although the research design demands of policy-related research may necessarily result in certain compromises in normative or conventional research methods, it may also require—and inspire—innovation and solution to methodological problems that simply might be avoided in "pure" basic research. The regression and typological method produced by this research are outcomes fruitful for both applied and basic research which are the direct outgrowth of an attempt to grapple with the breadth and scope of the policy research goal.

RESEARCH ISSUE II: SURVEYING ATTITUDES AS POLICY INPUTS. Policy-related research may sometimes identify new policy issues, thereby suggesting new directions further research should take; the second case study illustrates such research [2]. Upon completion of the research described above, both the planning agency for which it was performed and the researchers recognized that the attitudes and behavior of rural residents will play an important role in determining the success of future planning, not only for regional development but also in assuring compliance with future planning to conserve transportation energy. Thus completion of the initial study permitted the researchers to contribute to the further articulation of transportation policy needs and the information necessary to meet those needs.

This second case study illustrates a relatively inexpensive means for gathering attitude and behavior information from a large sample survey and the use of specific devices to elicit data from that sample for developing models of policy alternatives. The study describes the use of mail surveys among a sample of 7,086 residents of the regions studied in the earlier research.

This research effort well illumines the interplay of theoretically grounded "basic" research with "descriptive" efforts. The researchers believe that research addressing itself to advancing the frontiers of academic knowledge can often also be the research producing the most sensitive inputs for policy formulation.

Three theoretical issues are evident in the policy needs of this research. First, are the travel patterns of rural region residents consistent with those postulated by locational analysis and central place theory? These approaches posit a hierarchy of communities providing specific services to the area, attracting travel from their hinterlands. What impact does regional centralization and level of development of socioeconomic and transportation facilities, as identified in the earlier study, play in determining travel patterns and unmet transportation demand?

The second theoretical issue is directly occasioned by inadequacies of previous studies assessing public response to planned changes in transportation. To be blunt, asking: "If a bus came to your door, would you use it?"—or variations on that question—simply will not suffice. Various decision-making theories suggest that responses to that question are meaningless unless the respondent simultaneously is provided an indication of possible trade-offs between the many fuel conservation alternatives other than increased public transit. To meet this need, the "paired choice technique" was utilized to structure trade-offs between different dimensions of fuel policies [6]: supply constraint through rationing or pricing, use constraint through change in travel patterns, and so forth.

The third theoretical issue also addresses itself to the kinds of behavioral adjustments people may make in response to a change in fuel supply. Previous research has very well established two common-sense findings about public reaction to the fuel crisis. First, the public is not eager to "bite the bullet" by accepting the policy alternatives of very increased pricing or rationing. Second, people have made minimal adjustments to existing changes in fuel sales. If the sciences to which basic research contributes are truly cumulative, and if planners are to learn any more about the dynamics of public behavior and attitudes, the research design will have to permit fairly sophisticated and complex attitude measurement based upon reasonably subtle hypotheses out of the attitude-formation and decision-making literature.

The researchers designed their data analysis in such a way that these theoretical issues provided guidance for identifying contributions to regional transportation planning. For example, in dealing with the issue of regional travel patterns, questions were constructed and analyzed in such a manner that researchers could observe variations by trip purpose and salience (working, major and minor health service needs, major and minor retail shopping needs, etc.). Deviations detected in the classic hierarchical travel patterns permitted the researchers to delineate different transportation solutions appropriate to different "layers" in the travel hierarchy. Thus this theory provided guidelines for recommendations to meet transportation needs in the local rural community, the state planning region, the state, and multistate regions.

The "paired choice" technique of policy preference identification was coupled with an independent analysis of policy preferences related to energy-conserving behavior, attitudes about the shortage, and situational characteristics (e.g., age, income, car ownership). These analyses revealed patterns that permitted the researchers to identify factors salient in determining preferred policies. More importantly, these analyses indicated that transportation consumers were extremely aware of and responsive to the differential impacts of conservation practices in terms of their personal situation. Thus the young preferred different conservation policies than the aged.

Similarly, analysis of existing consumption practices indicated a a strong sensitivity to the transportation situation of the individual and a tendency for attitudes directly related to personal economic consequences of fuel savings, rather than ideology and beliefs, to be related to fuel savings. This finding regarding energy conservation preferences and practices permitted the researchers to designate more specifically the differential needs of various target groups of rural transportation consumers and to identify the kinds of concerns planners must address in garnering public support for fuel-conserving policies.

Innovations in Mailed Survey Techniques to Meet Policy Needs. This second case study illustrates another facet of research design for policy research not explicitly addressed by Eberts and Sismondo. Planners and other sponsors of research are becoming more assertive in demanding greater "bang for the buck" from their grants and contracts. This demand has two aspects: first, a desire for research results with specific payoff for policy development and second, a desire for more favorable cost/benefit ratios in the research process. The derivation of theoretical perspectives for investigation of the policy questions described above shows that the first of these demands can be met without sacrifice of academic integrity; indeed, the policy goals enhanced study of the theoretical questions.

In response to the demand for more efficient data gathering, the researchers sought an alternative to the highly expensive interview survey technique. (There was also a certain irony, not unrecognized among rural respondents, in sending fleets of single-occupancy cars to the far-flung corners of the state to ask people how they were conserving gas.) The possibility of mailed surveys was carefully considered before that choice was finally made. Despite the obvious cost advantage, such studies have traditionally been plagued by low response rates. Because these data were to be used in policy modeling, it was most desirable to obtain a high response rate from the sample chosen; a refusal rate, which represented the majority of the sample (not uncommon in mailed questionnaires) might represent sample bias intolerable for recommending policy alternatives purportedly applicable to a wide spectrum of society.

The technique utilized for this research involved careful and systematic organization of instrument format and item construction, as well as a program of follow-ups which minimized costs while expanding the likelihood of response.

A systematic procedure for stimulating response from large samples of the general public developed by Dillman [4] was used in this study. This procedure incorporates a variety of techniques dealing with the instrument format, item construction and ordering, and the content and formats for the initial cover and subsequent follow-up letters. These techniques have been tested by Dillman for their effect upon response rates.

Techniques used to enhance return and insure quality data centered upon a rational flow of thought, from the soliciting of participation in the cover letter to ordering of the items, and a stress upon personal identification with the goals of the research and the cooperation of the respondents. Every attempt affordable was made to avoid the stigma of a form letter. (For example, all cover letters directly addressed the specific family of each sample household and were signed individually by one of the project directors.) These measures were taken in the context of an instrument physically designed to maximize readability while simultaneously minimizing costs.

All the items to be surveyed could not be included in a single instrument without creating an impractical burden on each respondent. Therefore, the sample was divided into three equal portions; separate instruments were constructed for each subsample, with some overlapping items and common socioeconomic status questions.

A crucial feature of this survey method is the generating of waves of follow-up contacts with nonrespondents. A "thank you–reminder" postcard was sent one week after the initial mailing; three weeks later a letter and replacement questionnaire were mailed. Telephone calls were made to remaining respondents.

The combined effect of carefully orchestrated questionnaire construction, personalized soliciting of participation, and exhaustive follow-ups rewarded the researchers with a total response rate exceeding 70 percent at an estimated direct cost of $1.13 per useable instrument. A more detailed description of the use of the mailed survey technique applied to this project appears elsewhere [3].

This project illustrates the points made by Eberts and Sismondo cited earlier about several characteristics of policy research. First, the conceptual apparatus for seeking answers to policy questions displays the interplay between pure and applied research. Second, adherence to established canons of research procedures is apparent in the sampling, instrument construction, and data analysis phases of the research. Third, the demand for innovation in scientific methods for the conduct of policy research, especially when that research is to explore the parameters of policy needs, is illustrated in the use of the mailed survey instrument. This innovative thrust in meeting policy research goals is a particular feature of the third project to be described.

RESEARCH ISSUE III: INNOVATIVE RESEARCH TOOLS FOR FOR POLICY NEEDS. The third case study further illustrates how research design innovation can produce a solution to policy research needs while simultaneously addressing basic research needs.

In the course of performing the two projects described above, the researchers were attracted by the problem of eliciting responses to hypothetical situations (How will you adjust your travel patterns to future fuel scarcity?), given the absence of adequate information by which respondents can evaluate the consequences of their decisions.

The problem therefore becomes one of providing such information for respondents through a simulation of "real world" consequences that might follow from their conservation choices in terms of impact upon household financial and time budgets and social interaction. The approach taken captures the spirit of proactive research as described by Eberts and Sismondo:

> It is based on the concept of simulation. . . . It attempts to foresee problems policymakers will face and forewarn them. . . . it focuses on symptoms and causes of people's needs as well as on the needs themselves. It seeks to uncover the multiple and circular causation patterns of such needs, enabling policymakers to better understand them and to adjust their policies in such ways as to counteract deficiencies most effectively.

To achieve a research design appropriate to those tasks, the researchers are attempting to structure a "decision tree" that will provide a tracing of the "symptoms and causes of people's needs" as they move toward adjusting to decreased fuel supplies. To a large degree, the proposed process will represent a substantial improvement in validity over responses to items such as one cited earlier: "If a bus came to your door, would you use it?" The thrust of this question can be inserted into the decision tree model to illustrate how the process would result in more realistic answers—answers therefore of much enhanced utility to planners.

Simulation Procedures. The computer will be used to assist respondents in choosing between energy conservation alternatives to their present travel behavior by indicating the consequences of any alternative choice. These consequences will represent constraints in family money, time, and interaction budgets determined within the parameters of the respondents' resources and social needs. The degree of stricture in alternatives presented may be increased through several rounds of the decision-making process. Thus the researchers may simultaneously enhance the "reality quotient" of the attitude-tapping process and introduce greater precision in the prediction of behavioral responses to energy conservation practices varying in kind and degree.

One of the most important features of the simulation will be its data-gathering properties. As the respondent makes choices, ranks alternatives, and reorders priorities, the simulation will note and record the information. For the researcher, the results will resemble a map of the respondent's progress through the simulated world of shrinking transportation resources.[1]

The use of the computer in providing feedback, whereby respondents may evaluate realistic consequences of their responses to decreasing levels of fuel supply and transportation resources, is analogous to the logic of interactive computer games. Thus the several aspects of this design have been utilized independently of one another in previous work. Interactive computer simulation techniques have been used in the field via telephone-computer coupling to study public response to mass transit, but without use of the decision tree logic. The decision tree–simulation logic has been used without a computer. And, as pointed out above, the logic of the method derives from gaming, which is usually a heuristic device rather than a research tool. The social/psychological literature on attitude and attitude change as well as decision making provides ample theoretical guidance for structuring the decision tree and interpreting the resulting data. The innovative contribution of this research design is that it represents a comprehensive synthesis of these diverse elements to meet particular research goals.

The results of this research should provide policy planners with high-quality data whereby they may predict with greater precision public responses to alternative fuel conservation plans within various sectors of the population as it is sampled. For example, questions such as: At what point will lower middle class suburbanites turn to public transit? need not be given shot-in-the-dark answers.

CONCLUSION. There is one further point about the three case studies that policy researchers may wish to consider. Although the cases

1. This paragraph describing the computer decision tree format is slightly revised from a personal memo by Professor William F. Woodman, Department of Sociology, Iowa State University.

cited were interrelated in subject matter, and Case II was a direct outgrowth of Case I, each independently illustrates various aspects of the policy research process touched upon by Eberts and Sismondo. When viewed collectively, these projects represent common themes the authors believe will become increasingly prevalent in policy research of the future. In each case, the policy problem has been broad in scope; the theoretical perspectives employed have reached across diverse professions, from engineering to social psychology; the methodology has been eclectic; and the data analysis highly synergistic.

For better or for worse, the researchers are convinced that the diversity of perspectives, experiences, and orientations brought to bear on policy problems affords a distinct advantage; few regional development problems can be neatly categorized as economic, sociological, or engineering problems. Through extensive interaction and collaboration, the interdisciplinary approach has stimulated an integrated approach to generating research designs to meet the myriad challenges in transportation planning for regional development.

REFERENCES

1. Berry, Brian J. L. 1967. *Geography of Market Centers and Retail Distribution*. Englewood Cliffs, N.J.: Prentice-Hall.
2. Brewer, K. A., R. O. Richards, R. L. Carstens, S. L. Ring, M. L. Millett, Jr., W. H. Thompson, C. E. Dare, and B. D. Young. 1974. *Integrated Analysis of Small Cities' Intercity Transportation to Facilitate the Achievement of Regional Urban Goals*. Washington, D.C.: U.S. Department of Transportation.
3. Brewer, K. A., R. O. Richards, D. L. Butler, and B. D. Young. 1976. Mail survey design to acquire policy model inputs. Proc. 6th Annu. Pittsburgh Conf. on Simulation and Modeling.
4. Dillman, D. A. 1972. Increasing mail questionnaire response in large samples of the general public. *Public Opin. Quart.* 36:254–57.
5. State of Iowa Office of Planning and Programming. 1967. *A Regional Delineation for the State of Iowa*. Des Moines: Office of Planning and Programming.
6. Thurstone, L. L. 1959. *The Measurement of Values*. Chicago: Univ. of Chicago Press.
7. Zahavi, Y. 1970. Introducing the idea of the "K Distribution" to transportation patterns. *Highway Res. Rec.* 322.

CHAPTER EIGHT

LAND USE RESEARCH: A WORKSHOP REPORT

LAWRENCE W. LIBBY and RONALD L. SHELTON

THIS WORKSHOP SESSION was approached as an opportunity to share preferences and biases among generators and users of land use research. Participants were asked to resist the temptation to report specific results in detail. Perhaps by design of the conference organizers, participants were almost evenly split between university researchers and land use policy "practitioners" with a need for land use information. The latter group included staffs of regional planning agencies in the north central states, councils of governments, state planning offices, and Title V research coordinators.

Workshop leaders established the context for the ensuing discussion with brief opening comments. The conclusions that emerged from the discussion were summarized verbally for the full conference and are also presented here.

ISSUES IN RESEARCH STRATEGY AND METHODS. The research task in land use appears to have at least two major dimensions. The first involves the immediate, the short run, the "little picture." Policy choices *are* being made and hopefully better decisions may result from choices made with knowledge of consequences. There appears to be a substantial research task here in helping improve the process of constructing rules for public choice in land use. The second major category concerns the longer-run conceptual parameters

LAWRENCE W. LIBBY is Associate Professor of Agricultural Economics and Resource Development, Michigan State University.

RONALD L. SHELTON is Associate Professor of Resource Development, Michigan State University.

This chapter is a report on one of the five conference workshops. Major contributions by Dr. Raymond Vlasin, Chairman of the Department of Resource Development, Michigan State University, are gratefully acknowledged.

of land and water use. Researchers agree that we must have some better notion of where we are headed as a society before we tamper with the business of day-to-day decisions. These short-run choices, each rational and acceptable in itself, may lead to major dead ends for the human race. Economist-philosopher Heilbroner has said as much [2]. Both types of research are legitimate and critical, yet are often competing for scarce resources of research energy, time and dollars.

Workshop participants acknowledged that the chances for significant methodological breakthroughs in land use research during a two-hour workshop are pretty slim. But incrementalists as a breed of researchers or policymakers, are resigned to the fact that changes come in small adjustments—not major leaps, and insights that are truly significant in altering the course of public policy do come in small doses. Certainly, opportunities exist for major innovation in the technology of land use research—in data collection and processing. The crunch comes in the interpretation and weighing of that information by different political groups and subsequent action through mechanisms for public choice.

Researchers who focus on longer-run concerns are confronted with the need to integrate land use policy with policies pertaining to environmental quality, energy, resources and materials, food, population, growth, and development. What conceptual basis is there for treating them as a whole, and how might they be translated and implemented for policy and planning purposes? More particularly, what constraints do these longer-run considerations place on public choice?

The task for effective land use research was discussed in the following three categories, with varying perceptions among workshop participants:

1. Research *organization*. Applied land use research is not disciplinary. It is not even a well-defined set of issues. Varying skills and perspectives must be brought together in some fashion for usable research results. The question is—*how?*

2. Research *method*. Conceptual models encourage an efficient allocation of effort in dealing with complex researchable issues. Discussion of analytical constructs employed by researchers participating in the workshop was useful.

3. Most important researchable *issues*. These vary by time and place. Priorities are not stable.

Research Organization. On the matter of organization, the multidisciplinary university department is a research unit with apparently important advantages. The Department of Resource Development

(R.D.) at Michigan State University is such a department, and is offered here only as an example of this organizational approach. The full-time faculty includes resource economists, two lawyers, a hydrologist, three community development specialists, and several faculty members who deal with natural resource policy. Liberal use of joint appointments for R.D. faculty and for individuals with primary assignments in other departments has linked R.D. with departments of Agricultural Economics, Urban Planning, Forestry, Parks and Recreation, Fisheries and Wildlife, Human Ecology, Engineering, and even the College of Human Medicine. The structure and opportunity for multidisciplinary research are substantial. In addition, many of the faculty members have research/extension appointments, which both encourage problem-oriented research and facilitate distribution of results. There is just no substitute for the "real world" scrutiny of research methods, assumptions, and results that can be achieved by a link to the extension system.

An impressive roster of research disciplines does not assure effective problem-oriented research, but it is a good start. The chances for integrating the essential dimensions of research on land use problems would seem greater in a multidisciplinary department than in other organizational models we might consider. The multidisciplinary research team model has proved extremely successful when researchers can get released time from other university duties to concentrate their efforts for relatively short periods on a particular problem. Each participant must bring a special skill or disciplinary focus to the problem-solving activity. Research administration is critical in any such project to assure that the individual contributions add up to something. Professors Glenn Johnson and E. Rossmiller at Michigan State University have demonstrated the viability of this project model in their direction of major studies of agricultural development in Nigeria and Korea. Other examples could be noted from several of the north central states.

Research Method. Perhaps the most important land use research at this time falls into two categories: (1) diagnostic analysis of the decision process for particular areas of policy and (2) observation of institutional performance. Both are admittedly concerned with the "little picture" involving attempts by people with honest value differences to achieve some measure of control over their own lives. Both assume few if any absolutes, and both assume that all land use information has distributive implications. These are suggested in the context of generating inputs for the policy process.

The first category involves the study of institutional factors that influence and in some cases *determine* the outputs of a particular policy process. This research is at least partly descriptive. It is concerned with information flows, roles played by various participants in the system, their political access, apparent incentives, and opportunity for exercise of policy discretion. Studies in this category are concerned with what seems to happen in the policy process and why. Chapter 4 presents part of a diagnostic framework relating parts of a decision system. Political scientist Easton has presented a similar model, with emphasis on the screening mechanisms in public policy [1]. Ogden, of the University of Colorado, has contributed the useful notion of the political "power cluster" [3]. All these are methods of organizing observations about how policy options are generated, put on an agenda, and processed through a decision system. It is a critical type of policy research, geared to understanding real choices.

An example might be useful. A statewide comprehensive land use planning bill was proposed in Michigan in 1975. A complex mix of interest groups, state agencies, and local authorities is involved. *Any* new set of public rules for land use will shuffle the allocation of power among these participants. Some have better access to the key decision points than others. In this case, battle for authority among several state agencies may have more influence on the success of the proposal and ultimately the success of the planning system than any set of land use data we can identify. We can fret about the apparent irrationality of the system, but it just may be that each participant is perfectly rational, given the information and perceived consequences available.

Studies of institutional performance (the second type noted above) are concerned with the *implications* of different rules for guiding human actions with respect to land use. It seems to us that there is very little new under the sun in the list of techniques of land use control. The aspect we do not know much about is how these different rules actually affect use of resources, who bears the cost, and who gets the benefit.

The attempt to influence land use behavior by adjusting the tax bill of the owner is the prime example in this category. A remarkable variety of state programs preserve open land by lowering owners' taxes in various ways. There is little doubt that the tax load is redistributed, but these programs are seldom sold as income transfers. The impact on resource use is far less clear. Experiences with these programs now should be sufficient to permit empirical observation of performance under alternative sets of circumstances. For example, what difference does it make if a *full* rebate of taxes, plus interest, is required of the farmer who develops land that is already receiving special tax treatment for agriculture, as opposed to a *five-year rollback* of taxes avoided by such a program? What difference in land use results if farmers themselves initiate inclusion of land under a special tax program rather than giving that authority to a unit of government? These observations then become inputs in building new institutions elsewhere. In Michigan a unique open-space tax law permits eligible and interested farmers to receive a credit on state income tax for the amount by which their property tax bill exceeds 7 percent of household income. It is an intriguing law, but we have virtually no guesses on what will happen. We have little idea of cost to the public treasury, or incidence of that cost. More than that, we have little insight on the likely effect on land use.

As another example, what land use differences may be attributed to the fact that zoning is accomplished by townships rather than counties, or that counties may overrule township authority rather than vice versa? There are other such examples. To many, these questions of institutional performance seem hopelessly shortsighted and piecemeal. Perhaps they are, but one could argue that our policy process is basically of that character. Choices *are* being made constantly. Seldom do we have the luxury of careful contemplation of long-run possibilities. And even when we do, the problem of reconciling possible futures with present realities is handled very differently by different groups of people. Their judgment is usually influenced by the costs they are asked to bear *today* to avoid the possibility of far greater costs to all people in the future. There is nothing irrational about that. The important challenge, it seems to us, is to recognize the impact distribution implicit in land use rule changes and build that recognition into the process of forming institutions.

Research Issues. The research agenda in land use is virtually infinite. But in the spirit of doing something within the very real constraints of imperfect information and imperfect researchers, a number of key issues related to land use planning may be identified for priority attention.[1] Because of the relatively limited attention to rural land use planning as a guide to local decision making in the past, little serious research has been done at this level. Research has been concentrated mainly on urban area problems and on rural-urban transition problems. Notable exceptions are the research on land tenure and on the impacts of specific public projects such as highways and reservoirs. Issues cited here relate to planning in nonmetropolitan areas.

CHANGING ATTITUDES, VALUES, AND ETHICS AMONG "USERS" OF LAND. Changes are occurring in our attitudes about land resources and the way in which these resources are now used. We do not have clear

1. These issues were articulated by Dr. Raymond Vlasin, chairman, Department of Resource Development, Michigan State University. Editorial license has been exercised (cautiously) by the authors.

information on how and at what pace these attitudes are changing, what future changes are likely, how these changes differ among population groups, and the implications of these changes for the content and procedures in land use planning.

FORCES AFFECTING CONVERSION OF LAND FROM AGRICULTURE TO OTHER USES. Many economic and political forces affect the use of availability of land for agricultural purposes. They include inflation; the shifting of investment capital from other forms of investment to the best risk of all—rural land; migration of families to the country out of metropolitan areas; demands for seasonal and second homes; and increasingly critical demands for sites for urban services, such as solid and liquid waste disposal. These and other forces affect changes in ownership, size of holdings, and the supply schedule for land in production. We need better documentation of these forces and information on possible modification or augmentation to provide improved land resource planning.

SHIFTS IN THE ALLOCATION OF LAND RIGHTS BETWEEN OWNER AND SOME LEVEL OF GOVERNMENT. We are aware that state and local governments are reclaiming more of the discretion in how land will be used. The redistribution of land is coming about through various court tests of the bounds of ownership as defined in statute, weighed against constitutional safeguards. We need to study the *patterns* of this redistribution and the implications for resource use. Land use planning practice will clearly be affected.

SHIFTS AMONG ALTERNATIVE LEVELS OF GOVERNMENTAL ACTIONS WITH RESPECT TO LAND. There is considerable evidence that some of the authority for planning and for land use control previously retained at local governmental levels has been either poorly exercised or has proved inadequate to handle the scope or scale of the problems with which local governments must deal. Some of this authority has been shifting upward from municipalities and townships to counties, multicounty regions, and states to internalize the external impacts of local choices. Again, we need clear information on the nature and extent of these shifts, the purposes for which the shifts occurred, and the consequences or outcomes. Research here should explore the alternatives possible in the distribution of public authority in land use planning and control and should evaluate actual circumstances, through case analyses, where such distribution of public authority has operated.

SHARED RESPONSIBILITIES, NEW CONCEPTS, AND NEW ROLES. As various land use problems are evaluated, it becomes clear that some lend themselves to local management, some require multijurisdictional regional approaches, and some clearly are statewide matters and require corresponding state-level actions. In many instances *simultaneous* actions are required by two or more levels of government. Research could focus on instances in which shared responsibility and authority for land use planning and guidance has been attempted, and other instances in which sharing would be uniquely appropriate.

OPPORTUNITIES AND APPROACHES TO INTERGOVERNMENTAL COOPERATION. Experience has shown possible efficiencies and economies from intergovernmental cooperation in providing public services. For example, water supply, waste treatment, and police and fire protection arrangements have been forged among communities or counties with significant advantage to all parties. There are opportunities for economies in intergovernmental arrangements for resource inventory, land use problem analysis, land use planning, land use monitoring, and implementation of land use controls. We need further evaluations of the performance of these arrangements and the appropriateness of adopting them in other jurisdictions.

GOALS AND PROCESSES OF GOAL FORMATION DIRECTLY APPLICABLE TO LAND USE PLANNING. Clearly, land use planning is not an end in itself but is a means to some end. There is seldom consensus about what goals are appropriate. Planning must be done with awareness of the goal dispersion, and implications of these goals must be set for the selection of planning strategy and instruments of control. We need better documentation of the goal forming and articulating processes, perhaps with case studies of successful efforts.

DEVELOPMENT OF FEDERAL AND STATE GUIDELINES FOR LAND USE PLANNING. While counties, communities, and regional units likely will play the major roles in land use planning, they must neither inadvertently violate federal and state laws nor counter the policies emanating from them. Therefore, it is imperative that clear principles and guidelines be developed that help regional county and community planning units. These principles and guidelines might cover resource inventory systems to be used, comparability and additivity of plans, approaches to land use designation, and identification of land uses of regional, state, or national interest. They also might involve guidelines for designation of critical areas, unique and essential agricultural areas, and areas of multijurisdictional concern.

OPPORTUNITIES FOR INTEGRATING LAND USE PLANNING WITH LOCAL AND AREA DEVELOPMENT. Local agricultural production opportunities and sound local agribusiness are important to stability or growth of non-metropolitan communities. In times of economic stress, agricultural production and agribusiness opportunities serve to diversify the employment base and income opportunities of communities, regions, and states. Specific research on opportunities for integrating land use planning and local area development efforts could help document the economic relevance of agriculture as an input to the planning process.

LOCAL LAND PLANNING PROCEDURES. A major barrier to effective land use planning at any level is often the absence of a common vocabulary between planners and "plannees." People have problems, planners have procedures. Yet, successful planning requires local support that can come only through better understanding of the planning procedures and their implications for people. The procedures related to articulation of community preferences are particularly critical. Community leaders and citizens do not always have perfect agreement on key variables—both must be involved. Again, research in this area may be largely documentation (success stories and failures) to gain better insight into performance and help build better institutions.

INTEGRATION OF LAND POLICY WITH FOOD AND RURAL DEVELOPMENT POLICIES AT FEDERAL AND STATE LEVELS. Vigorous policy research is needed on ways to integrate emerging land use policy with rural development policy and food policy. Programs in the three areas appear not to be developing in a manner that would deliberately exploit the possible complementarities among them. We need to better clarify food demand and requirements for domestic purposes and for international trade and world food security. Food demands and the world food situation in general should then become a specific consideration in policies designed to encourage retention of farmland. We will not achieve a magic ratio between land and food, nor will we successfully assign land quotas for each state or region. But better information on food-land relationships could help focus attention on open-land planning programs. It is a relationship that often evades the planning process as each planning unit attempts to solve its own problems. A broader perspective is needed.

The same kind of policy integration is needed with other areas. Settlement patterns are both the cause and the result of major land use problems. Energy supply, transportation policy, and economic development efforts influence settlement. Study of the cause-effect relationships involved could substantially improve our capacity to respond to problems of location. The danger in any research of this type is the paralyzing complexity of it all. The research challenge is to identify parts of the policy-settlement pattern linkage that can be rigorously documented. Such information can then become input to further study and can influence the development of policy.

CONCLUSIONS. Despite our modest expectations for the workshop session, a number of significant conclusions emerged that are worth recording.

A major difficulty in dealing with land use policy in any cogent way is the baffling degree of issue complexity surrounding this area of concern. "Land use" is not a clear set of issues. In some sense it is the locational dimension of many social, economic, and political problems of the day. Practically any social issue, from busing to railroad abandonment, finds expression in the patterns that evolve on the landscape. Land is a quite different resource to the farmer than to the urban dweller, so "land use" also has a quite different meaning. Several workshop participants spoke to this complexity in the context of trying to undertake rational planning programs. There may be no satisfactory answer to the matter of policy "fuzziness" in this area, but sometimes it helps just to articulate it and be aware of it.

Significant advantages of a multidisciplinary university department were noted. With its own budget, faculty meetings, student programs, and other characteristics of a unit of academic production, the multidisciplinary department has a better chance of coping with the problems of disciplinary boundary maintenance than do many other organization types. Researchable problems seldom follow disciplinary lines. Useful research demands the insights of several scientific perspectives. The major challenge in the multidisciplinary model is to exploit the strengths of component disciplines by focusing clearly on problem solving. Research planners must avoid adopting the least common denominator approach to multidisciplinary studies where, in the spirit of compromise among disciplines, *no one* learns anything useful. Research must be more than a random statement of issues and recommendations with no perceptible conceptual basis.

Workshop participants noted dissatisfaction with the "research institute" model for land use research. In that system, each participant writes his chapter, defends the discipline, and seldom comes to grips with the true interdisciplinary character of the issue. By the same token, we should not overlook the utility of creative conflict among competent scientists.

The long-run/short-run phenomenon is particularly bothersome in land use policy research. A wise old philosopher is said to have noted: "In the long run, we are all dead." Many are concerned that the long-run approach may be shorter than we think. The difficulty for policy research is that different people or groups apply quite different discount rates to future eventualities. A person weighs the possibility of catastrophic consequence from depletion of the ozone layer against the problem of those messy roll-on deodorants every morning. The abstractions of this business are all perfectly acceptable (environmental quality, comprehensive planning); the crunch comes in weighing the personal costs of alternative methods for accomplishing those abstracts.

People basically *live* in the short run. Their actions are influenced by clear evidence of costs of failing to act. Our job as researchers is to assist in the identification of costs (long run and short run), of acting or failing to act in certain ways, and the distribution of those costs. Armed with more information on consequences of choice, our policy process may produce better decisions. We must acknowledge a considerable momentum to policy. Public agencies are living proof of Newton's laws about bodies at rest staying that way and those in motion continuing. The costs of action options must also be made clear to those agencies with authority to act in matters of natural resource management. Most planning agencies must make recommendations quickly, with whatever information is at hand. Problems are immediate and must be dealt with now. To be useful, information on the implications of choice must be available now— or yesterday. Planners become extremely impatient with the long-run type of research, even as they feel the frustration of their inability to have this kind of perspective.

As the major research centers in the United States, university departments may have difficulty striking a balance between the user-oriented studies that produce short-run answers and the longer-run needs of a graduate program. The historic pattern of departmental research has emphasized graduate training, answering immediate public questions only incidentally. Users of publicly financed research are frequently impatient with that approach. At the same time, research administrators, including advisors of graduate students, are often frustrated by their inability to accept specific projects, deliver information to the user in some reasonable time frame, and still be consistent with the needs of the graduate student.

Greater attention is needed in the articulation of research projects in ways satisfactory to a broader range of clientele. Public universities cannot assume unlimited financial support. Major research problems must be broken down into parts that are feasible to accomplish, satisfactory as graduate dissertations, and useful to somebody. This is *not* an unrealistic expectation on the part of the public. By the same token, users must acknowledge the role of research "over-head"—investigation of the methodological, design, and conceptual aspects of research.

REFERENCES

1. Easton, David. 1965. *Systems Analysis of Political Life*. New York: John Wiley & Sons.
2. Heilbroner, Robert. 1974. *An Inquiry into the Human Prospect*. New York: W. W. Norton.
3. Ogden, Daniel. 1971. How national policy is made. *Increasing Understanding of Public Problems and Policies*. Chicago: Farm Foundation, pp. 5–11.

CHAPTER NINE

A RURAL PUBLIC SERVICES POLICY
FRAMEWORK AND SOME APPLICATIONS

FRED HITZHUSEN and TED NAPIER

A WIDE ARRAY of public services exists in rural America, and the diverse socioeconomic problems associated with the delivery and financing of these services cannot be collapsed into a single public policy question. In addition, the authors represent disciplines (economics and sociology) that complement one another but differ in perspective. Accordingly, this chapter attempts to develop a general policy framework for rural public services and to make some applications of the framework for selected public services. Specifically, the subset of the policy framework dealing with determining desirable or adequate service levels is discussed primarily from a sociological perspective with respect to several public services, and the service of fire protection is discussed primarily from an economic perspective relative to several subsets of the framework.

Much has been written in recent years about public service problems in rural areas and the relationship of public services to the location of industry, quality of life, population migration, etc. The concern is not a new one. As early as 1927, rural health facilities served as the focus of a research project at the Ohio Agricultural Experiment Station [25]. Other states have similar early precedents in the analysis of public services and facilities in rural areas [9, 26].

Rural public services are generally presumed to be inadequate, but adequacy is a relative concept. According to Brunn, it is still an open question whether rural public services and facilities are inadequate relative to community preferences, undersupply, or extra-community (usually federal) standards [33]. In fact, some might ar-

FRED HITZHUSEN is Associate Professor of Resource Economics, Department of Agricultural Economics and Rural Sociology, Ohio State University.

TED NAPIER is Associate Professor of Developmental Sociology, Department of Agricultural Economics and Rural Sociology, Ohio State University.

gue that many rural public services and facilities are not inadequate, particularly when compared to central city areas.

For purposes of this chapter, public services are defined as the direct and indirect functions of government. The direct public functions or services include education, welfare, public safety, hospitals, highways, sanitation, water supply, public health, parks and recreation, and libraries. Indirect public functions or services are usually in the form of various regulatory or control measures that influence the type, quantity, quality, and price of goods and services in the private sector. Examples include land use controls, professional licensing, safety requirements, and utility regulation [16]. The emphasis in this chapter is on those public services provided at the local level regardless of source of financing.

The concept of "rural" has been defined in numerous ways. Rural in the context of this chapter will refer to nonmetropolitan counties as well as the small villages, towns, and open country of metropolitan counties that do not contain a city of 50,000 population. The terms "rural" and "nonmetropolitan" will be used interchangeably.

GENERAL POLICY FRAMEWORK. Figure 9.1 demonstrates the interrelationships of the major policy and decision-making parameters concerning rural public services. The framework delineates the basic types of rural communities; outlines the various types of public services; lists alternative approaches to resolving three primary service policy questions; and outlines some policy criteria, research designs, and measurement techniques for evaluating the policy alternatives. It represents a general synthesis of considerable theoretical and empirical literature in the community services area.

Rural Community Variation. Considerable variation in population size, growth and density, proximity to other communities, resource base, ethnic mix, organization, climate, etc., exists among rural communities. Several of these sources of variation between rural communities have important implications for public services and facilities.

In recent years, rural communities have experienced considerable variation in the magnitude and direction of population change. From 1940 to 1970 the most significant rural population declines occurred in the Great Plains, western Corn Belt, southern Appalachian coal areas, and the old Cotton Belt of the southern Coastal Plain. These rural areas experienced a 30 percent decline in population from 1940 to 1970. During the same period, the most significant rural popula-

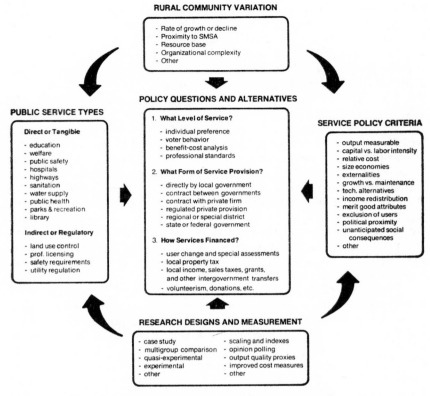

RURAL COMMUNITY VARIATION

- Rate of growth or decline
- Proximity to SMSA
- Resource base
- Organizational complexity
- Other

POLICY QUESTIONS AND ALTERNATIVES

PUBLIC SERVICE TYPES

1. **What Level of Service?**

   - individual preference
   - voter behavior
   - benefit-cost analysis
   - professional standards

Direct or Tangible

- education
- welfare
- public safety
- hospitals
- highways
- sanitation
- water supply
- public health
- parks & recreation
- library

2. **What Form of Service Provision?**

   - directly by local government
   - contract between governments
   - contract with private firm
   - regulated private provision
   - regional or special district
   - state or federal government

Indirect or Regulatory

- land use control
- prof. licensing
- safety requirements
- utility regulation

3. **How Services Financed?**

   - user change and special assessments
   - local property tax
   - local income, sales taxes, grants, and other intergovernment transfers
   - volunteerism, donations, etc.

SERVICE POLICY CRITERIA

- output measurable
- capital vs. labor intensity
- relative cost
- size economies
- externalities
- growth vs. maintenance
- tech. alternatives
- income redistribution
- merit good attributes
- exclusion of users
- political proximity
- unanticipated social consequences
- other

RESEARCH DESIGNS AND MEASUREMENT

- case study
- multigroup comparison
- quasi-experimental
- experimental
- other

- scaling and indexes
- opinion polling
- output quality proxies
- improved cost measures
- other

Fig. 9.1.   Rural public services policy framework.

tion growth was in the interstitial zones between the metropolitan areas of the Lower Great Lakes states, and the Northeast, in the Far West, the Florida Peninsula, and the textile areas of the Southern Piedmont. These rural areas experienced a 44 percent growth in population from 1940 to 1970 [3].

Rural communities also differ widely in their proximity to a Standard Metropolitan Statistical Area (SMSA) or central city of 50,000 or more population. For example, in 1960, out of a U.S. population of approximately 180 million, 20 million people were within 50 miles of an SMSA, 33 million resided between 50 and 100 miles from an SMSA, and 13 million lived more than 100 miles from an SMSA. The remaining were residents of an SMSA [34].

Considerable variation also exists in the size and composition of the human, natural, and fiscal resource base in rural communities. This is particularly true of per capita taxable property (real, public utility, and tangible personal) valuation. Even within Appalachian Ohio, rural counties show considerable variation in this measure of resource base. For example, Morgan and Adams counties had per capita taxable 1974 valuations of $7860 and $7300, respectively, the highest per capita valuations in Ohio. The lowest per capita valuations in 1974 were also in nonmetropolitan Appalachian counties. Perry and Meigs counties had per capita valuations of $2180 and $2200, respectively [32].

The organizational complexity of rural communities also varies widely. Organizational complexity is exemplified by the number and types of civic and social, economic, educational, religious, and governmental structures in the community. In the area of government, rural communities range from situations of long-standing political party dominance to those involving very competitive party politics. Much has been written on variation in power structures of rural communities which are generally classified as pyramidal, factional, coalitional, or amorphous [28]. Several other factors such as climatic variation may affect the type, levels, and relative costs of public services provided in rural communities.

The thrust of this discussion is to highlight some community characteristics relevant to decision making on public services and facilities in rural communities. Communities experiencing population growth, stability, or decline may have very different community service needs or demands. Close proximity to other communities, large or small, may facilitate arrangements for joint as well as specialized service provision. A rural community with a large property tax base (e.g., public utility installation) is in a position to demand and pay for more variety and/or a higher level of services and facilities than less-favored communities. Rural communities void of a competitive situation in local party politics may be less likely to change priorities on service levels, delivery mechanisms, or financing. A county in the Michigan Upper Peninsula will probably spend relatively more on snow removal, and a low-rainfall county in southwest Texas may spend relatively more for fire protection.

Key Policy Questions and Alternatives. The variability in rural communities and the wide range of public services and facilities in existence result in a large number of public policy problems and questions. A substantial literature has emerged on the problems of measuring output and quality of various public services [15, 23, 35, 36]; assessing the need or demand for various services [1, 4, 7]; evaluation of alternative service delivery mechanisms in terms of costs, accessibility, etc. [6, 10, 12, 29, 37, 43]; and financing of public services [38, 39, 40].

In spite of the breadth of literature and complexity of problems, it would appear that most rural public service problems can be grouped under three major public policy questions: (1) What level of service is desirable? (2) What is the optimal form of service provision or delivery? (3) How should the various types of services be financed?

Several alternative approaches address each of the foregoing policy questions on public services. The appropriateness of any given alternative is primarily a function of the characteristics of the community and the service under consideration. A more detailed discussion of some of the service characteristics and policy criteria for evaluating alternative approaches is reserved for the following section.

Determining a desirable level of service involves both the measurement of service level or output and a normative judgment on whether that level of service is desirable or adequate. At least four general approaches have been suggested by Hirsch and others for determining the demand for public services or for answering the question: "What level of service is desirable?" [13]. The approaches are: (1) individual preference, (2) voter behavior, (3) benefit-cost analysis, and (4) professional standards. Depending on the nature of the service, the individual preference approach is generally associated with the direct purchase of services (e.g., water supply); the use of associated or substitute private costs as proxies for demand (e.g., travel costs to public recreation facilities or private school costs); and the use of various types of gaming and constrained preference polling techniques.

The voter behavior approach is an expanded version of the individual preference approach and focuses primarily on issues or expenditure packages. It is concerned with better understanding the complex political process as opposed to a simple summation of individual preferences. This approach has involved analysis of voting issues (public school and utility bond issues); public service–related population migration ("voting with one's feet") [41]; and the study of legislative and bureaucratic behavior.

The benefit-cost approach is primarily an extension of welfare economics to determine who gains and who loses from various types of collective action. It can help identify the demand for various services, but the results may vary depending on which group is doing the analysis. Professional standards are usually concerned with minimums and maximums based on public safety, health, or well-being. Examples include teacher certification, minimum standards for the management of a sanitary land fill, and specifications for emergency medical service vehicles. Externalities are normally the reason for the standards.

A wide variety of forms provides for public services. Services may be provided directly by a local unit of government or by contract between local units of government. Local governments may also contract with private firms for a given service or regulate the private provision of a given service. Regional or special districts are also utilized for the provision of some services and facilities.

The considerable interest and concern regarding the financing of rural public services and facilities are not surprising, given man's insatiable wants and limited resources for both private and public consumption. The primary alternatives for financing rural public services and facilities are: (1) user charges and special assessments; (2) property, income, and sales taxes; (3) grants and other intergovernmental transfers; and (4) a complex array of voluntarism, donations, and fund-raising activities (carnivals, walkathons, bikeathons, etc.).

Numerous criteria have been proposed for evaluating various aspects of public services and facilities. The attempt here is to identify the primary criteria for evaluating the alternative approaches to the three public policy questions on rural public services and facilities identified earlier: (1) output measurability, (2) capital or labor intensity, (3) relative cost, (4) size or scale economics, (5) externalities or spillovers, (6) growth versus maintenance emphasis, (7) number and complexity of technical alternatives, (8) income redistribution, (9) merit good attributes, (10) ease of excluding users, (11) political proximity, and (12) unanticipated social consequences.

Public services vary widely in the amendability of their output (both quantity and quality) to measurement. Bish and Ostrom cite services with tangible physical benefits, such as water supply, snow removal, bridge construction, and garbage pick-up at one end of the measurement continuum [5]. The other extreme is represented primarily by those services involving personal interaction between public employee and citizen, such as police patrol, school teaching, and social casework. Gessaman and others have suggested a related but not identical criterion—the degree of labor or capital intensity of the service [33]. In either case, output measurability has important implications for questions on service level, form of provision, and financing.

Relative cost relates to the proportion of total service costs or expenditures represented by any given service. It is a measure of the relative value of resources consumed by or allocated to a given service. *Census of Government, 1972* data for all U.S. county area local governments per capita expenditures show a range from $3.70 for libraries to $239.38 for education [43]. Local governments in county areas of less than 10,000 population had 1972 per capita expenditures ranging from $1.06 for corrections to $221.07 for education.[1] Per capita expenditure data do not control for variation in output quality or take into account volunteer effort and other related private and joint public costs. Nevertheless, these data illustrate the considerable variation in the average level of public resources devoted to various local government services in the most rural U.S. county areas. Questions on the level, provisional form, and financing are particularly crucial on public services with high relative costs.

Economy of size or scale is a criterion frequently utilized in evaluating the provision of various public services. It simply states that unit costs of providing certain services decrease as the scale of service provision increases. Valid measurement of size economies is hampered by the difficulty of controlling (measuring) for variation in output quantity and quality of most services among communities. Capturing any actual size economies involves either significant growth of a small community or close proximity to other communities to facilitate consolidation, contracts, or other joint arrangements. Accordingly, many rural communities may have little opportunity for realizing size economies in public service provision [19].

In a strict sense, externalities or spillovers involve physical interdependence of the production or consumption functions of households, public agencies, and private firms [13]. Both external diseconomies (e.g., various types of environmental pollution from solid waste or sewage) and external economies (e.g., public primary and secondary education) are of concern in rural public service policy. To internalize the externalities from certain public services may require demand assessment, provision, and financing at a sufficiently aggregated level to encompass most of the "third party effects" of the externality.

Maki has suggested that certain public services and facilities, such as sewer, water, streets, schools, and zoning, are more oriented to growing rural communities, which tend to place more emphasis on infrastructure investment and land use controls [27]. In stable or declining rural communities, more emphasis is generally placed on maintenance-oriented services such as health and welfare.

Public services vary widely in the number and complexity of technical alternatives available for their provision. Technology has

1. The other service per capita expenditures in these rural county areas ranked as follows: highways ($55.71), hospitals ($24.09), public welfare ($13.08), police protection ($10.06), water supply ($8.86), natural resources ($5.74), public health ($3.08), sewage ($2.89), housing and urban renewal ($2.75), fire protection ($1.78), parks and recreation ($1.70), solid waste ($1.54), and libraries ($1.30) [43].

been relatively stable over time in service areas such as water supply and parks, but relatively dynamic in others such as health care and solid waste management. Rapidly changing or complex service technology increases uncertainty and thus increases the probability of making inefficient or dysfunctional decisions on rural public service level, provisional form, and financing.

Public services differ in their effect on income redistribution both in cash and in kind. For example, education, public welfare, and public health tend to have major income redistribution effects while most other local public services do not. Buchanan, Hirsch, and others have dealt with merit goods such as neighborhood parks and libraries [7, 14, 15]. Merit goods involve interdependencies in utility functions (i.e., citizens other than direct users receive utility from knowing that users of certain services consume more than if the marketplace alone determined distribution) [13]. Both merit goods and income redistribution considerations have important implications for the financing of public service.

The exclusion principle refers to the cost of excluding anyone from use of a good or service. Exclusion costs range from zero for a pure private good to infinite for a pure public good (i.e., the costs of excluding any one individual from enjoying a pure public good or service, without excluding all other individuals, are infinite) [13]. The degree to which the exclusion principle applies to any given public service has implications for both demand assessment and financing. For example, where users cannot be excluded (spraying for mosquitoes by air), financing by user charge is generally not feasible.

Political proximity has been proposed as a criterion for evaluating public services. An ACIR report recommended that "the performance of functions by a unit of government should remain controllable by and accessible to its residents" [2]. Hirsch elaborated on this and other recommendations by suggesting that local versus area-wide operation of various local government services is primarily a trade-off between political proximity and scale economies [14].

Unanticipated social consequences may result from altering the level and form of provision of some public services. For example, the development of park and recreation facilities in a community may attract outsiders with behavior norms quite different from the residents of the local community. Drinking and public displays of affection may not be acceptable forms of behavior in the local community and may result in a net decrease in utility for some local residents. Regional cooperation among community groups for the provision of public services could result in changing power or leadership structures or modification of community cohesiveness within the cooperating communities.

Ideally, the foregoing public service policy criteria or subsets of the criteria discussed are applied and weighted by decision makers (citizens, elected officials, bureaucrats) in making policy decisions on rural public service levels, form of provision, and financing. However, availability and reliability of decision-making information on these policy criteria vary considerably. For example, output measurability, capital versus labor intensity, and ability to exclude users all influence attempts to measure citizen preferences for various services. Public service data on relative costs and size economies generally either ignore measures of output and capital costs or make gross and often inaccurate assumptions about their inclusion [19]. Measures of related and joint private and public costs are usually not available. Likewise, data on income distribution and measures of various external effects (both economic and social) associated with some public services are generally not available. The following section suggests some research designs and measurement techniques for improving the information on these policy criteria.

Research Designs and Measurement. There are numerous ways of classifying research designs that may be employed for the analysis of public services, but the designs to be discussed here are: (1) case study, (2) multigroup comparison, (3) quasi-experimental, and (4) experimental.[2]

The choice of the most appropriate research design to be used in evaluating public services is dependent upon numerous considerations, such as type of service being evaluated, resource limitations, time restraints for decision making, as well as methodological appropriateness of the design. The utility of the research designs should be weighed against the limitations and constraining factors.

The case study has enjoyed a unique position within social science research. The approach consists of an in-depth analysis of some social unit of measurement such as an individual or a collective group. Minute details are frequently gathered about some social unit but often the data are very descriptive in nature. An example of its use might be an inventory of specific public service socioeconomic characteristics in a single community. Description of the situation over time would also be appropriate. A single community case study may be faulted in terms of not being representative of the public service situation in other communities.

2. An alternative approach might be to discuss descriptive, statistical, programming, and simulation methods relevant to rural public services and facilities research. Other authors have utilized variations of the latter categories to inventory the various quantitative methods with applications in rural development and community services research [24, 33, 42].

Multigroup studies are an improvement over a single case study since differences among groups may be observed, but often the causes of the differences are not identifiable. Several communities may be compared relative to specific socioeconomic aspects of their services and differences may be observed. The question then becomes: What factors caused the observed differences? Was it the form of organization, means of financing, consumer attitudes, conflicting value structures, or other factors? In essence, the observed differences could be a function of nonservice-related variables.

Quasi-experimental designs are an improvement over the preceding designs because they provide some control of exogenous factors, but they fall short of controlling all exogenous variables. Static group or time series comparisons may be incorporated into the design (similar to multigroup comparisons), but the unique characteristic of this type of research is the introduction of a stimulus of some type to the experimental group. It should be noted, however, that the researcher usually does not have control over the introduction of the stimulus. The design has its greatest utility when observations are made in both the experimental and control groups prior to the introduction of the stimulus and after it has been applied. The problem of assuming equality of the groups is a serious one with this design.

A further improvement in determining the impact of public services modification is the experimental design. Unlike the quasi-experimental design, experimental research consists of randomization to equate the experimental and control groups prior to the manipulation of the stimulus (researcher has control of stimulus). Some public services lend themselves to this type of research design. When the services are divisible and may be selectively applied to groups (some users can be excluded), experimental design may be applicable. For example, fire protection may be provided in many forms. If an innovative technique were developed, a selected group could be provided the modified service (experimental) while the existing system would be maintained for the others (control). Comparisons could be made between the systems to determine the differences (if any) in fire losses, direct service costs, etc., that emerged. The political process then determines if the new system will be adopted.

The difficulty of measuring the various service policy criteria is a recurring theme. Measurement is a complex issue with many theoretical and practical dimensions and limitations. For example, Hushak has discussed the output measurement difficulties inherent in the "flow" nature of most public services as contrasted to the "stock" aspects of most commodities analyzed by economists [21]. No conclusive literature has emerged to date, and what follows must be considered exploratory and suggestive. Given these qualifications, the measurement techniques and concerns discussed are: (1) attitude scaling and index construction, (2) constrained opinion polling, (3) output quality proxies, and (4) improved measures of and secondary data series on costs.

Attitudes and preferences of local people are extremely important in the decision-making process on various public services. The measurement of attitudes is not an easy matter if the researcher is concerned about validity and reliability of the measurement devices. Often researchers throw items together to evaluate attitudes of some group. Without good theoretical underpinnings the validity and reliability of attitude scales are questionable. One mechanism for increasing the probability that constructed scales will be valid and reliable measures is to use the following suggestions:

1. First construct a minitheory for each variable to be measured.

2. Build scale items from theoretical concepts used to build the theory in step 1 (Likert or Guttman scale items may be constructed).

3. Submit scale items to experts for evaluation of appropriateness.

4. Pretest scale on a group of individuals with characteristics similar to the universe being analyzed.

5. Reformulate scale after the data from pretest have been analyzed using factor analysis or item analysis.

6. Submit reformulated scale to subject population.

7. Analyze data with factor or item analysis and sum items in the final scale to produce the scale score per respondent.

8. Analyze scale scores relative to other variables determined by theory [30].

Another type of measurement device researchers may wish to consider is the construction of index scores using a continuum for each component to be measured. The techniques are presented below:

1. Select public services that are representative of all services available to people. Services provided on a local basis should be included with those provided on a regional basis.

2. Create a rating scale from excellent to poor with a range of scores, such as 0, 1, 2, . . ., N.

3. Select a representative sample or use total universe and have the subjects evaluate each of the services.

4. Submit the data generated from step 3 to factor analysis to determine clusters of services or use item analysis to determine the services that best differentiate the subjects.

5. Construct factor scores or sum the services that "load together," using item analysis for each subject.

6. Use the index scores for descriptive purposes and data input for analytical purposes.

Such procedures will produce a measure of some chosen variable (e.g., satisfaction with existing services or perceived need for services improvement) that is associated with service evaluation on an aggregate basis (grouped services), but the same data may be disaggregated into individual components by service areas.

Nonconstrained polling of public opinion on various public services is generally nonconclusive. Most people will opt for more of most services if the opportunity cost of doing so is zero. To derive information useful to policy on public services, some type of budget constraint must be incorporated into the public opinion poll. Crown and others have reported some interesting preliminary findings utilizing constrained preference assessment or opinion polling [8]. More of this type of analysis is needed, particularly on those public services that lend themselves to individual preference assessment.

Direct measurement of user assessment of output quality of some public services is inappropriate (due to externalities and cost of measurement) and problematic from the standpoint of interpersonal utility comparisons. One alternative is the development of output quality proxies, particularly for those services (e.g., fire protection) where professional standards are appropriate. There appear to be few generalizations possible in this area; thus one must proceed on a case-by-case basis. A later section of this chapter (on fire protection) illustrates the use of the American Insurance Association schedule for grading municipal fire defense as a proxy for fire protection, emergency ambulance service, and other selected services.

Some assumptions about or progress in measuring output quantity and quality are a necessary condition for improved measurement of public service costs. Valid cost measures (direct, joint and indirect, capital and operating) are generally not available in existing secondary data series. This is a function of both the divergence in definition of costs by accountants and economists and the difficulty of measuring the various dimensions of public service costs.

This data problem is particularly acute for small rural communities which are often omitted (because of size) from existing summary data series on expenditures, revenues, etc., published by the Bureau of the Census. As more precise and comprehensive cost analysis is completed for each of the public services, some reforms may be possible in the form and content of existing public service data series. A later section on fire protection develops several alternative measures of direct, joint, indirect, capital, and operating costs and discusses some of the policy implications for these alternative measures.

ASSESSING SERVICE ADEQUACY.

Criteria for Adequacy. A significant research problem in the assessment of rural public services is the relative lack of established criteria for determining the desirable level or adequacy of existing services. Variables such as physician-client ratios to assess the adequacy of medical care become quite arbitrary on the part of researchers, since service areas for health care are difficult to delineate except in a very general manner. Some medical care facilities, for example, serve multistate regions, but the physician-client ratio does not reflect this multistate service area. The ratio of teachers to students is not necessarily reflective of adequacy [22]. Other factors such as education facilities could serve to negate low student to teacher ratios.

Some authors have suggested that proximity to public health care is indicative of availability [11]; however, service personnel or agencies in close geographical proximity do not guarantee access to services. Socioeconomic status may operate to prevent use of medical care services, since people may be unable to pay for medical care even when the services are located in close proximity to them. Value structures of the people may prevent utilization of public health personnel except in emergency situations, since people may not value preventive health care.

The difficulty of isolating relevant criteria for determining adequacy of services, which in turn will provide a means of assessing how much and what type of services should be provided to a specific group, is further compounded by the problem of determining the proper social unit of measurement. Should emphasis be placed upon aggregations of communities or states or upon specific communities? Use of national averages on the surface may appear to be a reliable proxy, but in reality such averages are probably unrealistic since states and subareas within states may have different types of service needs. To assume that regions or states with disproportionately aged populations have the same service needs as relatively young populations is questionable. The same argument may be used relative to the use of aggregated state averages to evaluate services within local communities. The varying nature of the client populations makes such criteria much less useful to decision making.

What criteria should we use in determining how much of what service should be made available to people within rural areas? If agreed-upon criteria, shown to be reliable and valid measures of service adequacy, cannot be established, then little hope exists for easy answers to the question. If a model to be imitated is unrealistic and if researchers cannot use national or state average alone as the goal for communities to achieve without consideration of group variation, then an alternative is to seek part of the answer to the question on the local level. Local service area residents should have a significant role in the determination of what is adequate for their own perceived needs within certain parameters. As noted by Napier, service adequacy is a normative concept, and within certain limits the group being served is often in a better position to evaluate the relative adequacy of services [31].

Limitations of Individual Preference. Utilizing local consumer or citizen preferences for determining local service levels is not without some methodological problems. In the assessment of realistic needs, the potential exists for the local people to ignore externalities imposed upon other groups. Symbiotic relationships with other groups may be relegated to the background in favor of local preferences or lower direct costs, thus creating difficulties for one or more neighboring groups (externalities). A community may be unwilling to invest in a sanitation system, for example, to eliminate pollution for a community downstream, or a group may be content with the existing public services but ignore latent functions of their actions upon other groups. Educational systems that do not socialize the products of the system in such a way as to prepare migrants for rapid integration is another example.

Consumer preference assessment of service adequacy may be associated with unrealistic expectations on the part of local people. Every community may desire or feel a need for a public health nurse or physician to be in residence in the community or perceive a strong need for a resident fire department. In reality, the effective utilization of such services in many small communities is questionable. Surveys often only ask about desires and not commitment to achieving some desired end, and thus the phenomenon in question may not be evaluated. The people may abstractly desire a new or expanded service but not be willing or able to finance it. It is also possible that the technology does not exist on a level that may be adaptable to the group or may prove to be so costly that groups cannot realistically be expected to finance its introduction.

An exception to the general assertion that standards are very difficult to establish is the role of professionals in the establishment of minimum standards. Professionals should be able to aid groups in the establishment of minimum health and safety standards in terms of water supply, sanitation, hospitals, solid waste disposal, and so forth. These standards are and should remain minimum, or they could become rather arbitrary.

A technique frequently used by community development agencies is a panel of experts who monitor the situation and make suggestions to decision makers relative to the service needs of the people they represent. This technique is relatively inexpensive and can produce results reflecting the attitudes of the population being studied, but the technique is subject to methodological criticism. The primary obstacle to valid and reliable findings is the representativeness of the panel members. A common practice is to use leaders of communities to represent the interests of all people, but differing socioeconomic status, vested interest, and other factors tend to reduce the representative nature of the leadership.

As noted earlier, one source of evaluation is professionals or representatives of external groups. When externalities are operating (e.g., pollution due to sewage leakage), it may be necessary to impose norms (internalize an externality) of the larger social system upon a lower-scale component. Public health or environmental protection agency personnel may alert communities that certain services are not adequate in terms of symbiotic relationships with other groups.

This section discussed the concept of service adequacy and basically suggests that a single criterion for evaluating public services does not exist. Depending on the type of public service, several types of assessment may be required with particular emphasis placed upon local citizen assessment. The assessment, however, must take into consideration the symbiotic relationships with other groups. Data from national and state social units may be compared with data from comparable local sources, but expert opinion (e.g., professional standards), local perceptions and attitudes, and leadership assessments should also be utilized.

AN APPLICATION TO FIRE PROTECTION. Alternatives for determining the level of and providing and financing fire protection can be better evaluated utilizing improved measures of the policy criteria developed in the foregoing policy framework.[3] In output measurement difficulty, fire protection probably falls somewhere between water supply and waste disposal at one extreme and education and health services at the other. In terms of relative costs, fire protection ranks ninth among local government services, based on *Census of Government 1972* per capita expenditures for all county area local governments [43]. However, there appear to be substantial indirect public and private costs related to fire protection including water supply and volunteer effort [18]. Accordingly, per capita ex-

---

3. The conceptual and empirical work summarized in this section is part of an unpublished Ph.D. dissertation [20].

penditures probably understate the relative importance of this public service. In addition, there is conflicting evidence on the existence and significance of size or scale economies in this service, which leads to some confusion on the optimal form of provision [19].

Hirsch has concluded that fire protection generally does not generate major externalities or income redistribution consequences, but that political proximity is important in this service [14]. It would appear that fire protection does not have major merit good overtones, and it is generally not easy to exclude users from this service. These attributes suggest why fire protection is generally provided at the local level and typically does not employ a user charge for financing.[4]

Although fire protection is usually associated only with the fire department, a complete view of fire protection must include public water supply, building code enforcement, and fire prevention activities. In addition, private fire prevention equipment and activities and private fire insurance represent very important aspects of total fire protection output and costs. Finally, examination of the unusual trade-off relationship between public fire protection expenditures and practices and private fire insurance costs requires a more comprehensive view of fire protection costs.

A General Cost-Output Model. On the basis of several theoretical and methodological considerations and criticisms of previous research, some general directions in specifying a cost-output model for fire protection emerge. First, it is possible to delineate closer approximations of quantity and quality dimensions of fire protection output than has been done heretofore. Output quantity can be thought of as either total number of people or total value of property protected. To define unidimensional fire protection output quantity would require a common denominator (preferably monetary) for human lives and real property. This is a difficult task from both a measurement and a human values standpoint.

One approach to resolving this problem is to look at the number of people protected as fire protection output quantity holding constant the value of real property per person protected. Alternatively, one might consider a given unit of property value protected as output quantity and hold constant the number of people per unit of property

4. Public fire protection is usually heavily supported (with the exception of fund-raising volunteer departments) by the property tax at the local level. Thus one encounters a relatively unique and direct relationship between costs and benefits even though the fire protection service does not typically utilize a user charge. There are isolated cases where the service is provided privately and financed by user charge for relatively homogeneous residential areas through forced compliance [20].

value protected. Unlike some other local government services, fire protection does provide more benefits to those who own more property. In addition, one might argue that protection of burnable property from fire loss is crucial to protection of human life. Thus the importance of property in defining output quantity must be emphasized.

Given these two alternative definitions of output quantity, output quality is how well people and property are protected. Some exogenous factors (such as adverse climate, structural age and type, etc.) add to the difficulty of defining output quality of public fire protection. However, most of these factors can be identified and held constant in any analysis. Thus it would seem possible to use the American Insurance Association (AIA) schedule for grading municipal fire defense and setting fire insurance rates as a guide for defining the quality of public fire protection or fire department output.

The AIA Grading Schedule has been utilized with modifications since 1916 and is composed of six major features of municipal fire defense quality: water supply, fire department, fire alarm, fire prevention, building department, and structural conditions. Grading engineers assess deficiency points within each of these major features based on potential loss of property and life from fire. Total deficiency points are utilized to arrive at a final AIA classification number for a municipal fire defense system. Thus it is possible to get a fairly objective evaluation of an individual municipal fire defense system's output quality based on over fifty years of municipal grading and associated fire loss experience.

A more comprehensive concept of costs is needed. None of the previous fire protection cost studies have attempted to impute a value to volunteer effort, and only one or two of the studies have given any consideration to related local government (e.g., water supply) and private (e.g., fire insurance) costs of fire protection. Accordingly, this general cost-output model incorporates a relatively comprehensive concept of fire protection costs.

The general cost-output or average-cost model might be stated as follows:

$$C_i/O_j = f(O_j, Q, X_1, X_2, \ldots, X_n, U)$$

where C_i represents five alternative definitions of fire protection public and private costs, U is a disturbance term reflecting the stochastic nature of the relationship, O_j is an independent variable representing the two measures of output quantity or size, and Q is an independent variable reflecting output quality as determined by the AIA Grading Schedule. Independent variables $X_1, \ldots, X_n$ represent other factors affecting fire protection unit costs one wants to estimate and hold constant in examining the net relationship between output quantity and unit or average costs.

Based on a review of previous theory and research, and numerous discussions with local, state, and national fire protection personnel, several factors or independent variables emerge as important in explaining the variations between communities in average fire protection costs. The factors include population and dwelling density, income and wealth, urbanization, proportion of population transients, proportion of multiunit and older housing, percent of property commercial, percent of population Negro or of German or Mexican origin (hypothesized effect on fire losses),[5] adverse climatic conditions (high winds, hot, dry weather, etc.), base salary differentials, and amount of state and federal aid received by other local government services (a "substitution" effect). Other factors, such as whether the fire department is part paid, full paid, or volunteer, are mainly the result of improper measurement of costs.

Empirical Results. The cost-output conceptual model for fire protection was empirically tested with a stratified random sample of fire departments in 140 Texas municipalities. The data collection procedure and final statistical model and results have been reported elsewhere [19]. In general, the individual cost equations had a higher R^2 value when expressed in terms of property value protected rather than population protected. In addition, where property value protected was the unit of output, the cost equations had progressively higher explanatory power as the definition of fire protection unit costs became more comprehensive. The opposite was generally true where population protected was the unit of output. The implication seems to be that value of burnable property in Texas is generally more closely correlated with fire protection intercommunity cost differentials than is population.

Taking the cost-output equations with the most comprehensive measure of public and private fire protection costs (fire department adjusted operating and capital expenditures, volunteer effort, water supply, and private fire insurance costs) and utilizing the relative size of the beta coefficients as a criterion, one can draw some conclusions about the relative importance of the various independent variables.

5. Discussion with several fire grading engineers in Texas led to the inclusion of these ethnic variables. They had observed higher fire losses in communities with a high proportion of Negroes and lower fire losses in communities with a high proportion of residents of Mexican or German origin. Very strict fire laws in Mexico and Germany were cited as a possible factor. Discrimination in housing and in actual public fire protection provided may be intervening factors, particularly with the Negro population.

With public and private costs on a per capita basis, property value per capita was the most significant explanatory variable (positive), followed by population size (negative) and adverse climatic conditions (positive). All these significant factors reflect the sources of rural community variation (e.g., resource base, population size, climate) from the public services policy framework discussed earlier.

There were generally "size" economies (i.e., more populous and higher burnable property value communities tend to have lower unit costs) in the provision of fire protection in the Texas communities sampled. However, contrary to the empirical findings by Hirsch and Will, most size economies were exhausted at a population protected of around 10,000 people [13, 44]. Up to a population of approximately 10,000, the magnitude of the size economies tended to increase when the unit costs of fire protection included (in addition to fire department operating costs net of ambulance activities) an annual cost for fire department capital, an imputed value for volunteer effort, a charge for water supply, and an estimate of private fire insurance costs. In other words, when the more comprehensive measures of fire protection costs were utilized, the unit costs were not only higher in the smaller communities, but the differential between small and large communities was much greater. Further, adverse climatic conditions, value of property per person protected, and percent of structures built in 1939 or earlier tended to be positive unit costs.

Some Policy Implications. A small community located in close proximity to another community may be able to realize reductions in both public and private fire protection unit costs via consolidation or contractual arrangements for fire departments as well as water supply, inspection, and other components of the total fire protection system. In other cases it may be possible for adjoining communities to share or for smaller communities to lease or secure certain types of specialized and relatively expensive communications, fire fighting and emergency equipment, inspection personnel, and training programs from larger adjoining communities. Some small isolated communities may not be able to work out cooperative or contractual arrangements. Further, the potential size economies in fire department operating and capital costs appear to be quite limited without improving the water supply and fire prevention components of the fire protection system and imputing a value to volunteer effort.

The most comprehensive fire protection unit cost measures had mean values over three times higher than those for the least comprehensive measures. Other local government services may have significantly related (particularly inversely related) public and private costs. Thus the impact of increasingly more comprehensive measures of costs on the unit cost differentials between different sizes and types of communities may have some applications for other public services. Prime examples of some of these related costs are the services of volunteer hospital workers, private health insurance costs, private transportation and other costs incurred in securing public services, and expenditures for private and parochial schools. Even simple comparisons of unit costs of various local government services between communities of like size and type would gain considerable validity and usefulness if more comprehensive and precise cost and output measures were utilized.

Similar geographic and technological constraints to those discussed in the case of fire protection complicate implementation of consolidation and contractual arrangements to realize size economies in existence with other local government services. Some qualifications are also necessary in generalizing to other services the fire protection findings on unit cost differentials between various measures of public and private costs. However, more comprehensive and precise definitions of costs and output may lead to quite different conclusions on both relative costs and size or scale economies for services other than fire protection. To the extent that various measures of local government service unit costs reflect or are utilized to establish criteria for the allocation of state and federal money and in-kind grants, these findings may be quite significant [17].

SUMMARY AND CONCLUSIONS. This chapter has attempted to develop and make selected applications of a general conceptual framework for rural public service policy. The "state of the art" currently limits rigorous determination of the direction and significance or weighting of relationships among the various factors of the framework. While researchers can continue to improve the conceptualization, measurement, and generation of improved information on the various factors in the framework, the weighting of factors remains primarily in the domain of the political decision-making process. It is hoped that the framework is sufficiently comprehensive and the applications sufficiently specific to be suggestive and helpful to the total decision-making and research process on rural public services.

The conceptual framework focuses attention on the interaction between the type of community and public service, various service policy criteria, and research design and measurement techniques in addressing some key policy questions and alternatives on rural public services. The applications are intended to be pragmatic and suggestive of specific research design and measurement applications of the framework for evaluation of specific policy alternatives.

A recurring problem throughout this analysis is the difficulty of conceptualizing and measuring valid policy criteria, including service adequacy, output quality, full costs, scale economies, and various economic and social external effects. One of the first research tasks for any decision-making group is to determine what constitutes adequacy for its clientele within given constraints, and then to evaluate the existing services in this context. Constrained opinion polling should prove useful in this regard.

The fire protection application was an attempt to illustrate the development of a proxy for output quality and alternative measures for the direct, joint, indirect, and capital and operating costs of fire protection. The policy implications from this analysis are at least suggestive for other services. Thus from an economic perspective, it would appear that similar detailed cost-output analyses of other services could do much to overcome the overall measurement problem.

When these basic measurement questions have been at least partially resolved, it may be feasible to consider improved secondary data series on rural public service adequacy, quality, cost, etc. Furthermore, these improved data should facilitate more effectual measures of size economies or diseconomies, intercommunity service quality, and fiscal effort differentials between various types (county versus municipal) and sizes (SMSA versus non-SMSA) of communities. From these improved measures, it should be possible to generate more valid policy recommendations on professional standards for selected services, local government consolidation, contractual and leasing arrangements, and state and federal grant-in-aid and revenue-sharing formulas.

REFERENCES

1. Adams, Robert. 1965. On the variation in the consumption of public services. *Rev. Econ. Stat.* 47(4): 400–405.
2. Advisory Commission on Intergovernmental Relations. 1963. *Performance of Urban Functions: Local and Area-wide.* (M-21 rev. Sept.)
3. Beale, Calvin. 1974. Rural development: Population and settlement prospects. *J. Soil Water Conserv.* 29(1).
4. Birdsall, William C. 1965. A study of demand for public goods. In Richard A. Musgrave, ed., *Essays in Fiscal Federalism.* Washington, D.C.: Brookings Institution, pp. 235–94.
5. Bish, Robert L., and Vincent Ostrom. 1973. *Understand Urban Government.* Washington, D.C.: American Enterprise Institute for Public Policy Research.
6. Breton, Albert. 1965. Scale effects in local and metropolitan government expenditures. *Land Econ.* 41(4):370–72.
7. Buchanan, James M. 1968. *The Demand and Supply of Public Goods.* Chicago: Rand McNally.

8. Crown, Robert. 1973. A survey of 550 households in a 10-county area in northern Iowa. (unpublished) Center for Agricultural and Rural Development, Iowa State University.

9. Curtiss, W. M. 1936. Use and value of highways in rural New York. Cornell Univ. Agric. Exp. Stn. Bull. 656.

10. Hady, Thomas F. 1969. Cost of local government services. *Agric. Finance Rev.* 30 (July): 11–20.

11. Hassigner, Edward W., and Robert L. McNamara. 1971. Rural health in the United States. *The Quality of Rural Living.* Washington, D.C.: National Academy of Sciences.

12. Hein, Clarence J. 1960. Rural local government in sparsely populated areas. *J. Farm Econ.* 42 (Nov.): 827–41.

13. Hirsch, Werner Z. 1970. *The Economics of State and Local Government.* New York: McGraw-Hill.

14. ———. 1964. Local vs. areawide urban government services. *Nat. Tax J.* 17 (4): 331–39.

15. ———. 1962. Quality of government services. In Howard G. Schaller, ed., *Public Expenditure Decisions in the Urban Community.* Washington, D.C.: Resources for the Future, pp. 164–79.

16. Hitzhusen, F. J. 1973. Community services in rural Ohio. *Ohio Rep.* 58 (5): 99–102.

17 ———. 1974. Federal revenue sharing: Some implications for rural communities. Presented at Meet. Am. Agric. Econ. Assoc., College Station, Texas.

18. ———. 1973. Public-private fire protection cost trade-offs in Texas and New York: A benefit-cost analysis. Agric. Econ. Res., pp. 7–9, Cornell University.

19. ———. 1973. Some measurement criteria for community service output and costs: The case of fire protection in Texas. *South. J. Agric. Econ.* (July): 99–107.

20. ———. 1972. Some policy implications for improved measurement of local government service output and costs: The case of fire protection. Unpublished Ph.D. diss., Cornell University.

21. Hushak, Leroy. 1970. The measurement of output in the service industries: With special reference to formal schooling. ESO 15. Department of Agricultural Economics and Rural Sociology, Ohio State University.

22. Isenberg, Robert M. 1971. Quality of rural education in the United States. *The Quality of Rural Living.* Washington, D.C.: National Academy of Sciences.

23. Kiesling, Herbert J. 1967. Measuring a local government service: A study of school districts in New York State. *Rev. Econ. Stat.* 49 (Aug.): 356–67.

24. Leadley, S. M., ed. 1971. Working papers on rural community services. National Workshop on Problems of Research on Delivery of Community Services in Rural Areas, Lincoln, Nebr.

25. Lively, C. E., and P. G. Beck. 1927. The rural health facilities of Ross County, Ohio. Ohio Agric. Exp. Stn. Bull. 412.

26. Lutz, E. A. 1941. Rural public-welfare administration and finance in New York. Cornell Univ. Agric. Exp. Stn. Bull. 760.

27. Maki, Wilbur R. 1974. Local funding of rural public services. *Am. J. Agric. Econ.* 56 (5): 946–52.

28. Mitchell, John B., and Sheldon Lowry. 1973. Power structures, community leadership and social action. North Cent. Reg. Ext. Publ. 35.
29. Morss, Eliott R. 1966. Some thoughts on the determinants of state and local expenditures. *Nat. Tax J.* 19 (1): 95–103.
30. Napier, Ted L. 1975. Assessing the social impact of natural resource development: A research overview with commentary about contemporary uses of research methodologies. Proc. Environ. Des Res. Assoc. 6 Meet., Lawrence, Kans.
31. ———. 1975. Evaluation of service provision to rural community groups: Is there a service delivery problem and how do we research it? Econ. Sociol. Stud. 521, Department of Agricultural Economics and Rural Sociology, Ohio State University.
32. Ohio Public Expenditure Council. 1974. Real estate, public utility and tangible personal property taxes for Ohio's 88 counties, calendar year 1974. *County Data*, 75–7. Columbus, Ohio: OPEC.
33. Public services for rural communities: Some analytical and policy considerations. 1975. (Compiled by R. Beto Brunn) Great Plains Agric. Counc. Publ. 70.
34. Rainey, Ken. 1973. Public services in rural areas. *Manpower Services in Rural America.* East Lansing: Center for Manpower and Rural Public Affairs, Michigan State Univ.
35. Ridley, C. E., and H. A. Simon. 1943. Measuring municipal activities. Int. City Managers' Assoc. Meet., Chicago.
36. Schmandt, Henry J., and G. Ross Stephens. 1960: Measuring municipal output. *Nat. Tax J.* 13 (4): 369–75.
37. Shapiro, Harvey. 1963. Economies of scale and local government finance. *Land Econ.* (May): 175–86.
38. ———. 1963. The finances of local governments. *A Place to Live. The Yearbook of Agriculture, 1963.* Washington, D.C.: U.S. Government Printing Office, pp. 260–67.
39. ———. 1962. Rural government structure: Its relationship to service levels and revenues. *Agric. Finance Rev.* 23 (April): 15–23.
40. *Supplying and Financing Public Services in Rural Areas of the Midwest.* 1966. Proc. North Cent. Land Econ. Res. Comm., Chicago.
41. Tiebout, Charles M. 1956. A pure theory of local expenditures. *J. Polit. Econ.* (Oct.).
42. Tweeten, Luther, ed. 1972. Research application in rural economic development and planning. Res. Rep. P-665. Department of Agricultural Economics, Oklahoma State University.
43. U.S. Department of Commerce. Bureau of the Census. 1972. *Census of Government, 1972.* Washington, D.C.: U.S. Government Printing Office.
44. Will, Robert E. 1965. Scalar economies and urban service requirements. *Yale Econ. Essays* 5 (Spring).

CHAPTER TEN

RURAL HOUSING: IMPLICATIONS

WILLIAM J. ANGELL, CURTIS L. SIPPEL, and B. WARNER SHIPPEE

DURING THE PAST fifty years, the federal government has assumed primary responsibility for housing policy. Recently, however, a trend toward greater local and state involvement has clearly emerged. Although housing policy continues to involve all levels and branches of government, the quality of local and state policy assumes more significance. In this context, there is a unique opportunity for social scientists to support a more explicit and systematized analysis of causal variables and policy alternatives, thereby strengthening local and state policy determination and implementation relative to housing.

The purpose of this examination, then, is to encourage an interface between the policymaker and the social scientist. To fulfill this purpose, a number of factors influencing rural housing, and thus local and state policy issues, will be explored. More specifically, the following areas will be reviewed:

1. *Basic trends and relationships,* including a discussion of changing housing conditions and standards, the relationship between

WILLIAM J. ANGELL is Assistant Professor and Extension Specialist in Housing, Agricultural Extension Service and Design Department, University of Minnesota.

CURTIS L. SIPPEL is Extension Research Specialist in Housing, Agricultural Extension Service and Design Department, University of Minnesota.

B. WARNER SHIPPEE is Director of Housing Project, Center for Urban and Regional Affairs, University of Minnesota.

The authors are currently involved in the "Housing System Development Program: A Pilot Study," a research project (Minn 20–53) funded by the Agricultural Experiment Station, Agricultural Extension Service, and the Center for Urban and Regional Affairs, University of Minnesota. The major purpose of this exploratory research has been to develop a framework for more effective housing research, education, and policy.

housing deprivation[1] and poverty, and the subsequent evolution of housing policy in the United States.

2. *Basic nature of housing,* including a brief examination of the interrelationship of housing with variables of the quality of life.

3. *Distinctive housing characteristics,* including an examination of ten factors inherent to housing, and thus to housing deprivation and policy.

4. *Dimensions of rural housing,* including a review of indicators of rural housing problems and the interrelationship between housing and rural development.

5. *Models of housing,* including a delineation of structural-functional (descriptive) frameworks and simulation approaches to housing.

6. *Housing policy strategies,* including examination of basic policy questions and local strategies of housing.

BASIC TRENDS AND RELATIONSHIPS. From a cursory review of statistics, it is apparent that housing conditions in the United States have been improving. Amidst this advancement, however, housing deprivation has endured despite technological, economical, and political progress. For a significant portion of the population, housing remains a highly visible symbol that society's progress is not evenly distributed.

Housing deprivation is relative, in part reflecting ascending perceptions of housing quality.[2] With rising incomes, contemporary societal standards have changed earlier concepts of adequate/inadequate housing. Living arrangements perceived as sufficient a few years ago may now represent substandard, deprived environments. Indicators employed in the decennial census (between 1940 and 1970) of housing reflect the elastic nature of housing standards [21].

1. Housing deprivation is a relative state determined by comparison with the greater affluence of others. An individual may occupy a dwelling which is adequate and sound, yet feel deprived if he or she has not achieved the perceived standard of his or her reference group. Societal housing norms represent nearly a universal standard reinforced through popular media, policy, and other instruments of society [21].

2. Perceptions of adequate/inadequate housing may vary between individuals or groups. The least amount of variance is found in scientific standards of housing (structural, mechanical functions, flamability, etc.). These standards are generally exceeded even in the worst housing in the United States. Personal standards, on the other hand, are highly variable. This fact may create conflict among consumers, public officials, and other housing decision makers. For instance, an individual may perceive a mobile home as a desirable standard, yet be unable to obtain a zoning permit or reasonable financing because key local decision makers perceive mobile homes as inadequate [19].

Increasing societal norms and absolute improvements in housing have been the result of dramatic changes in production techniques, mortgage financing, state statutes, and extensive federal intervention,[3] as well as increases in real income. Not all the change, however, has been positive. Land prices, construction costs, financing charges, and purchase prices have risen sharply. During 1974, for example, the homeownership index and purchase price of a new house rose faster than both the consumer price index and per capita disposable income [2]. Despite tremendous price increases, consumers feel that on the average, the quality of new houses has declined [13].

While societal housing concerns are relevant, the relationship between housing deprivation and poverty deserves special consideration. Grigsby and Rosenberg noted: "Poor families suffer housing deprivation not because of low income alone, but because of the interacting network of negative variables which collectively constitute poverty" [12, p. 5]. Poverty and housing deprivation are so closely interwoven that it is best to approach housing problems as both cause and effect.[4] To ameliorate situations of housing deprivation and poverty, the network of negative variables must be altered.

While there is serious question as to the compatibility of specific housing policy objectives, the explicit intent of housing policy has remained basically the same:[5] to eliminate or greatly reduce substandard housing threatening a large segment of the population, especially the middle class. As early as 1638, local regulations were enacted in an attempt to improve community safety by reducing the threat of fire caused by thatch roofs and wooden chimneys. During the midnineteenth century, investigations into the relationship of substandard housing with epidemics, prostitution, crime, and other social ills led to the establishment of local building codes and eventually,

3. Reflecting these changes are mobile homes, FHA-VA mortgage insurance and guarantees, secondary mortgage markets, landlord-tenant statutes, state mortgage funding, and federal subsidy (approximately 25 percent, 1968–1972) of residential construction.

4. On one hand substandard housing is one of the most visible indicators of poverty and may increase respiratory ailments, safety hazards (fire), vermin infestation, poor school performance, and family conflict and dissolution. Likewise, households spending a major proportion of their income for shelter may be forced to sacrifice other necessities, such as medical and dental care and food.

5. While the basic intent of housing policy has remained fundamentally the same over the years, the specific focus and effects of individual policy action have varied and often appear contradictory. For instance, recent increases in FHA, FmHA, and VA interest rates and adoption of stringent local zoning have adversely affected housing. While these policy actions have dealt directly with broader economic and environmental questions and thus are not explicitly housing policy, their impact is substantial. The lack of clear housing policy goals and the apparent conflicting objectives of implicit housing policy is a major problem.

in 1901, to housing codes [8]. A national forum of concern for decent housing was also advanced with the emerging women's suffrage movement and the writings of Jacob Riis and others.

The depression of the 1930s produced the most significant national commitment to housing. From this era a broad and diverse federal policy evolved which revised residential mortgage practices, stimulated employment through construction, initiated urban renewal, established rural resettlement efforts through the development of new towns, created publicly subsidized housing, developed secondary mortgage markets, and so on [8].

Significant policy developments such as clarifying landlord-tenant relations, creating statewide building codes, establishing state bonded mortgage pools, and facilitating condominium and cooperative developments have been more recently incorporated in state legislation. During the past ten years, regional government has begun to gain substantial planning and implementation power over land use and public services that directly affect housing (transportation, water, sewer, etc.). The courts have likewise rendered quasi-policy decisions altering such basic concepts as implied warranties of habitability and definition of reasonable public purpose through the power of eminent domain.

BASIC NATURE OF HOUSING. The diverse character of policy action evolving within all levels and branches of the American political system underscores the importance attached to the perceived interdependence between housing and the quality of life, as well as to the perceived need to manipulate the complex and ill-defined processes of housing production, distribution, and consumption. The fundamental nature of housing within the context of the quality of life, whether approached from the individual consumer's perspective or examined from a rural development objective, is indicated by several important relationships.

Consumer Relevance. Housing has special sociopsychological and financial importance to consumers. While conclusive research is lacking, the symbolic quality of housing appears to have significant influence on the individual's perceived quality of life [1, 5, 7, 10, 19, 21, 29, 32]. Compounding this characteristic are two additional trends. First, for the average family, housing is the largest single financial commitment and represents the greatest proportion of its budgetary expenditures [32, p. 376]. The cost of construction and home ownership has consistently increased faster than the Consumer Price Index [2]. Second, housing is a dominant area of consumer frustration and complaint [13]. Thus housing is not only important symbolically and financially to the consumer but also a likely source of dissatisfaction.

Economic Importance. In terms of the nation's economy, housing is both an important source of employment and income and a major vehicle for the use of credit. More than 3 million jobs are directly associated with new residential construction alone,[6] in addition to the employment in the supportive wood products, household equipment, textiles, home furnishings, mobile home, remodeling, transportation, banking, and real estate industries. The relevance of credit for residential mortgages is illustrated by the 770 percent growth in the aggregate mortgage debt between 1950 and 1973, which represents a growth rate twenty times greater than the federal debt [32, p. 459].

Environmental Consequence. Housing also has a tremendous environmental impact from the standpoint of land use, energy, and natural resources. On the average, housing dominates the single largest proportion of community land area (about 40 percent in larger cities and considerably more in small rural communities). Enormous quantities of extracted resources, including three-fourths of the lumber and plywood consumed in the United States, are used for residential purposes [33]. Housing also directly accounts for more than 20 percent of the nation's energy consumption, an amount significantly greater than agricultural consumption [32, p. 517].

Governmental Significance. Finally, housing is an important variable in local government fiscal policy. More than 80 percent of tax revenues collected by local government originate from the property base [32, p. 245]. Conversely, local expenditures for such capital improvements as schools, roads and streets, and water-sewer systems are directly related to housing development. Also, evidence suggests that the ability of a community to attract business, industry, and employment opportunities is influenced by housing.[7]

Approaching housing with an appreciation for the complex interrelationships that exist with quality of life variables or indicators is an important step toward effective policy analysis. Such an understanding alone, however, will not result in better policy decisions. In order to explore basic issues and alternatives, it is necessary—or at

6. The direct employment figure offered here is based upon the labor requirement of 217 man hours per 100 square feet divided by 1,920 hours per man per year (240 days times 8 hours) for the construction of 1.8 million dwelling units.

7. In case studies of four local housing systems in Minnesota in 1974, several community leaders indicated that the lack of an adequate housing stock led industries to seek other locations.

least extremely desirable—to delineate the fundamental characteristics of housing.

DISTINCTIVE HOUSING CHARACTERISTICS. The basic question of why government should intervene in the private housing market can be answered from two philosophical prospectives: (1) the fundamental interrelationship of housing with the quality of individual life and (2) the distinct nature of housing processes, which are often conflicting and therefore not harmonious with basic societal goals [19]. Since the private housing market is unable to respond effectively without public intervention [7, 29, 32], the latter philosophical perspective will be examined in preparation for subsequent analysis of policy alternatives. Based upon this emphasis, ten interrelated, distinctive characteristics of housing are noted.

Political Interdependence. More than any other consumer commodity or service, the basic nature and distribution of housing is ingrained in the fabric of public policy. For instance, fee-simple, condominium, cooperative ownership, and rental tenancy, including consumer rights to privacy and safety, are grounded on state statutes and encouraged or discouraged by federal income tax and monetary and fiscal policy. Locally, zoning regulations, housing codes, and property taxes shape the distribution and cost of housing. At the least, housing is accidentally the by-product of policy decisions.

Durability. Individual and societal housing decisions represent a significant influence on future as well as present life styles. In contrast with the mobility of households in the United States (five years), housing represents a capital investment with a primary economic life range from an estimated 80 [23] to 150 [27] years for single-family dwellings to 15 years for mobile home [19]. Initial decisions regarding location and design involve future societal investments of natural (land, energy) and financial (public service) resources. Furthermore, as many as thirty different families will occupy a specific dewlling[8] and attempt to adapt it to their specific needs and life-styles. These facts are true of no other commodity in our society.

Inelasticity of Supply. Because of the durability of housing and its basic fixed location to the site, the supply of housing is extremely inelastic. During the short run, qualitative changes realized through remodeling and additions do little to improve the overall quality of the housing stock. Likewise, quantitative changes in the housing

8. This is based upon an average length of tenure of 5 years and a primary economic life of 150 years.

stock are incremental and sluggishly respond to demographic variables. The annual production of new dwellings seldom exceeds 2 percent of the existing stock nationally. In the short range—five to ten years—the nation's housing stock is largely inherited.

Obsolescence. The combination of technological advances in building materials and production, changing consumer market preferences, and demographic alterations reduces the utility or service consumers receive from dwellings over time. These facts appear to have a greater impact on housing than natural decay, which may be minimized with normal maintenance. Although restoration may be becoming more popular, demographic, consumer (market), and technologically induced obsolescence remains the rule. In fact, new forms of housing production appear to intensify obsolescence. Mobile homes, with a primary economic life of 80 to 90 percent less than other single-family dwellings, are a growing proportion of residential construction, especially in rural areas [1].

Filtering. With the exception of short-lived federal subsidies, low- and moderate-income families have obtained housing through filtering. In the classical sense, filtering occurs as previously occupied dwellings produce less relative utility and thus are placed on the housing market at prices affordable by lower income households. Many housing authorities contend that filtering does not satisfactorily upgrade the housing situation of lower income families because of population growth (especially household formations)[9] and the inelastic nature of supply (modest production and rehabilitation and fixed location). Recent examinations of filtering indicate other limitations of the effectiveness of filtering. Lansing et al. noted: (1) families often remain in large dwellings after family size decreases; (2) contrary to popular opinion, approximately half the moves are initiated by death of previous occupants, subdivision of existing dwelling units, or emigration rather than new construction; and (3) housing markets are segregated by age, social status, and race [15]. Furthermore, contrary to the classical concept of filtering, new construction is added over a wide price range, not just at the top of the cost-quality profile. The cost of moving, including buying and selling, causes additional frictions in filtering.

9. Housing demand is directly associated with the rate of household formation rather than absolute population growth. The relevance of this distinction is illustrated in many rural areas where population may be declining, whereas demand for housing is increasing. In such situations, households are generally becoming smaller and more numerous.

Abandonment. At the end of the economic life cycle, housing abandonment and eventually destruction occur. While this process is frequently desirable from the standpoint of removing grossly inadequate dwellings from the housing stock, abandonment often produces undesirable effects (precipitates rather than follows community decay). Moderately obsolete but sound dwellings are frequently abandoned (perhaps following being vacated and vandalized) when the investment stream is insufficient. It is often hypothesized that better individual and community management could reduce undesirable abandonment.

Management. The way in which housing is managed appears to have a substantial influence on the stream of utility received by consumers. Prudent management of both owner- and renter-occupied dwellings minimizes physical decay. Exploitive management, on the other hand, especially in rental units with absentee landlords or publicly subsidized structures, produces greater tenant dissatisfaction (lower utility) and higher operating costs. While evidence is not incontestable, there appears to be reason to believe that serious mismanagement, especially inadequate maintenance, may underlie the problem of premature abandonment. For example, during extended periods when dwellings stand vacant (following death or illness of occupants or during mortgage or tax foreclosure), maintenance often declines and exposure to vandalism increases. In marginal communities, it is easier and less expensive to abandon the dwelling than to remedy deficiencies that may be intensified during vacancy.

Instability of New Production. As a durable product, short-term housing demand is largely unstable, sharply fluctuating with overall economic changes. Unlike perishable commodities, housing is a sizable financial commitment representing discounted future consumption. Construction of dwellings produces marginal results in terms of the total demand for housing. For instance, to satisfy a 1 percent change in aggregate consumer demand, a 50 percent change in the rate of construction would be needed (assuming the average rate of construction is 2 percent of the total housing stock).

Capital Interdependence. Consumer housing decisions are especially dependent upon the availability and cost of credit. As a durable capital good, housing is sensitive to fluctuating demands for capital, as reflected in mortgage interest rates and savings deposit rates. With recent massive government borrowing (fiscal policy) and unstable savings deposits, residential mortgage interest rates have risen. Government monetary policy, including Federal Reserve Bank regulations, deposit interest restrictions, FHA and VA fixed rates, and state usury laws have increased short-run instability in the housing market. Furthermore, "red lining" practices by lenders, offering less favorable mortgage terms to selected areas (core cities and many rural areas), have depressed housing markets.

Externalities. Community facilities and services, neighborhood composition (social and physical), environmental amenities, and other factors strongly influence the utility and value of housing, although these items are largely beyond the control of individual consumers. Individuals, on the other hand, have a significant influence on the utility—and economic value—of the dwellings in immediate proximity to their own property. Attempts to manage the external character of housing are represented by local policies, including zoning, building, subdivision, and housing regulations. There is serious question, however, concerning the ability of such policies to effectively involve public participation, reflect intangible externalities, and effectively account for even quantifiable externalities without intensifying segregation and discrimination.

Composite. These ten interrelated characteristics of housing underscore the importance of explicit systematized policy analysis, development, and implementation. Furthermore, these factors should serve as testimony to the policymaker that housing problems defy simplistic solutions (i.e., policy). To the social scientist, these distinctive characteristics of housing represent possible variables for analysis and simulation.

DIMENSIONS OF RURAL HOUSING. In rural areas the need for effective policy analysis, development, and implementation is critical. Housing deprivation, obsolescence, ineffective filtering, marginal production, insufficient credit, and undesirable abandonment indicate the magnitude of this need. In this section, indicators of rural housing problems and the interrelationship between rural housing and rural development are reviewed.

Rural Housing Indicators. In a report to the Senate Committee on Rural Development [26], it was noted that nonmetropolitan households lacked complete plumbing facilities at a rate four times greater than metropolitan households. For rural elderly households, the lack of complete plumbing was even more prevalent; one-third of the rural units without complete plumbing were occupied by elderly, although elderly accounted for only 23 percent of all rural households. While plumbing facilities are only one indicator of inadequate housing, other variables support the contention that rural housing is more likely to be older, deteriorated, and a burden rather than an asset to rural people and communities [4, 6, 26, 28].

As Cochran, of the Rural Housing Alliance summarized: ". . . by deliberate Congressional policy we have facilitated . . . out-migration [and] have created a crisis in the cities without curing the rural housing problem; rural deficiencies are so severe that the out-migration did not make available decent housing even to those who remained" [6, p. 53]. The comparative substandardness of rural housing adds support to the belief that public policy, instead of intentionally and effectively dealing with these problems, has dealt with symptoms and therefore has often compounded rural housing problems because of externalities or unintended consequences.

While causes of rural housing problems are as complex as the problems themselves, many authorities contend that a lack of adequate residential financing is an important variable. Data from 1971 reflect that rural home buyers are twice as likely as metropolitan buyers to finance their homes on a contract for deed basis or to obtain a mortgage from a commercial bank [26, 28]. In the case of mortgage financing, average rural home buyers encountered higher interest rates and shorter terms than their metropolitan counterparts. For instance, the difference in average rates and terms for a $24,000 mortgage would cause rural buyers to pay 35 percent more per month than a metropolitan buyer. Additional evidence suggests that significant rural and urban differences in income elasticities for shelter, household operations, and total housing expenditures may also explain the rural consumer's lower rate of housing consumption [17].

Although adequate data are not available, it appears that rural housing problems may be intensified by both the lack of residential financing and the greater unwillingness of rural consumers to obligate themselves to long-term debt when income streams are less stable and predictable over time.

Even if more favorable financing were provided and consumers were willing to make greater use of financing, housing deficiencies would probably not disappear in rural areas due to (1) the limited ability of the private market to respond to isolated and scattered demand (i.e., difficult to achieve scales of economy) and (2) the shortage of skilled local labor, the lack of successful entrepreneurial models, and the substantial costs of transferring labor, material, and services to distant areas. The prevalency of owner-building in rural areas, at a rate three times greater than in urban areas, reflects the limited ability of the production systems to meet rural demand.

A more complete analysis of a hypothetical "average" rural community could logically include a quantitative examination of the ten distinctive characteristics of housing: political interdependence, durability, inelasticity of supply, obsolescence, filtering, abandonment, management, and externalities, as well as capital interdependence and instability of new production. In terms of these characteristics, several recent studies indicate that many rural communities engender housing situations which could be summarized as follows [4, 5, 6, 12, 20, 26, 28]:

1. Filtering is extremely limited due largely to low rates of housing construction, especially in communities with declining populations (demand).

2. Obsolescence is most severe among elderly homeowners who cannot liquidate the financial assets they have in the home.

3. Management and maintenance are common problems (inadequate) among low-income renters as well as homeowners, especially elderly lacking financial and physical resources or friends or relatives to assist in upkeep.

4. Abandonment may be primarily positive inasmuch as the most substandard portions of the housing stock are removed.

While this analysis is hypothetical, it illustrates a fundamental descriptive approach to housing policy. Effective policy must emerge from a sound, explicit understanding of existing problems, conditions, and trends. Furthermore, since each community is unique in terms of its housing situation, it is important to realize that (1) local analysis is essential for effective local policy action and (2) the larger context in which local policy makers operate, namely federal and state policy, should be flexible in allowing local application.

Housing and Rural Development. To effectuate meaningful rural development, it is particularly useful to clarify the interdependence between rural development and housing. The basic purpose of rural development is to maximize the quality of life through efficient use of resources. Housing, within this concept, involves organizing the human resources of the housing system with the capital, natural, and man-made (e.g., utilities, streets, parks) resources of the rural community. Because of the interrelationship between housing and rural development, housing may be treated either as: (1) An independent variable or a tool to stimulate rural development (e.g., to create additional local employment and income) or (2) A dependent variable or a goal or result of rural development (e.g., to provide independent living arrangements affordable by elderly).

When variously employed as either a dependent or independent variable, the nature of housing may produce conflicting policy action. As noted, one objective may involve stimulation of jobs and income through construction, while another may encourage lower consumer housing costs through automation of construction and thus reduced labor costs and contractor overhead.

MODELS OF HOUSING. In addition to understanding the distinctive nature of housing in general and important aspects of rural housing, effective public policy must reflect an explicit awareness of housing itself. Such an awareness involves both a theoretical understanding of the housing system and its specific performance in a specific community.

The potential usefulness of a housing model for policy formation and management purposes rests upon accurate delineation of functions, roles, and interdependencies comprising the system of housing. Unfortunately, much of the simplification of the housing system has been informal and implicit on the part of policymakers. The product of unsystematic analysis has been generally ineffective policy. Even where individual policy action has been successful, the lack of an adequate description of the situation has limited application to similar problems in other communities. Consequently, wasted efforts (e.g., inconclusive, expensive market surveys) continue to pile on the shelf, contributing little more than dust to the foundation of policy development.

It should be noted that poorly conceived research also damages the credibility of social scientists to the housing policymaker. Comments such as: "Give me the money they are going to spend on that survey and I'll build fifty houses" are not uncommon.

The product of a rigorous descriptive analysis, however, can be a policymaker with a more accurate understanding of the critical problems, the causes, the policy alternatives to ameliorate the problems, and the techniques to evaluate and manage policy action. Structural-functional models of housing offer a framework through which desired policy action may evolve.

Typifying the structural-functional approach is the examination of housing problems and needs by the President's Commission on Urban Housing. In technical appendices of the commission's report, it was noted that "Since [housing] is a flow as well as a stock, the industry . . . may be viewed as a process subject to its own structure" [30]. In this context, the functions of the housing industry and institutional factors affecting the production, distribution, and consumption of housing in any community can be examined:

Functions
1. Production
    a. site identification
    b. site preparation
    c. construction
2. Distribution
3. Consumption and redistribution
Institutional Factors
1. Public or quasi-public
2. Private

Building upon this structural-functional perspective, major participants in any local housing situation may be assessed in terms of individual performance or interdependent conflicting-complementary roles in the four phases of the housing process: (1) preparation, (2) production, (3) distribution, and (4) service (Table 10.1).

A number of studies have used this approach, concentrating upon the influence of functional actors within the housing system. For example, Nenno examined the individual roles of five key actors in the implementation of regional and state housing strategies: housing developer, chief political executive, comprehensive planner, development administrator, and consumer advocate [25]. In another study, Thee hypothesized that a rural community's housing situation is largely dependent upon the perception of relevant participants in the housing process, including: builders, real estate agents, lenders, and community leaders with political or social influence [31].

Another possible approach to analyzing and describing local housing situations was advanced by a group of educators and researchers participating in a NASA-ASEE fellowship program at Auburn University [29]. Employing a systems approach, the Auburn group explored a structural-functional framework with seven housing elements, accentuating outputs (desired performance or objectives in contrast to existing performance), constraints (interfunctional or intrafunctional limitations), and requirements (management and resources needed to achieve desired outcomes):
1. Capital
2. Public services
3. Land use
4. Natural resources
5. Housing production
6. Market characteristics
7. Research

Treating each of the seven elements as subsystems, however, the Auburn group concluded their examination with emphasis upon housing production and consumption (market characteristics). The remain-

Table 10.1. Housing process: participants and influences

Phase	Participants	Influences

1. Preparation
  A. Land acquisition
  B. Planning
  C. Zoning
	Land owners
	Developers
	Real estate brokers
	Title companies
	Attorneys
	Engineers,
	  architects
	Surveyors
	Planners
		Real estate laws
		Recording regulations
		  and fees
		Banking laws
		Zoning
		Subdivision
		  regulations
		Public services
		Deed restrictions

2. Production
  A. Site preparation
  B. Construction
  C. Financing
	Developers
	Lenders
	Mortgage insurers
	Contractors, sub-
	  contractors
	Tradesmen (including
	  union)
	Material manufacturers,
	  suppliers
	Building code officials
	Insurance companies
	Architects, engineers
	Developers
	Real estate brokers
		Transportation
		  regulations
		Banking laws
		Subdivision
		  regulations
		Building codes
		Trade, professional rules
		Union rules
		Insurance regulations

3. Distribution
  A. Sale
  B. Resale
  C. Financing
	Lenders
	Mortgage insurers
	Title companies
	Attorneys
	
	Owners, occupants
	Maintenance firms
		Real estate laws
		Recording regulations
		  and fees
		Banking laws
		Transfer taxes
		Professional rules
		Property and
		  income taxes

4. Service
  A. Maintenance,
    management
  B. Repairs
  C. Improvements,
    additions
	Management firms
	Utility companies
	Tax assessors
	Tradesmen (including
	  union)
	Lenders
	Architects, engineers
	Contractors,
	  subcontractors
	Material manufacturers,
	  suppliers
	Zoning officials
	Building code officials
		Housing and
		  health codes
		Banking laws
		Utility regulations
		Building codes
		Zoning
		Trade, professional
		  rules
		Union rules
		Insurance regulations
		Transportation
		  regulations

Source: A decent home [7].

ing five elements were examined in terms of their influence upon production and consumption. From the standpoint of generating a descriptive model of housing, the systems approach used by the Auburn group provides a complementary method to the functional emphasis advanced by the President's Commission on Urban Housing.

Other descriptive modeling efforts have utilized Critical Path

Method (CPM) or Performance Evaluation and Review Technique (PERT) methods to delineate microsystem structural and functional dimensions of housing. Within the consumption subsystem, for instance, Morris and Winter advanced a theory of family housing adjustment composed of three major forms: residential mobility, residential adaptation, and family adaptation [21, 22]. Based upon this theory, Angell expanded the concept of consumer housing alternatives to include: form of tenure, type of construction, and type of residential structure (Fig. 10.1) [1]. Both of these efforts, to a limited extent, delineate the interrelationship of consumption with housing production and policy.

In terms of production, numerous CPM or PERT diagrams have also been developed to describe the sequence of activities in residential construction. Angell and Olson, for example, employed PERT techniques to examine owner-built housing (Fig. 10.2) [3].

Despite the relative abundance of descriptive models using the structural-functional approach, few studies have adequately integrated production, distribution, and consumption of housing with the distinctive character of housing variables. Consequently, to what degree descriptive studies have resulted in effective public policy to the extent that would be possible with further integration of production, distribution, and consumption is seriously questioned.

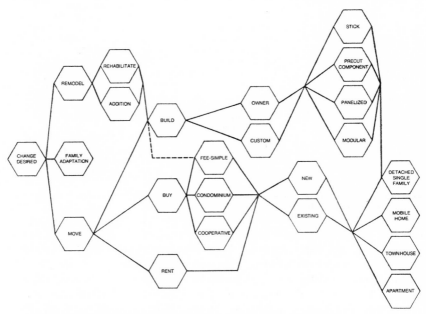

Fig. 10.1.   Paradigm of consumer housing alternatives.

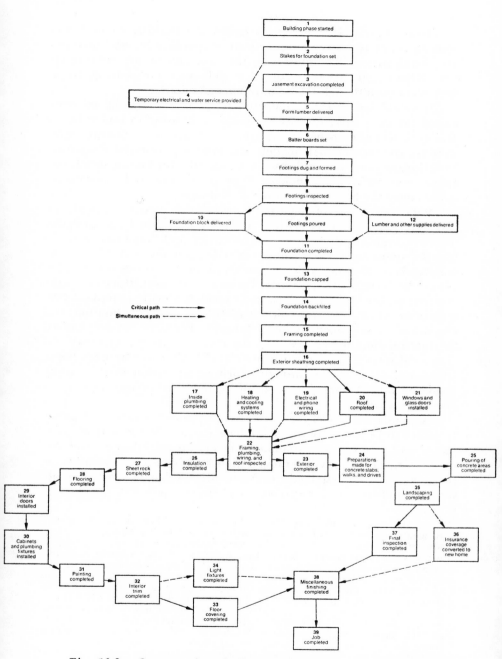

Fig. 10.2. Construction (building) phase of owner-built housing.

Thus an initial challenge to researchers desiring to deal with housing policy issues is the refinement of qualificative and quantitative descriptive models integrating the functions of the housing system. Existing structural-functional models offer a reasonable beginning point even though there are inherent limitations.[10]

It would be extremely unfortunate, however, if social scientists waited for the *perfect* descriptive model of housing to evolve before dealing with policy issues (see Chap. 4). While many housing problems are complex enough to defy the most sophisticated descriptive model, many housing problems can be solved with known social, economic, and political technology—if properly employed. Descriptive models offer the first step toward this realization.

Policy analysis evolving from a descriptive model implicitly involves some degree of simulation. At the most informal and probably the most common level, policy generation and implementation is founded upon an implicit conceptualization on the part of the most policymakers. Significant developments in more rigorous policy simulation, however, have evolved. Forrester [9], notwithstanding the criticism of Lee [16], Garn [11], and others, has made important contributions simulating dynamic relationships between housing and community development policy. Basically, Forrester has emphasized the interrelationship between (1) the cycle of growth, maturity, decline, and stagnation frequently associated with a community's population and (2) a system through which policy action may be simulated and thus evaluated in terms of hypothesized or intended effects and externalities.

A simulation model such as Forrester's allows a variety of policy variables to be tested prior to implementation. While a descriptive model and, eventually, a simulation model are useful, one must recognize a model is only a representation and is never as complete as the system being described. Consequently, a balance between objectivity and intuition is necessary for effective policy.[11]

10. Abe Farkas and Curt Sippel, in an unpublished paper (Structural-Functional and Contextual-Process Approaches for a Housing Model, 1974. University of Minnesota), observed that structural-functional frameworks (1) tend to assume a single-value system and organized structures; (2) are incapable of dealing with major structural change (i.e., are static); and (3) emphasize only interactions and roles that are functionally relevant (i.e., supportive of the structure). Thus Farkas and Sippel advanced a contextual process approach to account for differing situations, objectives, values, interests, and relationships that may occur in housing.

11. Some questions can legitimately be raised as to how a comprehensive housing policy can ever be formed. Given the complexity that exists even in descriptive models of a housing system and the substantial variance in that system between market areas, public policy seeking both broad application and inclusive effects may well be doomed to failure. Substantial evidence of these failures, especially among the federal housing programs of the 1950s, is abundant. What we are suggesting is that a more comprehensive *understanding* of the

HOUSING POLICY STRATEGIES. Thus far, housing characteristics, problems, and policy issues have been examined from largely an academic perspective. This approach, however, may not be politically acceptable. As Harris observed: ". . . policy analysis is concerned with large steps in dealing with a social problem; it relates the large steps to quantitative measures of what will happen if things are done, how they can best be done, and how much they will cost. Political constraints are explicitly taken into account. . . ." [14].

Basic Policy Questions. The nature of the constraints Harris mentions is largely related to questions about focus, time frame, resources, and feasibility of anticipated policy. In further detail, these parameters include the following questions [12, 14, 18].

HOUSING OR NONHOUSING FOCUS? The potential competition between housing and nonhousing policy for rural development resources may be resolved through analysis of marginal benefits of these two alternatives. The effectiveness of nonhousing policy, such as employment, training, health, and income-maintenance programs, as an indirect approach to solving rural housing problems is a remaining question. The results are largely unknown, although a superficial examination may indicate that nonhousing policy alternatives do not offer immediate, visible, and material relief to housing deprivation. More income or better health care may be more important to a family than fixing up a sagging porch.

These facts support the contention that local policymakers should concentrate directly upon identified housing problems rather than rely upon a chance that other policy action may produce secondary housing benefits. At the very least, nonhousing policy should be assessed as to its impact upon housing.

POVERTY OR LOW INCOME? Housing deprivation is fundamentally interrelated with poverty as both a cause and an effect. Considerable evidence suggests that improved income alone will not significantly

process of housing by those decision makers in the housing system will lead directly to not only effective policy but *better* policy, in the sense that the interests and objectives of these actors (including the consuming public) will have been considered and, hopefully, when in conflict, resolved. We believe that the modeling process in its various forms (qualitative/quantitative, descriptive/simulation, etc.) is an appropriate tool to aid this understanding. In sum, while we advocate a direction of effort that stresses comprehensive modeling, and therefore we hope the development of more holistic policy that will be effective, we also recognize an alternative. Policy action directed at solving complex social problems may indeed have to become much more flexible in its application than has been true in the past. This would be particularly appropriate for federal and state housing policies, where the effects of implementation are very local.

improve housing situations because of the inelasticity of supply (construction), imperfect filtering (segregation, elderly remaining in large homes after children have left, etc.), the lack of capital, insufficient management-maintenance, and so on.

This situation suggests that local policymakers should deal with the interrelationship of poverty and housing deprivation and the variables limiting improvement rather than dealing with problems of low income alone. Greater individual financial resources alone may result in purchasing the same degree of housing quality (deprivation) at a higher cost.

INTERMEDIATE OR LONG-TERM ANALYSIS? The delivery of results over the intermediate term is generally more politically acceptable than continued promises of future results. Policymakers are generally seeking programs to deal with problems for which they have no obvious answers. Thus incremental change offers the greatest likelihood of political acceptance. This change includes both alteration of existing policies (property taxes, zoning, building codes, etc.) and additional policy implementation.

This situation suggests that relevant policy analysis at the local level will be continuous and involve both policy management and development.

LIMITED OR UNLIMITED RESOURCES? Within the intermediate term, resources must be assumed to be severely limited, especially for expensive policy alternatives. For instance, in the short term, new construction, intensive rehabilitation, and related capital improvements may quickly consume available policy resources while directly serving only a minority of the households in need. Unless these expenditures can be justified in terms of their leverage or multiplier effect, they must be seriously questioned.

It is extremely important for the policy analyst to understand the limitation of resources available to the local policymaker. When possible, it is desirable to weigh policy alternatives according to their cost-benefit. It must be emphasized, however, that quantification of cost-benefit is difficult at best and, without acknowledging underlying assumptions, may be misleading.

POLITICAL OR TECHNICAL FEASIBILITY? Policy alternatives are seldom rejected or accepted on the basis of technical feasibility (e.g., Operation Breakthrough) alone. Rather, the political environment of vested interests, competition, and compromise serve to restrict alternatives that appear to shift power or influence. As Nelkin noted, it makes little sense to develop technically acceptable alternatives without dealing with political acceptability [24].

Policy analysis needs both a technical competence of subject matter and an awareness of politically relevant or acceptable alternatives. This situation may be encouraged by greater contact and interaction with policymakers.

Nelkin offers the policy analyst a valuable perspective of major barriers to effective housing policy: first, housing is composed of many vested interests which are often in opposition and conflict; second, housing policies frequently lack clear, measurable objectives, which makes evaluative and simulation research difficult; third, housing problems are generally complex and multifaceted; and finally, the housing system operates primarily upon practical experience rather than research [24]. The logic of research, development, and application cannot be equated with the political process of dealing with broad and complex issues and, in turn, select the least disagreeable and risky compromise.

Local Policy Strategies. Local policymakers and decision makers are faced with a problem of quite different scale than are policymakers at the state or federal level (Table 10.2). They must make choices between alternatives seen as achievable with present or potential resources and within the parameters of currently existing programs. While they may involve themselves in attempts to change the nature

Table 10.2. Primary levels of public policy affecting housing

---

Federal
Fiscal policy (including reliance on capital markets)
Monetary policy (including reserve requirements; discount rates; FHA, FmHA, VA terms)
Technological research and development (National Bureau of Standards)
Tax policies (Internal Revenue Service)
Energy distribution

State
Income tax credits and policies
Banking regulations (including usury limits)
Insurance regulations
Utility (rate) regulations
Land division and sales regulations (condominium statutes, transfer taxes)
Landlord-tenant rights
Manpower training
Property tax equalization

Local (including Regional)
Comprehensive plan (including capital improvements)
Zoning codes
Subdivision regulations
Building codes
Housing codes
Property tax
Municipal services (safety, water, sewer, etc.)
Special services (watershed, mosquito control, parks and recreation, etc.)

---

of housing programs at the legislature or in the Congress, these efforts can only pay off in a fairly remote future.

With the availability of community development funds, a limited resource to be sure, local decision makers do have the opportunity to influence the local housing system and to choose between various available courses of action. They also may have the opportunity to attract resources from both the private and public sectors at higher geographic levels (regional, state, or federal), although these resources may be tied to specific programs. For example, a state housing finance agency may have funds for new construction but not rehabilitation. The decision then is not whether to use these resources for new construction or rehabilitation but rather between types and levels of construction.

Knowing the level of resources available and the limitations on their use is obviously a first order of business for the local policymaker. Among other limitations is the reliability of the funds and the assurance of their continuance. A one-time resource will be used quite differently than the same resource that is either available incrementally or on a continuing basis. Beyond knowing whether capital or start-up funds are available, the local decision maker needs to know whether continuing resources will be needed for program operation or maintenance and where these may be coming from. Local municipal officials have long been accustomed to looking a gift horse in the mouth. A park or playground without resources for maintenance and program frequently becomes an albatross around the neck of the local administration, likewise, a housing development for the elderly.

Looking at the output side, a major advantage of explicit systematic analysis is that it allows for careful consideration of both leverage and feedback effects. The direct or obvious output of a program may be far less significant than the secondary effects induced or "levered" by it (e.g., the improvement of the worst houses on the block through subsidized rehabilitation may give heart to surrounding owners and inspire them to make improvements in their own buildings).[12] On the other hand, a building which in itself may be an asset for the local fiscal situation may play havoc with surrounding property values and discourage investment in them so that the long-

12. Probably the easiest, most direct, and least costly subsidy to manage locally is a real estate or property tax credit. For instance, a property tax freeze or a one-time tax credit could be given to property owners rehabilitating obsolete or substandard dwellings. A similar subsidy could also be directed toward new construction in vital communities with low vacancy ratios. A strong incentive for such (local) programs would be state revenue disbursement to match foregone property tax revenue.

run tax effects are negative. Most of these kinds of results are predictable and can be taken account of explicitly by a descriptive model. Their presence as implicit fears or expectations in the mind of the policymaker is a much less reliable basis on which to make decisions.

The descriptive model can also order inconsistent or even conflicting objectives and allow them to interact in advance of commitment of resources. This may be particularly important when housing problems are approached indirectly through programs having other direct objectives: health, employment, income maintenance, and so forth. For example, increasing income may reasonably be expected to result in more expenditures for housing by some housing-deprived persons. The amount may not be known but can be investigated. William Grigsby, using a Maslow type hierarchy of needs-analysis for housing, indicates that additional income may be applied by poor people to many other needs before housing, depending on specific circumstances [12]. A housing allowance to a man with unfed children will be spent for food.

Both employing local labor and providing better housing to the housing-deprived may be objectives of a rural development program. The best housing at least cost, however, may result from using modular dwellings manufactured in a nonlocal plant. Choice then must be made between the two objectives and should be made on an explicit rational basis or at least in light of specific facts rather than on the basis of hunch and guesstimate.

An explicit descriptive and systematic analysis can allow these and many other factors to be taken into consideration objectively. While it may not be possible to quantify each variable, it does encourage identification of symptoms, problems, and underlying assumptions.

CONCLUDING OBSERVATIONS. In general, this examination has suggested that public policy directed toward ameliorating housing deprivation would be strengthened considerably by usable, appropriately based academic research. Benefits would accrue to both public policy and research institutions. This examination stresses that policy analysis in housing should be virtually a foregone conclusion.

The key factors for a more mutually beneficial relationship are largely cooperative in scope. On one hand, policymakers and agencies should seek to strengthen general communication with the social science researchers and to disseminate research beyond the infrastructure. On the other hand, academic researchers need to strengthen their own functions, especially (1) adherence to rigorous methodological and analytical standards, (2) patience and persistence to stay with a problem as policy considerations slowly and sporadically evolve, and (3) nonabstract, simplified communication with decision makers.

In terms of housing policy specifically, several key questions and strategies have been noted. While the authors have indicated general biases, it should be emphasized that the uniqueness of local housing markets necessitates individual analysis. A rational approach using a content (housing) and policy (Eberts and Sismondo, Chap. 4) framework offers the tool for such an analysis.

REFERENCES

1. Angell, William J. 1976. A context of consumer housing alternatives. In Carol S. Wedin and Trudy Nygren, eds., *Housing Perspective: Individuals and Families.* Minneapolis: Burgess.
2. ———. 1975. Housing costs in the mid-seventies. Univ. of Minn. Agric. Ext. Serv. Folder 315.
3. Angell, William J., and Phillip S. Olson. 1975. Owner-built housing. Univ. of Minn. Agric. Ext. Serv. Spec. Rep. 53.
4. Bird, Ronald. 1973. Inadequate housing and poverty status of households. USDA, Rural Dev. Serv. Stat. Bull. 520.
5. Building the American city. 1969. Report of the National Commission on Urban Problems, Washington, D.C.
6. Cochran, Clay. 1971. The scandal of rural housing. *Archit. Forum* (March): 52–55.
7. A decent home. 1969. Report of the President's Committee on Urban Housing, Washington, D.C.
8. Ford, James. 1936. *Slums and Housing.* Cambridge, Mass.: Harvard Univ. Press.
9. Forrester, Jay W. 1968. *Urban Dynamics.* Cambridge, Mass.: M.I.T. Press.
10. Friedman, Lawrence M. 1968. *Government and Slum Housing: A Century of Frustration.* Chicago: Rand McNally.
11. Garn, Harvey A., and Robert H. Wilson. 1970. A critical look at urban dynamics: The Forrester model. Washington, D.C.: Urban Land Institute.
12. Grigsby, William G., and Louis Rosenberg. 1975. *Urban Housing Policy.* New York: APS Publications.
13. Harris, Lewis. 1973. The Lewis Harris survey: Product quality doubted. *Minneapolis Star,* Nov. 29, p. 6.
14. Harris, Robert. 1973. Policy analysis and policy development. *Soc. Serv. Rev.* (Sept.): 360–72.
15. Lansing, John B., Charles Wade Clifton, and James N. Morgan. 1969. New homes and poor people: A study of chains of move. Institute for Social Research, University of Michigan.
16. Lee, Douglass B., Jr. 1973. Requiem for large-scale models. *J. Am. Inst. Planners* (May): 163–78.
17. Lee, Fang-Yao. 1971. Regional variations in expenditure patterns in the U.S. *J. Reg. Sci.* (March): 359.
18. de Leeuw, Frank. 1974. What should U.S. housing policy be? *J. Finance* (May): 699–721.

19. The mobile home market. 1972. *Appraisal J.* (July): 391–411.
20. Mollenhopf, John, and Jon Pynos. 1973. Boardwalk and park place: Property ownership, political structure and housing policy. In Jon Pynos, ed., *Housing Urban America.* Chicago: Aldine.
21. Morris, Earl W., and Mary E. Winter. 1978. *Housing Family and Society.* New York: John Wiley & Sons.
22. ———. 1975. A theory of family housing adjustment. *J. Marriage Fam.* (Feb.): 79–88.
23. Musgrave, John C. 1974. New estimates of residential capital in the United States, 1925–1973. *Surv. Curr. Bus.* (Oct.): 32–38.
24. Nelkin, Dorothy. 1971. *The Politics of Housing Innovation.* Ithaca, N.Y.: Cornell Univ. Press.
25. Nenno, Mary K. 1973. Housing in metropolitan areas: Roles and responsibilities of five key actors. National Association of Housing and Redevelopment Officials, Washington, D.C.
26. Schusshiem, Morton, Joshua M. Kay, and Richard L. Wellons. 1975. Rural housing: Needs, credit availability and federal programs. Congr. Res. Serv., Libr. Congr. for Senate Subcomm. Rural Dev., 94th Congr., Washington, D.C.
27. Smith, Wallace F. 1973. Should a house last 300 years? *Socio-Econ. Plann. Sci.* (July): 723–37.
28. Spurlock, Hughes H. 1975. Differences in housing credit terms and usage between metro and non-metro areas. USDA, ERS, Agric. Econ. Rep. 305.
29. STARSITE—Toward a decision making mechanism for housing. 1972. NASA-ASEE Summer Faculty Fellowship Program, School of Engineering, Auburn University.
30. Technical Studies, volume 2. 1969. Report of the President's Committee on Urban Housing, Washington, D.C.
31. Thee, Robert. 1973. Approaches to measurement of housing environments in rural non-farm communities. Unpublished thesis, Iowa State University.
32. U.S. Department of Commerce. Bureau of the Census. 1974. *Statistical Abstracts of the United States,* 95th ed. Washington, D.C.
33. U.S. Forest Service. 1965. Timber trends in the United States. Forest Resour. Rep. 17.

CHAPTER ELEVEN

USE OF SIMULATION IN PLANNING

W. R. MAKI, R. A. BARRETT, and R. J. BRADY

SIMULATION is a technique for representing the workings of a complex system such as the governmental activities of a large city or the total economy of a multicounty region. Three types of simulation are identified in this presentation: computer simulation, games, and gaming simulation.

Computer simulation is based on the manipulative capabilities of modern computers to explore complex mathematical models of urban and regional systems. In games, on the other hand, the behavior of decision makers is simulated by condensing their roles into a few representative forms and by applying rules that closely depict their real life constraints. In gaming simulation, however, the computer provides both an environment for the game and a laboratory for experimentation. Operational gaming, finally, includes both games and gaming simulations and hence involves the playing of games with or without use of a computer.

Our intent is to relate the three types of simulations to planning. We are trying to attain a better understanding not only of *what* happens (which, for a complex system, is already a difficult task), but also *how* and *why* these happenings occur. Our goal, therefore, is to identify practical uses of simulation in coping with and

W. R. MAKI is Professor, Department of Agricultural and Applied Economics, University of Minnesota.

R. A. BARRETT is Director, Institute for Urban and Regional Studies, Mankato State University, Mankato, Minnesota.

R. J. BRADY was formerly Research Specialist, Department of Agricultural and Applied Economics, University of Minnesota.

The authors gratefully acknowledge the assistance of Dr. Yashwant Junghare in literature review of the development and use of computer simulation and operational gaming games.

understanding problems of local and regional change and development.

Our presentation is in two parts. Computer simulation models are presented first, starting with the Chicago Area Transportation Study (CATS) Model as a prototype of the special-purpose planning model [14, 66]. Computer model characteristics are described further with reference to the recently implemented Minnesota Regional Economic System Simulation Laboratory (SIMLAB). User and operator manuals for SIMLAB (graded by learning proficiency level grades 11 to 14, 15 to 17, and 18 and over) are being developed in collaboration with computer and educational systems specialists [9].

Operational gaming models start with Community (previously Cornell) Land Use Game (CLUG) and Metropolis as precursors of the operational gaming models [22, 29]. The City Model, which is being used for teaching planning courses at the University of Minnesota and Mankato State University, is one of the most recent versions of computer-based games [5]. Another version is the River Basin Model, which is used in watershed research at North Dakota State University, the University of Oklahoma, and also the urban and regional studies program at Mankato State University.

Planning applications of simulation models will vary with the style of planning [7, 8, 17, 18, 19, 30, 33, 35, 37, 38, 45, 48, 52, 53, 54, 63, 71, 74, 75, 82, 84, 92, 95, 96, 98, 99, 108, 113, 114]. Three planning styles are presented here as options to highly centralized command planning [60]. For the latter, simulation models provide scenarios and projections of what is likely to happen.

In policy planning, limiting factors in local and regional change are identified and alternative approaches for moving away from an unsatisfactory social or economic situation are devised and tested [94]. Knowledge of relationships between policy incentives and their outcomes (which is essential in knowing when and how to manage policy changes) is acquired by technical analysis, controlled experiments, projective techniques, and economic and social indicators. Uses for both computer simulation and operational gaming are found in policy planning.

Corporate planning, in contrast, is identified as a structured variation on politics-as-usual; it involves negotiation among representatives of major interest groups—a process which is readily simulated in a variant of operational gaming. The aim of the corporate style of planning is a temporary "mutual adjustment" of interests in which government planners perform the role of brokers among a small number of competing interests.

Participant planning refers to community forms of decision making which can involve neighborhoods, cooperatives, or voluntary organizations. Spatial contiguity of individuals in the participant style of planning is an important though not necessarily essential requirement [78]. Again, a simulation approach may be used to help professional as well as participant planners in learning about the problems they are facing and the available methods for dealing with them and in providing relevant information about the external environment.

The three planning options are incorporated in what Kalba calls competitive planning, in which motivation for public sector participation occurs because of its reliance upon private compliance [60]. The private and public sectors try to expand the scope of decision making in return for a reduction of uncertainty concerning the decision-making environment. Again computer simulation approaches may be used to show citizen and special interest groups how to reduce the adverse local impacts, for example, of a large suburban commercial or rural industrial development program. Simulation also may be used to show the local impacts of alternative income redistribution, service delivery, and public financing strategies.

COMPUTER SIMULATION. Use of computer simulation in planning is colored currently by the widely held view that large-scale models are unmanageable because of their excessive comprehensiveness and data requirements, coupled with grossness of spatial detail [59, 69]. For our purposes, however, computer simulation is viewed as an increasingly efficient and accessible means for understanding the processes and directions of local and regional change.

We identify a representative series of computer simulation models and assess their strengths and weaknesses in helping both professional and participant (citizen) planners to develop values, knowledge, abilities, and skills for the different styles of planning that occur in the public sector (Fig. 11.1). Indeed, we recognize a shift away from authoritarian and hierarchical planning to varieties of participant planning for which computer simulations can provide alternative scenarios of the external environment. The simulations can also show the economic constraints on equality of access to jobs, income, and services in the regional community. Likewise, they reveal the dynamic interrelationships between the private and public sectors [70].

Transportation. Computer simulations of regional transportation development are cited first because of their early occurrence [58]. They also illustrate the limitations of large-scale models that are goal-oriented optimizing models rather than role-oriented simulation models.

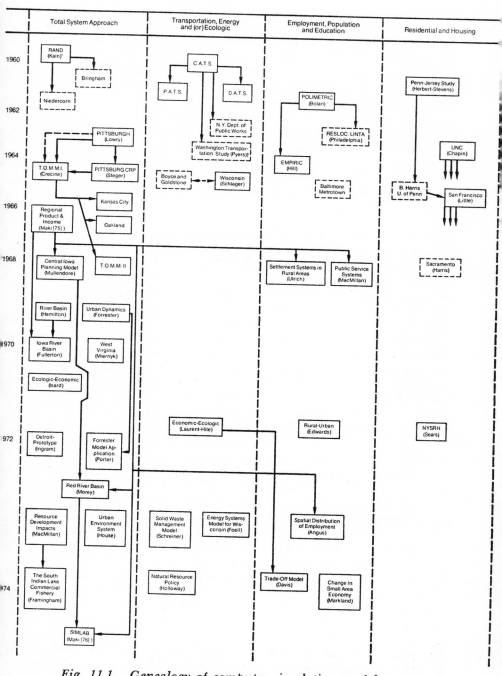

Fig. 11.1. Genealogy of computer simulation models.
* Because of space limitations, in some instances only first (or senior) authors are cited. See the reference listing at the end of the chapter for complete reference citations.
† The Washington Transportation Study (Pyers) is included in this figure but was not completely documented in Nagelberg [87], the major source for this figure.

The CATS Model is the precursor of the Pittsburgh, Detroit, and and other large-scale transportation models [13, 14, 66, 89, 100]. Land use is based on a probabilistic allocation of activities to land parcels. Projections of population and growth in open space and transportation, commercial, residential, and industrial activities are data inputs for the transportation forecasts.

Most recent efforts in transportation systems modeling deal with state and multicounty regions in the national economy [21, 96]. The U.S. input-output model provides the national economic constraints in the programming of least-cost interregional commodity shipments in one study [90]. A rent-maximizing model is used in allocating national employment levels among urban regions in another study [39].

Population and Employment. Subarea changes in residential population and employment as a function of migration and areawide growth are simulated in a large-scale model of Empiric. This is a linear programming simulation of five "located" variables (types of population and employment) in twenty-nine subareas, on which constraints are imposed by fourteen to twenty-two "locator" variables (types of social and private overhead capital) [44, 45].

State-level simulations of population and employment are provided in a nonoptimizing system model of the Iowa economy [75]. Here, an input-output submodel is used primarily as an accounting framework for achieving internal consistency in the projection series. A related set of multivariable equations is used recursively to make the model dynamic and to provide for public (or "outside") interventions in regional development activities.

Residential and Housing. Again, a microsystem approach is used in the residential and housing models of which the Penn-Jersey Transportation Model is a prototype [43, 103]. Market demand for land is determined for the highly disaggregated residential sector by linear programming solutions which yield optimal location patterns for housing by maximizing "rent-paying ability," that is, the difference between the available household budget for housing and transportation and the market costs, if sites were free.

Later variants include models of land use succession and housing renewal [13, 71]. Construction, deterioration, and modification of housing in urban districts and conversion of rural to urban land are simulated by these models.

Total Systems Approach. Interdependence of transportation development and land use changes was recognized in the large-scale modeling efforts of the 1960s, particularly in the urban development models [58, 59, 72, 87]. The earliest models were theoretical, not empirical. However, the Pittsburgh Urban Simulation Model was empirical and descriptive in its representation of several of thiry-nine computer subroutines; a variant of this model was incorporated into Michigan Effectuation Training and Research Operation (METRO) (discussed in the next section). Later, the Iowa, the Susquehanna Basin, the West Virginia, the Urban Dynamics, and also the rural urban and resource development models were developed to simulate the regional impacts of urban-industrial change [2, 4, 6, 15, 25, 31, 32, 38, 55, 56, 57, 65, 67, 73, 76, 77, 83, 85, 86, 91, 97].

Recent efforts in modeling a total regional system include SIM-LAB (the Minnesota regional system model) and the input-output based models used in state energy and economic development planning [30, 32, 36, 75, 79]. Also relevant here is the reconciliation of large-scale system orientation with local perspectives on the incidence of state and regional development impacts [11, 51, 55, 81].

We present SIMLAB now to illustrate the use of a computer-interactive approach in regional systems modeling and evaluation. A series of interdependent subsystems is identified in the basic model:

1. Markets—export and local—and respective roles in private sector planning
2. Investment—output-expansion, pollution abatement, and regional infrastructure, including energy and transportation facilities
3. Demand—household, business, and government—and role in "driving" production
4. Production—both goods and services, private and public, current and capital
5. Value added—household and business income and its distribution and deployment in the economy
6. Employment and labor force—in terms of production requirements and existing labor force of given skills distribution
7. Population and households—growth dynamics and dependency on jobs and overall role in "driving" demand
8. Fiscal and ecologic—public revenues and waste emissions and their relation to the production system

Each submodel is linked to the preceding and succeeding submodels by a feedback loop. A series of nine parameters is presented initially for review and adjustment in a particular sequence by the model operator. Each variable, however, is determined endogenously, except for the starting input variables. Eventually the input and output variables will be linked to a regional development game (patterned after the City Model cited earlier).

In addition, a series of submodels is being developed that will be linked to the preceding system model. The submodels are treated as separate modules in an expanded system model.

The additional computer simulation modules are identified, therefore, as follows:

1. Transportation and land use—their interdependence and interaction with markets, production, and population and with the ongoing activities in the economic, governmental, and social sectors of the local community and/or regional community

2. Energy allocation, conservation, and development—their interaction with demand and production and with economic, governmental, and social sectors in the community

3. Economic development—alternate strategies for economic base expansion to support essential environmental and human services

4. Housing and environmental services—impacts of providing, using, and financing residential units and related public infrastructure on economic, governmental, and social sectors

5. Human services delivery—impacts of providing, using, and financing essential social services on economic, governmental, and social sectors in the community

Each module thus will provide data that can be used in the community and regional development games and will receive data from each of the three community sectors. Initially, however, the computer modules will be linked only to the basic system model.

Proposed, therefore, is a modularized computer capability for simulating the local and regional incidence of economic development impacts. Such a capability is being developed in the use and extension of SIMLAB as a laboratory setting for experimentation with a regional system model. For example, a majority of high schools and all institutions of higher education in Minnesota are already linked to the central computer facility holding the SIMLAB programs. Actual data for selected areas in Minnesota are also available for use in the computer simulations. The next step is to introduce the planning student and practitioner to SIMLAB and its potential capabilities for experimentation in regional economic systems.

OPERATIONAL GAMING. Current operational gaming models used in planning have evolved from the two models cited earlier—CLUG and Metropolis (Fig. 11.2). Weaknesses and strengths of these models are presented in terms of our current experience with the City Model in college classrooms and planning workshops.

A primary distinction occurs between the early games and the more recent gaming-simulation models, that is, use of the computer in decision simulation [26]. The manual games differ further in the

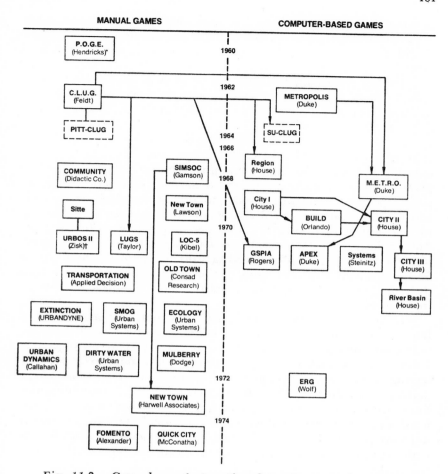

Fig. 11.2. Genealogy of operational gaming models.

* Because of space limitations, in some instances only first (or senior) authors are cited. See the reference listing at the end of the chapter for complete reference citations.
† Urbos II (Zisk) is included in this figure but was not completely documented in Nagelberg [87], the major source for this figure.

use of a grid playing board to represent a geographical area. CLUG, for example, is played on a grid board while Metropolis is not. CLUG is more systematic while Metropolis is more role playing. The two approaches are incorporated in the several versions of the City Model.

Manual Games. CLUG [28, 29], Land Use Gaming Simulation (LUGS) [104, 105], and New Town [40, 41, 68] illustrate the manual grid board games. The designer's objective in each game was education.

Because these games are played in planning courses in North America and Europe, they are presented here [74, 77, 106, 107]. Metropolis [22, 24] is not played on a grid board, but it, also, is a manual game.

Each of the manual games is differentiated according to three characteristics: player objectives, amount of economic growth, and locational pattern. Planning uses for the manual games evolve from the three characteristics.

PLAYER OBJECTIVES. In CLUG, the player objectives are to build, operate, and maintain the community and to make money. The players make all employment and commercial decisions. Profits depend upon location with respect to other businesses, households, and utilities. Government decisions are made by majority vote and include setting the local tax rate and expanding utility services. Sale of heavy industry output to national markets brings money into the local system. Money leakages occur out of the local system for government expenses, construction costs, land purchases from the bank, transportation charges, and purchases of goods and services from outside the community.

LUGS is a modified version of CLUG, but certain distinct differences occur in the two games. Making a business profit and providing adequate government services are important player objectives. Private decision makers develop heavy industry, commercial business-serving households, and housing, while government decision makers develop municipal services, parks, terminals, and communication links. Income in the private sector is totally a function of employees hired and determined by distance to a terminal. Owners of housing units are penalized by lower income if the residences are not located within a certain distance of commercial businesses, municipal services, and parks.

New Town is still another adaptation of CLUG. Four versions of the game are available. Version I provides for a specified objective—to achieve the highest ratio of total revenue to total land cost. Players roll dice to decide the type and density of development units they may place on owned or rented land. Bonuses in the form of increased incomes are provided for retail agglomerations, retail neighborhoods, industrial sites adjacent to the rail or river, and resident sites adjacent to the lake. In version II, money is introduced as a medium of exchange. Bidding of retail and industrial units, taxation, and redevelopment of property occurs to maximize rate of return. Additional bonuses are awarded to the teams (up to four in total) with the largest amount of industrial income and with homogeneous land uses on a parcel. The public sector is introduced in version III.

Here the planners' objective is set by the system or self-established in such a way as to serve or shape future development. Bonuses are affected by the placement of utilities, parks, and schools. Finally, version IV expands the range of government activity. Economic bonuses now reflect sociologic and aesthetic benefits. New public land uses include fire stations, health clinics, town halls, sewage plants, institutions, civic centers, refuse disposal plants, and airports.

In Metropolis, a real metropolitan area is used in simulation. The gaming activity focuses on the Capital Improvement Program for the single political jurisdiction represented. The players, in their various roles, are forced to choose between alternative courses of action on three capital improvements per round at the same time they are trying to achieve personal objectives. In each round, the administration prepares the capital improvement program, the politicians decide the annual budget, and the land speculators try to influence the formation of the capital programs so that increased profits accrue to them.

GROWTH AND LOCATION. Community growth in CLUG and LUGS is determined by the players and limited by cash balances. In New Town, however, growth is determined by dice roll. Before parcels can be developed, they must be served by utilities that emanate from the utility plant and run along the edge of the parcels.

In Metropolis, growth depends upon the resolution of community issues in each round. The gaming focus here of course, is the capital improvement program.

Natural features, such as a lake or river, influence the locational pattern of CLUG and LUGS. Three zones are delineated on the board in New Town; these represent the downtown, the transitional area, and the suburbs, and they are determined by dice role. Precise location of development within each zone, however, is based upon ownership and location relative to other units and natural features. Locational features are not important in Metropolis.

Use of the grid board is essential in achieving a locational perspective in a community development game. For this reason particularly, CLUG has been most widely modified and extended for land use and environmental teaching and planning purposes.

Computer-Based Games. METRO [23, 60], City I [26, 27, 31], Air Pollution Experiment (APEX) [15], and City Model [26, 47, 50] illustrate the computer-based games. The two city games, unlike METRO and APEX, make use of a grid board, but they were not constructed with real data. Both METRO and APEX deal with the real data base of Lansing, Michigan. Again, the three criteria cited earlier are used in illustrating the content and use of the computer-based games.

PLAYER OBJECTIVES. In METRO, players are assigned as members of two types of teams: a functional team—a politician, planner, school board member, and land developer; and a locational team—central city, suburbs, or urbanizing township in which each player has a role and a jurisdiction to represent. Household, industrial, and commercial behavior is simulated by the computer, which also serves as a data bank and processes the inputs and generates outputs. The computer also controls the simulated population which elects politicians to office. Politicians are in charge of the budget for their jurisdictions, some public land purchases, zoning, and carrying out specific capital improvement projects. Land developers attempt to relate to the politicians in trying to make successful land purchases and building decisions for the growth that is generated each round by the simulated land users, that is, industry, commerce, and households. School decision makers try to improve schools and get reelected; they set school tax rates, purchase land, allocate a budget, and make capital improvements. Finally, planners work one year ahead of the politicians and try to plan future programs; their task is essentially one of trying to persuade the community to accept their suggestions.

APEX is an extensively modified version of METRO. The Lansing data base is still employed, but the number of analysis areas (which are not located on a game board by coordinates) has been reduced from forty-four to twenty-nine. Players no longer make school decisions, but the six local industrialists and a county air pollution control officer (APCO) assume air control roles. The county APCO is the only player concerned exclusively with air pollution conditions of the simulated area. The other players are concerned with air pollution only insofar as the costs of controlling pollution affect them, the impact of regulations affect them, or the simulated electorate become vocal in their opposition to undesirable pollution levels. Players who are land developers buy, sell, and develop land in response to a simulated market. Simulated developers take up any remaining demand the gaming developers do not need. Success of the county APCO depends on his ability to persuade other local decision makers of the worth of his programs.

City I is an extension of CLUG and Metropolis; hence, a decision-making environment is provided in which the interrelatedness of decisions across the urban system and over time can be experienced and observed. Nine teams of from one to five members per team are the decision makers who effect land use and urban development on a 25 x 25 grid on which the game is played. Nine types of private land use are developed: heavy industry, light industry, business goods, business services, personal goods, personal services, high-income residences, middle-income residences, and low-income residences. Each of the nine teams is elected or appointed by elected officials to assume the duties of one of nine governmental functions which are performed simultaneously with the entrepreneurial functions common to all teams. Teams set their own objectives for both the public and private actions they undertake.

City Model is an extensive evolution beyond the City I model. The social sector is added to the system, which provides for multiple jurisdictions; also, the transportation component is expanded to include commuter bus and rapid-rail travel. Economic teams begin play with some developed property and certain amounts of cash and undeveloped property. To develop new parcels of land, however, zoning and utilities and highway access must be secured from the government sector. Social decision makers provide for the population units in the area. Time allocation and boycotting decisions are made for the three major socioeconomic classes of residents in the community. Governmental decision makers are elected by the social players or are appointed by the already elected officials to assume the duties of one of the governmental functions, which are performed simultaneously with economic and social functions. They make service delivery, policy, and capital improvement decisions. Players set their own objectives for both the public and private actions they undertake.

GROWTH AND LOCATION. Community or area growth depends on the resolution of the decision-making processes among the several sectors in each of the four illustrated games. Rules and regulations established and maintained by the governmental sector have a decisive impact influence on growth.

Locational questions are handled by game players in the two city games in a variety of decisions that have their outcomes represented on the gaming board. Capital improvement decisions, on the other hand, are not place specific. Neither are the air pollution controls place specific within the larger metropolitan area.

PLANNING APPLICATIONS. Computer simulation and operational gaming models are viewed, finally, in the context of planning and planning education. The elected models are compared and evaluated according to certain planning-related criteria cited earlier. These criteria relate to both the issues and the tools involved in urban and regional development planning in the United States. Their usage

Table 11.1. Comparison of selected evaluation techniques and processes in the use of technical and regional knowledge and system design features*

	Conventional Benefit-Cost Analysis	Modified Cost/Effectiveness Approach	Computer Interactive Programming and Simulation	Dialectical Scanning and Operational Gaming
Aggregate monetary impacts	M	U	U	U
Scaled measures of nonmonetary impacts	O	M	U	U
Spatial disaggregation of impacts	V	V	M	U
Subjective weighting of various impact criteria	O	U	U	U
Intangibles (nonquantified impacts)	O	V	V	U
Contextual specificity (inclusion of unique local phenomena as planning referents)	O	V	V	M
Easily incorporates new performance criteria	O	O	O	M
Encourages generation of new program alternatives	O	O	U	U
Provides rapid assessment of options by multiple criteria	O	O	M	M

* Listing of items and evaluation techniques are adapted from Hudson, Wachs, and Shofer [51, p. 26]. Symbols used in body of table denote importance of knowledge or design attributed as follows: M—major strength of method; U—usual characteristic; V—variants of method might incorporate the one characteristic; O—lack of characteristic.

offers considerable potential to develop values, knowledge, abilities, and skills of professionals and participants in the planning process.

The uses of knowledge and the flexibility of system designs are noted in the review of evaluation techniques and processes by Hudson, Wachs, and Shofer [51, p. 260]. The simulation approaches are viewed as part of an evaluation process, which allows for the use of both technical and personal knowledge in formulating alternative approaches to regional development that are sensitive to local values and concerns (Table 11.1). Unlike the conventional economic approaches (e.g., cost-benefit and cost-effectiveness analysis), both personal and technical knowledge and system design features can be handled in the computer simulation and operational gaming approaches.

Regional systems design solutions may be sought by use of one or more of several complementary evaluative techniques, such as benefit-cost and cost-effectiveness analysis [12]. Computer-based interactive programs (e.g., Intuition and Evaluation [INTU-VAL]) are also available for local proponents or opponents of change to determine the local impacts of regional development alternatives and to develop a set of inputed weights for each criterion used in the evaluation process [62]. SIMLAB is being developed as a computer-interactive programming technique that provides for facilities and related instructional resources.

Finally, "dialectical scanning" has been suggested as a viable structure for citizen participation in planning [51, p. 262]. In this approach, agreement is sought on whether conflicts exist and whether the counter disagreements are properly assigned with their opposites. Differences thus determined are to be reconciled in the second stage of dialectical scanning [64]. Operational gaming approaches are included with the dialectical scanning approach suggested by Hudson, Wachs, and Shofer.

Because of the multiplicity of goals and interest groups in state and regional planning, the several simulation approaches are viewed as being useful in identifying critical decision constraints and variables. The intent is not to prescribe certain development alternatives but to explore the implications of each alternative for the relevant interest groups (which may approve or oppose these alternatives, depending upon their respective goals and values). Sought here is a composite technical and organizational capability for facilitating dialogue and interaction between planners and interest groups involved in formulation of policies on state and regional development.

REFERENCES

1. Alexander, Ernest R., and Richard L. Meier. 1974. Fomento. (Mimeo.) Baltimore: Academic Games Association.

2. Angus, James E. 1973. Spatial distribution of employment: Alternatives for a metropolitan region. Ph.D. diss., University of Minnesota.
3. Applied Decision Systems, Inc. 1970. Transportation planning simulation. Presented at Environ. Urban Syst. Res. Conf., Dep. Transp., Washington, D.C.
4. Barnard, Jerald R. 1967. Design and use of social accounting systems in state development planning. Bureau of Business and Economic Research, University of Iowa.
5. Barrett, Robert. 1971. Mankato State: City Model usage in the urban studies institute. An environmental laboratory for the Social Sciences. Washington, D.C.: U.S. Environmental Protection Agency, pp. 75–82.
6. Belkin, Jacob. 1972. Urban dynamics: Applications as a teaching tool and as an urban game. *IEEE Trans. Syst. Man Cybern.* SMC-2 (2): 166–69.
7. Berger, Edward, Harvey Bouley, and Betty Zisk. 1970. Simulation and city: A critical overview. *Simulation Games* 1 (4): 411–48.
8. Bolan, Richard S., W. B. Hansen, N. A. Irwin, and K. H. Dieter. 1963. Planning applications of a simulation model. Prepared for Fall Meet., New Engl. Sect. Reg. Sci. Assoc., Boston College.
9. Brady, R. J. 1975. User manual for program SIMLAB: A computer simulation model of demographic and economic activity. (Staff paper) Department of Agricultural and Applied Economics, University of Minnesota.
10. Callahan, Loel A. 1971. Urban dynamics. Chicago: UrbanDyne.
11. Carruthers, Garrey E. 1968. An analysis of public investment in Iowa state parks and recreation areas. Ph.D. diss., Iowa State University.
12. Cartwright, T. J. 1973. Systems, solutions and strategies: A contribution to the theory and practice of planning. *J. Am. Inst. Plann.* 39 (3): 179–87.
13. Chapin, Stuart F., Jr. 1962. UNC Model, University of North Carolina.
14. Chicago Area Transportation Study. 1960. *Final Report. Vol. 2, Data Projections.* Chicago: CATS.
15. Cochran, Anne. 1969. Introduction to APEX—A gaming simulation exercise. Environmental Simulation Laboratory, University of Michigan.
16. Consad Research Corporation. 1971. Old town: A simulation about model cities. Pittsburgh: Consad Research Corporation.
17. Crecine, John P. 1969. *Governmental Problem-Solving: A Computer Simulation of Municipal Budgeting.* Chicago: Rand McNally.
18. Davis, R. M., G. S. Stacey, G. I. Nehman, and F. K. Goodman. 1974. Development of an economic-environmental trade-off model for industrial land-use planning. *Rev. Reg. Stud.* 4 (1): 11–26.
19. Didactic Games Company. The community. (Mimeo.) Chicago: Science Research Associates.
20. Dodge, Dorothy. 1971. Mulberry. Department of Political Science, Macalester College.
21. Douglas, P. G., and J. A. MacMillan. 1972. Simulation of economic impacts of highway expenditures. Univ. of Manitoba Cent. Transp. Stud. Res. Rep. 9.
22. Duke, Richard D. 1964. Gaming-simulation in urban research. Institute of Community Development and Services, Michigan State University.
23. ———. 1974. *Gaming: The Future's Language.* New York: Halsted Press. (Div. of John Wiley & Sons)

24. ———. 1966. METRO report on phase 1. Tri-County Reg. Plann. Comm. METRO Proj. Tech. Rep. 5, Lansing, Mich.
25. Edwards, C., and R. De Pass. 1971. Rural-urban population, income, and employment: A simulation of alternative futures. USDA, ERS, Agric. Econ. Rep. 218.
26. Environmetrics. 1969. City manual. (Mimeo.) Washington, D.C.: Environmetrics.
27. ———. 1971. City Model player's manual. (Mimeo.) Washington, D.C.: U.S. Department of Commerce, National Bureau of Standards.
28. Feldt, Allan G. 1966. The community (Cornell) land use game (CLUG). Department of City and Regional Planning, Cornell University.
29. ———. 1966. Operational gaming in planning education. *J. Am. Inst. Plann.* 32 (1): 17–23.
30. Foell, W. K. 1973. Simulation modelling of energy systems: A decision-making tool. Presented at Conf. on Energy and Environ. Long-Term Decision, Organ. Econ. Coop. Dev., Paris.
31. Forrester, Jay H. 1969. *Urban Dynamics.* Cambridge: M.I.T. Press.
32. Framingham, C. F., J. A. MacMillan, and J. Craven. 1974. Simulation of alternatives for the South Indian Lake commercial fishery. Manitoba Department of Mines, Resources and Environmental Management.
33. Fullerton, H. H., and J. R. Prescott. 1975. *An Economic Simulation Model for Regional Development Planning.* Ann Arbor, Mich.: Ann Arbor Science Publisher.
34. Gamson, William A. 1969. *SIMSOC: Simulated Society.* New York: Free Press.
35. Greenblatt, Cathy S. 1972. Gaming and simulation in the social sciences. *Simulation Games* 3 (4): 477–91.
36. Grubb, Herbert W. 1973. The structure of the Texas economy. Office of Information Services, Office of the Governor, Austin, Tex.
37. Guetzknow, Harold S., Philip Kotler, and Randall L. Schultz. 1972. *Simulation in Social and Administrative Science: Overviews and Case Examples.* Englewood Cliffs, N.J.: Prentice-Hall.
38. Hamilton, H. R., ed. 1969. *Systems Simulation for Regional Analysis: An Application to River-Basin Planning.* Cambridge: M.I.T. Press.
39. Harris, Curtis C., Jr. 1973. *The Urban Economies, 1985: A Multiregional, Multi-Industry Forecasting Model.* Lexington, Mass.: Lexington Books.
40. Harwell Associates. 1973. New Town. Convent Station, N.J.: Harwell Associates.
41. Hebert, Budd. 1972. The New Town game. *Simulation Games* 3 (3): 349–60.
42. Hendricks, Francis H. 1960. Planning operational gaming experiment (P.O.G.E.). Presented at AIP (N.C. chap.) Meet. on New Idea in Planning.
43. Herbert, John D., and Benjamin H. Stevens. 1960. A model for the distribution of residential activity in urban areas. *J. Reg. Sci.* 2 (2): 21–37.
44. Hill, Donald M. 1965. A growth allocation model for the Boston region. *J. Am. Inst. Plann.* 31 (2): 111–20.
45. Hill, Donald M., and Willard B. Hansen. 1968. Prototype development of a statistical land use prediction model for the greater Boston region. *Highw. Res. Board Rec.* 114:51–70.

46. Holloway, Milton L. 1974. An economic simulation model for analyzing natural resource policy. (Mimeo.) Office of Information Services, Division of Management Sciences, Austin, Tex.
47. House, Peter. 1969. The simulated city: The use of second generation gaming in studying the urban system. *Socioeconomic Plann. Sci.* 4 (1).
48. ———. 1973. *The Urban Environmental System: Modeling for Research, Policy-Making and Education.* Beverly Hills: Sage.
49. House, Peter, and Allan Feldt. 1968. Manual for REGION: An Urban development model. Washington, D.C.: Washington Center for Metropolitan Studies, Urban Systems Simulations.
50. House, Peter, and Phillip D. Patterson. 1969. An environmental gaming simulation laboratory. *J. Am. Inst. Plann.* 35 (5): 383–88.
51. Hudson, B. M., M. Wachs, and J. L. Shofer. 1974. Local impact evaluation in the design of large-scale urban systems. *J. Am. Inst. Plann.* 40 (4): 255–65.
52. Hufschmidt, Maynard M., and Myron B. Friering. 1966. *Simulation Techniques for Design of Water-Resource Systems.* Cambridge, Mass.: Harvard Univ. Press.
53. Inbar, Michael. 1970. Participating in a simulation game. *J. Appl. Behav. Sci.* 6 (2): 239–44.
54. Inbar, Michael, and Clarice S. Stoll. 1972. *Simulation and Gaming in Social Science.* New York: Free Press.
55. Ingram, G. K., John F. Kain, and J. Royce Ginn. 1972. *The Detroit Prototype of the NBER Simulation Model.* New York: National Bureau of Economic Research.
56. Isard, Walter. 1972. *Ecologic-Economic Analysis for Regional Development.* New York: Free Press.
57. Kadanoff, Leo P., and Herbert Weinblatt. 1972. Public policy conclusions from urban growth models. *IEEE Trans. Syst. Man Cybern.* SMS-2 (2): 159–65.
58. Kain, John. 1964. The development of urban transportation models. *Pap. Reg. Sci. Assoc.* (Univ. Pa.) 14: 147–73.
59. Kain, John, and John R. Meyers. 1968. Computer simulations, physioeconomic systems and intraregional models. *Am. Econ. Rev.* 58 (1): 171–81.
60. Kalba, Kas. 1974. Postindustrial planning: A review forward. *J. Am. Inst. Plann.* 40 (3): 147–55.
61. Kamnitzer, P. 1969. Computer aid to design. *Archit. Des.* 39 (Sept.): 507–9.
62. Kibel, Barry M. 1969. Gaming simulation of urban spatial processes. Proc. 9th Annu. Symp. Natl. Gaming Counc.
63. Kilbridge, M. D., R. P. O'Block, and P. V. Teplitz. 1970. Urban analysis. Division of Research, Graduate School of Business Administration, Harvard University.
64. Knight, D. E., H. W. Curtis, and L. J. Fogel. 1971. *Cybernetics, Simulation and Conflict Resolution.* New York: Spartan Books.
65. Kurtzweg, Jerry A. 1973. Urban planning and air pollution control: Research. *J. Am. Inst. Plann.* 40 (2): 82–92.
66. Lathrop, George T., and J. R. Hamburg. 1965. An opportunity-accessibility model for allocating regional growth. *J. Am. Inst. Plann.* 31 (2): 95–103.
67. Laurent, E. A., and J. C. Hite. 1971. Economic-ecologic analysis in the Charleston metropolitan region: An input-output study. Water Resources Research Institute, Clemson University.

68. Lawson, Barry R. 1969. New Town: An urban land use and development game. Convent Station, N.J.: Harwell Associates.
69. Lee, Douglass B., Jr. 1973. Requiem for large-scale models. *J. Am. Inst. Plann.* 39 (3): 163–78.
70. Lewis, Darrel R., and Donald Wentworth. 1971. Games and simulations for teaching economics. Center for Economic Education, University of Minnesota.
71. Little, Arthur D., Inc. 1966. Model of the San Francisco housing market. San Francisco Community Renewal Program, Tech. Pap. 8.
72. Lowry, Ira S. 1964. *A Model of Metropolis.* Santa Monica, Calif.: Rand, RM-4033-RC.
73. MacMillan, James, A. 1968. Public service systems in rural urban development. Ph.D. diss., Iowa State University.
74. Maki, Wilbur R., and J. E. Angus. 1973. Development planning. In G. C. Judge and T. Takayme, eds., *Studies in Economic Planning Over Space and Time.* Amsterdam: North Holland.
75. Maki, Wilbur R. and Ernesto C. Venegas. 1974. State regional economic models for long range energy planning. (Staff paper) Department of Agricultural and Applied Economics, University of Minnesota, pp. 24–27.
76. Maki, Wilbur, R., R. E. Suttor, and J. R. Barnard. 1966. Simulation of regional product and income with emphasis on Iowa, 1954–1974. Iowa Agric. Exp. Stn. Res. Bull. 548.
77. Markland, Robert E., and Peter J. Grandstaff. 1974. Analyzing change in a small-area economy using computer simulation. *Simulation Games* 5 (3): 291–315.
78. Maruyama, Magoroh. 1973. Human futuristics and urban planning. *J. Am. Insti. Plann.* 39 (5): 346–58.
79. Matson, R. A., and J. B. Studer. 1974. Simulating the prospective impact of coal development in Wyoming. Presented at 6th Annu. Meet. Mid-Continent Reg. Sci. Assoc., Urbana.
80. McConatha, Douglas. 1975. Quick city. Department of Sociolgy, University of Utah.
81. McLeod, John. 1968. *Simulation: The Dynamic Modeling of Ideas and Systems with Computers.* New York: McGraw-Hill.
82. Meier, Richard L., and Richard D. Duke. 1966. Gaming simulation for urban planning. *J. Am. Inst. Plann.* 32 (1): 3–17.
83. Miernyk, William H., Kenneth C. Shellhammer, Ronald L. Coccari, Wesley H. Wineman, Charles J. Gallagher, and Douglas M. Brown. 1970. *Simulating regional economic development: An interindustry analysis of the West Virginia economy.* Lexington, Mass.: Heath.
84. Morey, R. V., and N. E. Valentine. 1972. A simulation model for studying policy alternatives in a rural region. Proc. Int. Symp. on Syst. Eng., Purdue University.
85. ———. 1973. Systems models for studying rural development problems. Presented at Meet. Am. Soc. Agric. Eng., Chicago.
86. Mullendore, Walter E. 1968. An economic simulation model for urban regional development planning. Ph.D. diss., Iowa State University.
87. Nagelberg, Mark, and Dennis L. Little. 1970. Compiled bibliography: Selected urban simulations and games. *Simulation Games* 1 (4): 459–81.
88. Orlando, J. A., and A. J. Pennington. 1969. BUILD: A community development simulation game. Presented at 36th Natl. Meet. Oper. Res. Soc. Am., Miami Beach.

89. Pittsburgh Area Transportation Study. 1963. *Forecasts and Plans,* vol. 2. Pittsburgh: PATS.
90. Polenske, Karen R. 1970. A multi-regional input-output model for the United States. EDA Rep. 21, Harvard Econ. Res. Proj.
91. Porter, H. R., and E. J. Henley. 1972. An application of the Forrester Model to Harris County, Texas. *IEEE Trans. Syst. Man Cybern.* SMC-2 (2): 180–91.
92. Robinson, I. M., H. B. Wolfe, and R. L. Barringer. 1966. A simulation model for renewal programming. *J. Am. Inst. Plann.* 31 (2): 126–34.
93. Rogers, Clark D. 1970. Manual of operations: GSPIA decision exercise II. Department of Urban Affairs, University of Pittsburgh.
94. Rondinelli, Dennis A. 1973. Urban planning as policy analysis: Management or urban change. *J. Am. Inst. Plann.* 39 (1): 13–22.
95. Scheidell, John M. 1972. A dynamic simulator for economic forecasting and decision-making. *Simulation Games* 5 (2): 168–85.
96. Schlager, Kenneth J. 1965. A land use plan design model. *J. Am. Inst. Plann.* 31 (2): 103–11.
97. Schreiner, D., G. Muncrief, and B. Davis. 1973. Solid waste management for rural areas: Analysis of costs and service requirements. *Am. J. Agric. Econ.* 55 (Pt. 1): 567–76.
98. Scott, Andrew M. 1966. *Simulation and National Development.* New York: John Wiley & Sons.
99. Sears, David W. 1971. The New York State regional housing model: Simulation for public policy-making. *Simulation Games* 2 (2): 131–48.
100. Shubik, Martin, and Garry P. Brewer. 1972. Reviews of selected books and articles on gaming and simulation. (Mimeo.) Santa Monica, Calif.: Rand, R-732-ARPA.
101. Simile II. SITTE. LaJolla, Calif.: Western Behavioral Sciences Institute.
102. Steinitz, Carl, and Peter Rogers. 1970. *A Systems Analysis Model of Urbanization and Change.* Cambridge: M.I.T. Press.
103. Stevens, Benjamin H. 1961. Linear programming and location rent. *J. Reg. Sci.* 3 (2).
104. Taylor, John L. 1971. *Instructional Planning Systems: A Gaming Simulation Approach to Urban Problems.* Cambridge, England: Cambridge Univ. Press.
105. ———. 1968. L.U.G.S. Mark II (introductory version). Univ. of Sheffield (England), Dep. Town Reg. Plann., Discuss. Pap. 3.
106. ———. 1969. Some aspects of an instructional simulation approach to the urban development process. Unpublished Ph.D. diss., University of Sheffield, England.
107. Taylor, John L., and K. R. Carter. 1971. Gaming simulation. *J. (Royal) Town Plann. Inst.* 57 (1): 25–34.
108. Ulrich, Martin A. 1968. Optimal settlement systems in rural areas. Ph.D. diss., Iowa State University.
109. UrbanDyne. 1971. Extinction. (Mimeo.) Chicago: UrbanDyne.
110. ———. 1971. Dirty Water. (Mimeo.) Cambridge, Mass.: Urban Systems.
111. ———. 1971. Ecology. (Mimeo.) Cambridge, Mass.: Urban Systems.
112. ———. 1971. Smog. (Mimeo.) Cambridge, Mass.: Urban Systems.
113. Wilson, A. G. 1968. Models in urban planning: A synoptic review of recent literature. *Urban Stud.* 5 (3): 249–76.
114. Wolf, Lyle P., and Robert E. Laessig. 1973. ERG-energy resources game: Simulation gaming of regional energy management. *Simulation Games* 4 (3): 315–23.

CHAPTER TWELVE

COSTS AND BENEFITS OF ALTERNATIVE DATA-GATHERING TECHNIQUES

ROY D. HICKMAN and RICHARD D. WARREN

IN THE DESIGN and management of policy research, a major purpose is to provide quality information about social and economic situations to decision makers. Valid and reliable information is essential for the development and implementation of effective programs based on the problems and needs of people. This information is useful in describing past and current situations, examining alternative strategies and programs, reflecting the attitudes and opinions of persons involved, and providing a basis for projection of outcomes for various alternative programs.

In Chapter 4, Eberts and Sismondo discuss five categories of policy research and their respective roles: descriptive research, public opinion research, evaluation research, basic research, and proactive research. The range of informational needs suggested under these categories includes quantification of situations and problems, opinions and preferences of people for alternative means and programs, evaluation of programs and projects, proposition examination and theory development, methodological issues and questions, and projections and simulations under varying conditions.

For building theoretical and statistical models of relations among variables, it is necessary for policy researchers to collect, store, and process data that reflect information at the federal, state, county, municipal, and community levels. In making policy decisions and recommendations, sets of relevant policy variables are usually interrelated. Information may thus be needed in several related areas when programs are being developed in a single given area. Informa-

ROY D. HICKMAN is Associate Professor of Statistics in charge of the Survey Section, Statistical Laboratory, Iowa State University.

RICHARD D. WARREN is Professor, Department of Sociology and Anthropology and Department of Statistics, Iowa State University.

tional areas of concern for policy researchers include economics, transportation, land use, public service, housing, and population.

SELECTING DATA COLLECTION METHODS. Alternative research techniques are available for obtaining information needed by decision makers to develop policies. Requisite information can range from opinions about alternative solutions to problems expressed by individuals to data obtained through very sophisticated data collection and analysis techniques. Varying levels of both accuracy and cost must be compared with the policy problem under investigation, which will in turn reflect the accuracy and degree of precision necessary. Specific research procedures and techniques should be selected on the basis of the problem considered, degree of precision necessary for estimates required for the solution of the problem, geographical areas involved, theoretical models and propositions to be tested, resources available, and skills of personnel.

Likewise, the costs and benefits of alternative data-gathering techniques must be considered relative to the accuracy and precision in the estimates needed. In other words: How necessary is it to obtain very accurate and precise information for examining relations among variables to make recommendations, form inferences, and test propositions? Related to this question are the geographical areas designated for inclusion in data collection. For instance, policy decisions for a given region may be influenced by other regional situations. Multiregional data systems may be necessary. Also, it may be desirable for planning units in one location to share information with those in other locations. Thus the variables and measures used, along with the data-gathering techniques selected, may need to allow for interregional transfer of data as well as use in comparability studies of one region to another. One of the objectives of the policy researcher will be to ascertain the requirements necessary to determine the specific data-gathering techniques to be used under existing cost and benefit constraints. For purposes of discussion, data-gathering techniques are divided into two major categories: existing data sources and field data collection methods.

In many cases, data pertinent to the problem may have been collected and stored, but the researcher finds a need for more detail in terms of measurement of the concept or in terms of specific geographical areas. For instance, the researcher may need more specific and detailed information on additional variables when studying education systems, or the researcher may need it at the community level while it has been stored and available only at a county level. Also, supplemental data may be necessary for monitoring purposes or for updating existing data bases. If information on opinions and attitudes is essential, field data collection procedures will usually need to be utilized. The policy researcher in many instances may find it necessary to utilize both existing data sources and field data collection techniques.

USE OF EXISTING DATA SOURCES. For policy researchers, both published and unpublished data available at the federal, state, county, township, or municipal level will be extremely useful in many problematic situations. The Bureau of the Census, Department of Health, Education and Welfare, United States Department of Agriculture, and the Bureau of Labor Statistics are among the many federal sources that have considerable information in published form. Information also is available at colleges and universities, area and local school districts, state and local government agencies, and certain private organizations. Many of these are excellent data sources and have relatively high quality data that will be useful for policy research for a given problem area.

Problems of data usage that may be encountered include: (1) subdividing aggregated data to the geographical area desired or into the component dimensions making up the measure as reported, (2) aggregating existing data to larger regions or across time, (3) determining specification or definitional bias, (4) accuracy and precision of the existing data base, and (5) availability of the data to the policy researcher. One of the major decisions of policy researchers will be the general applicability of existing data to the problem under investigation. Will the data provide the accuracy, precision, and specific variable measures required to test the models to be developed and provide recommendations to the policy decision makers? Have the data been updated? If not, what are the possibilities for update? Are the operational definitions consistent with the research needs? Have the data been collected for those people or agencies for whom inferences, generalizations, and projections are to be made? If so, the cost-benefit ratio for the use of existing data in conducting policy research will usually be very desirable.

Available data must first be secured, then put in usable form for analysis and made available to the policy researcher. In many instances where multivariate models are to be used in planning and development, joint activities among personnel in adjacent geographic areas may be desirable or perhaps even necessary, especially for those problems where policy decisions made in one area will possibly influence social and economic conditions in adjacent areas.

FIELD DATA COLLECTION METHODS. In those cases where supplemental data are needed for updating or monitoring, or when additional basic data are required, the researcher will need to choose among various field data collection procedures. Also, data collection will be necessary in informational areas such as opinions and attitudes, interaction patterns among individuals, relationships among organizations, personal preferences, and certain social and economic conditions, especially at the household or individual level. Since a detailed discussion of various data collection methods would involve considerably more space than available here, cost-benefit considerations for three specific techniques are included in outline form.

    I. Face-to-face interview
- A. Involves highest costs of all methods
- B. Requires fairly complex field organization and control
- C. Sometimes difficult to guarantee anonymity to satisfaction of respondent
- D. Physical presence of interviewer allows stimulation of respondent and control of progression through questionnaire
- E. Allows collection of detailed and more complicated information

    II. Telephone interview
- A. Primary difference from face-to-face interview is lack of physical presence of interviewer
- B. Sometimes used to advantage in combination with other self-enumerative methods
- C. Generally less costly than face-to-face method
- D. For sensitive questions, respondent provided with greater anonymity
- E. Requires some degree of supervision and field control
- F. Somewhat easier for respondent to refuse since less personal contact involved
- G. Questionnaire must be relatively brief and straightforward
- H. Use of visual aids (flash cards, exhibits, etc.) limited
- I. Sampling frame problems usually arise
- J. Information for data base can be collected in relatively short time

    III. Self-enumeration—delivery of questionnaire to respondent by mail or in person
- A. Relatively low cost, at least by mail
- B. Anonymity guaranteed to a greater degree
- C. Questionnaire design restricted
  1. Simplicity of questionnaire construction and organization a must

2. Since questionnaire must be relatively short to maximize response, amount of information collectable limited
3. Depth of the subject matter limited—no involved skip patterns
4. Open-ended questions may not be practicable since probes not possible

D. Interaction between interviewer and respondent eliminated
   1. No assistance in question interpretation possible
   2. Probing not possible
   3. Possibility of interviewer bias eliminated
E. Nonresponse usually a major problem
F. Incomplete questionnaires may complicate coding and analysis
G. For mail method, sampling accomplished from some type of list frame, most of which are incomplete and contain errors or inconsistencies
H. Investigator has very limited control over who in sample unit (e.g., the household) responds to questions

SUMMARY. Some of the factors to be considered in the selection of alternative data sources are: (1) the problem under study, (2) geographical areas that are relevant, (3) the precision and detail of data needed for applied or theoretical models, (4) the stage of planning and implementation process, (5) resources available, and (6) skills of personnel. The physical costs of acquiring the data must be matched with the required information base in terms of the problem under investigation, the scope of inferences and recommendations to be made, and the precision required for estimates of propositions, inferences, and models to be tested.

For many problems in policy research, existing data available from various federal, state, and county agencies will provide relevant information of the precision and detail necessary. For other policy research, alternative field data collection procedures must be selected to supply supplemental data for updating existing data, provide additional information and data on variables not included in the data set, or monitor during the planning or implementation process. For information such as opinions, attitudes, perceptions, and preferences, field procedures will generally need to be used for data collection. The time frame in which data must be collected and analyzed will influence the technique(s) selected. Detailed information may need to be sacrificed to provide timely information for the decision-making process. In selecting data sources, an additional consideration is the time and effort required for "cleanup" and making the information usable for the current investigation.

There is no quick and easy answer to which data collection technique(s) should be used in a particular research situation. The policy researcher must consider several pertinent factors in a cost-benefit framework for the specific problems consistent with time and resource constraints.

CHAPTER THIRTEEN

FEASIBILITY STUDIES AS A TOOL FOR RURAL DEVELOPMENT

RICHARD J. MIKES

ECONOMISTS and other social scientists have developed a vast array of methodology useful in feasibility studies. The question is: Will this methodology be applied constructively to rural development research? Opportunities exist in every rural community for improving the quality of life; professionals concerned with achieving this goal have the techniques at hand for identifying and implementing viable alternatives. It is imperative to investigate and design practical strategies for rural development. In large measure, feasibility analysis is an integral aspect of unanswered research needs in rural America.

The discussion in this chapter will focus on three areas: (1) a historical critique of feasibility research, (2) the explicit recognition of the requirements for feasibility research in the Rural Development Act of 1972, and (3) the possible role, objectives, users, and techniques of feasibility studies.

ACADEMIC PERSPECTIVE. Obviously, feasibility studies can be and are conducted by a diverse range of individuals and public and private institutions. The land grant universities and the U.S. Department of Agriculture have played the major role in agricultural development in the nation's history. They have developed a massive research base and effectively extended it to their rural clientele. The vital role of educational institutions in rural development was furthered in Title V of the Rural Development Act of 1972.

RICHARD J. MIKES was Associate Professor and Coordinator, Marketing and Utilization, Rural Development Center, University of Georgia. He is now Assistant Controller, Ruan Transport Corporation and Ruan Leasing Company, Des Moines, Iowa.

Rural Development Act—Title V. The Rural Development Act of 1972 explicitly recognizes feasibility studies and an audience for these studies. Feasibility studies as defined in the act should be related to enhancing opportunities for income and employment expansion in rural areas. This major purpose of the act was described as follows: "Its major thrust is rural job creation and increasing of rural farm and nonfarm income and business activity" [7]. The purpose of Title V of the act is to encourage the creation of jobs and incomes by providing the knowledge necessary for successful rural development programs. Specifically, rural development extension programs under this act are charged as follows:

> Rural Development Extension Programs shall consist of a collection, interpretation, and dissemination of useful information and knowledge from research and other sources to units of multi-state regional agencies, state, county, municipal and other units of government, multi-county planning, development districts, organizations of citizens contributing to rural development, business, Indian tribes on federal or state reservations or other federally recognized Indian tribal groups or industries that employ or may employ people in rural areas. These programs also shall include technical services in educational activity, including instructions for persons not enrolled as students in colleges or universities, to facilitate and encourage the use and practical application of this information. These programs also may include feasibility studies and planning assistance [7].

Feasibility studies are more explicitly treated in the Rural Development Research Aspects of Title V, which states:

> Rural development research shall consist of research, investigations, and basic feasibility studies in any field of discipline which may develop principal facts, scientific and technical knowledge, new technology and other information that may be useful to . . . [those] involved in rural development programs and activities in planning and carrying out these programs and activities or otherwise very practical and useful in achieving increased rural development [7].

Feasibility Research Critiques. The lowly place of feasibility research was discussed several years ago by Polopolus: "While questions of economic feasibility have been answered by economic practitioners for many eons, feasibility research, as such, has not achieved any degree of respectability among theoreticians and academicians [4]. Recent criticism of the failure to apply these techniques stems from diverse sources. Hightower, in *Hard Tomatoes, Hard Times,* wrote: "Research on people and places in rural America is not geared to action. Projects tend to be irrelevant studies of characteristics and they tend to stem more from curiosity than a desire to change conditions" [3]. Tefertiller, as president of the American Agricultural Economics Association, noted:

> State universities have completed only a few thorough economic analyses for specific rural development areas. It seems that it has been easier for agricultural economists to concern themselves with organization and with defining or redefining the problem. . . . It will no longer be acceptable to deal solely with problem identification and organization. It is time for some solid research and extension accomplishments by agricultural economists. The university can and must package its expertise, technology, and research to assist rural areas in reaching social and economic goals [6, p. 776].

A study by the General Accounting Office in 1974 for the U.S. Senate Committee on Agriculture and Forestry documented the meager level of rural development research efforts by the USDA, fifty-three state agricultural experiment stations, and twenty-five other cooperating state institutions in the last few years. This was accomplished through a broad-based search of the Current Research Information System (CRIS) to retrieve research projects pertaining to rural development. The January 1974 search covered projects terminated from July 1, 1971, to March 1974, and active projects with a termination after March 31, 1974. The search revealed 575 projects related to rural development in three high-priority subject matter components: (1) community services and facilities (2) job and income creation, and (3) general purpose planning. Slightly over half (296) of the projects were related to job and income creation, as shown in Table 13.1. Projects related to program evaluation accounted for 18 percent of the total with the balance being general research projects.

Table 13.1. Number of projects by topic related to rural development, type of research, and status

Topic and Research	Number		
	All	Active	Terminated
All	575	362	213
Program evaluation	181	106	75
General research	394	256	138
Job creation and income improvement	296	188	108
Program evaluation	53	25	28
General research	243	163	80
Community services and facilities	161	106	55
Program evaluation	96	65	31
General research	65	41	24
General purpose planning	118	68	50
Program evaluation	32	116	16
General research	86	52	34

Source: Current Research on Priority Rural Development Topics [2].

This was strictly a quantitative search; no attempt was made to identify qualitative parameters.

Table 13.2 details the distribution of active research projects on job and income creation by type of economic activity. Over a third of the projects are related to farming, the traditional area of interest to most agricultural economists. Only 8 percent of the projects are related to industry, manufacturing, and assembly. The projects identified or pertaining to rural development represent only a small fraction of the research projects in CRIS, and of these only one-half are related to job and income creation, with the greatest number of these related to traditional agricultural pursuits.

Ample occasion remains for fruitful research in this subject area. If the active research projects related to farming are excluded, an average of only slightly over two projects per state are left. Universities possess the resources capable of answering the broad needs of rural America and can respond positively to this challenge. Applied feasibility studies no longer can afford to be viewed as "second class" research but rather as an opportunity to respond to the changing nature of rural America to enhance its qualities of living. Societal pressures are being felt by the academic community as its concern for relevance and accountability is increasing. Increased emphasis on applied studies related to rural development may be forthcoming.

FEASIBILITY ANALYSIS. The term "feasibility study" has many connotations. Generally, it is an analysis to determine if a given course of action is practical, possible, or workable. The dictionary's definition of feasible is "capable of being used or dealt with successfully." Feasibility studies cover a broad spectrum of possible applications and alternative procedures. For example, a firm is interested in the most profitable enterprise or combination of enterprises given its available resources. The methods employed could range from a simplified costs and returns budget to a profit-maximizing linear program of its total existing and proposed operation. Alternatively, a multistate development organization, such as the Appalachian Regional Commission, could be interested in determining what types of industry would offer maximum employment and income opportunities compatible with the region's resources. These could be identified through a general inventory survey method or by developing an input-output model for the region.

There is no standard or generally accepted objective or format for a feasibility study. The challenge is to construct a research package that will address the problem and provide the needed information in a useful and reliable manner.

Table 13.2 Distribution of active program evaluation and general research projects on job and income creation by type of economic activity related to rural development

Type of Economic Activity	Program Evaluation (Number)	(Percent)	General Research (Number)	(Percent)	Total Projects (Number)	(Percent)
All types	25	100	163	100	188	100
Cooperatives	0	0	1	1	1	1
Employment services	4	16	20	12	24	13
Farming	7	28	62	38	69	37
Fishing and fisheries	0	0	9	6	9	5
Forestry	1	4	5	3	6	3
Forest products processing	0	0	2	1	2	1
Industry, manufacturing, and assembly	1	4	14	9	15	8
Insurance	0	0	0	0	0	0
Mining	0	0	2	1	2	1
New town development	0	0	0	0	0	0
Outdoor recreation enterprises and tourism	4	16	17	10	21	11
Vocational education and manpower development	6	24	2	1	8	4
General economic development	2	8	29	18	31	16

Source: Current Research on Priority Rural Development Topics [2].

Objectives of a Feasibility Study. A clearly defined objective for every feasibility study is absolutely essential. Two guiding questions are: What is the ultimate purpose of the study? To what audience is it addressed? It must be determined if the objective of the study is to develop a strategy for a region's growth and development to be used by a regional planning group, or if it is a preliminary examination of a possible investment opportunity designed to attract the interest of a potential investor. As noted in Title V, the potential audience is varied, as can be the ultimate use of a study. For example, an individual firm may be interested in the feasibility of a specific type of manufacturing operation, or they could be interested in determining what type of manufacturing operation is feasible in their local area.

Without defining the objective of a feasibility study, it is impossible to rationally choose appropriate research techniques. Every researcher in contemplating a feasibility study either implicitly or explicitly answers several questions about the intended use of his study results. Obviously, we can conduct feasibility studies before explicitly considering how the results will be used; however, such an approach raises serious questions regarding research efficiency and resource utilization. Professional industrial developers have recognized the varied nature of a feasibility study. Cassell notes:

> For his promotion and developmental efforts, the most useful feasibility studies are those which accomplish one of two objectives. In some situations, the industrial developer may need and may seek advice and guidance as to what might be the soundest industrial opportunities for his area. Such direction can give him definite pointers for aiming this overall solicitation program. But, in contrast to given situations where an established company is searching for another branch plant location, the developer may be confronted with trying to evaluate the profit potential of a venture which is proposed by a single individual who is concentrating on a specific type of manufacturing operation [1].

Studies related to the first objective attempt to obtain a better utilization of regions' resources by identifying the types of industrial and business operations that could operate profitably in a region. After identifying these potentials as specifically as possible, the subsequent task is to be prepared to demonstrate the viability of a venture to potential investors. The users of such a study may range from multistate regional commissions to state, multicounty, and local groups with ultimate users being the decision-making firms.

Studies related to the second objective are more specific if their focus and their ultimate user is a firm or group of firms. They are generally designed to evaluate investment opportunities, which can be categorized as internal and external. An increased level of investment may result from expansion of existing plants and businesses or relocation of plants and businesses from outside to within the area. This potential investment could be stimulated by similar or dissimilar circumstances to which firms respond. Some possible circumstances to which firms respond. Some possible circumstances are: (1) An increase in demand for the goods or services being supplied by the firm. The current production capacity could be at its limit and the firm must decide whether to expand its facilities in a particular location or start a new plant in another location. It may need to balance diverse factors such as increased economies of scale that could be achieved by expanding the existing plant, contrasted to decreased transport cost by locating a plant in another geographic area closer to its market. (2) A firm is considering adoption of new technology. The existing plant might be obsolete, and the firm is confronted with renovation or relocation. 3) Other circumstances include: acquisition or mergers, expanding products or service lines (perhaps to achieve diversification), or a desire for expanded geographic market areas.

Selection Criteria for Feasibility Studies. The research program of most organizations is determined by (1) pressures of clientele needs on researchers, (2) the willingness of researchers to respond to these needs, (3) the available resources, and (4) the source of funds.

These are obviously interrelated elements. Should researchers respond to specific requests or should they exert independent initiative in undertaking investigations? This is a classic dilemma of reaction and action. Given the resource constraints of any research organization, whether it consists of an individual industrial developer in a rural area or a large land grant university, selection of projects requires careful consideration. A decision must be made on whether a study will be undertaken and the amount of resources to be committed to it.

Some general criteria for selecting and ranking projects include: (1) Who are the clientele and what are their major concerns? (2) What is the probable economic and social impact? (3) What is the probability of a project's success? These criteria are essentially judgmental in nature and require deliberation by both the researcher and potential clientele.

Some guidelines for screening subject areas for feasibility studies have been advanced by industrial developers [1]. First, requests for information on specific categories of products often prove a useful tool for identifying development possibilities. Repetitive inquiries to a development organization or a university researcher can reveal the need or desire for such a product. A cursory inquiry into such prod-

ucts may identify directions for further analysis. A second guideline
is investigation of the possibility for developing ancillary or satellite
operations which can match with the existing industrial complex (the
so-called forward or backward linkage). Third, investigation of the
amount or extent of an area's resources, including mineral, forestry,
agricultural, tourist, and human resources, may identify opportunities for expansion of the economic base. Fourth, identifying opportunities for development primarily through analysis of published materials by attempting to identify growth industries, industries oriented
to regional markets, and industries exhibiting a preference for rural
location is helpful. Fifth, development agencies may have already
selected a particular kind of industry they desire to encourage, based
on favorable primary and secondary impacts on the local economy.

**DESIGNING FEASIBILITY STUDIES FOR SPECIFIC PROJ-
ECTS.** Once potential development opportunities have been identified for a particular region (where rather simple or sophisticated
techniques are used or a potential firm has a specific project in mind),
the subsequent task is to design a feasibility study of a specific venture
or industrial class. An investment is made only after either an informal or formal investigation has been made of the feasibility of
the proposed venture. Generally, as the size of the investment increases, so will the depth and formality of the feasibility study. The
research team and its diversity of disciplines also will likely enlarge
in scope.

Generally, it is assumed that the overall objective of the firm is
profitability within the framework of acceptable societal standards,
such as concerns with the environment. That is, a firm would not
undertake capital expenditure if over time the stream of revenue
generated did not exceed the associated costs. The estimation of cost
and revenues can be accomplished by several alternative methods.

For example, a feasibility study on a proposed processing or
manufacturing decision can be viewed in three major components.
These include the supply of raw products used in manufacturing or
processing, the processing or manufacturing operation itself, and
marketing of the product.

Consider, for example, a feasibility study on an agricultural processing operation as it relates to these components. The analysis could
entail three phases: (1) availability and costs of raw product supplies, including any cost of assembly to the processing plant; (2) the
technical engineering components of the plant and associated input-
output data; and (3) the demand for the particular product and associated transportation and marketing alternatives. Any of these components could be a complete study in itself, requiring inputs from a

wide range of disciplines. It behooves the research manager to develop an interrelated and coordinated approach to undertake a truly comprehensive feasibility study.

Various questions need exploration in each of these components. What is the existing production level of a commodity in an area, and its historical trends? What share of the production could be assured the plant over time? What is the seasonality of this production? Estimating supply could come from a simple delineation of the plant's anticipated supply area and determination of historical production levels in that area using census data, a detailed survey of producers in the area, or a study indicating the amounts producers should be willing to supply given alternative resource utilization opportunities.

The second phase involves an investigation of the facility itself. This may require development of an engineering model or securing accounting data from existing plants to estimate input requirements. Typical questions are: What are the various levels of inputs and associated levels of outputs? Are there economies of scale? What are the requirements for buildings, equipment, labor, utilities, supplies, and services?

The third phase may entail answering: What is the demand for the product? What are costs associated with moving the product through marketing channels to the ultimate consumer? What is the normal channel of distribution for the product? How is market entry achieved? What pricing and selling arrangements are required?

Techniques for Evaluating Investment Opportunities. Once cash flows are estimated, we could apply any number of methods for ranking or evaluating investment alternatives familiar to potential users. Cash flow is defined as the net income before depreciation and after taxes that results from an investment. This is equivalent to the operating revenues less the sum of cash operating cost interest on debt capital, and noncash expenses (depreciation) less the income tax. The following four represent some commonly used methods: (1) payback method—the number of years required to return the original investment; (2) net present value method—present value of future returns discounted at the appropriate interest rate minus cost of the investment; (3) the internal (or discounted) rate of return method—interest rate that equates the present value of future returns to the investment outlay; and (4) modified benefit cost ratio—present value of future returns divided by present value of the investment outlay. All these methods assume, of course, that it is possible to accurately estimate cash flow for each year in the period under consideration.

The payback method is widely used by firms and criticized by academicians. The payback period is the number of years it takes the firm to recoup its initial investment. This method is criticized because it fails to consider income flowing from a project beyond the payback period, and it ignores the time value of money. Two investments may have identical total cash flow in a payback period, with one exhibiting a larger cash flow initially and the other at the end of the period. The payback method would rank the projects as identical. It is obvious that the investment with the large initial cash flow would be preferable.

The payback method has been criticized because it is biased in favor of short-lived alternatives. It is often defended on the basis that returns beyond a few years are difficult to accurately predict. Smith notes that:

> despite its limitations, the payback period is not totally lacking in conformity with the other methods but when one compares (1) rate of return against a predetermined minimum or (2) payback period against a predetermined maximum the conclusions tend to be identical if the interest rate is high and the period is long [5].

The net present value method is the present value of future returns, discounted at a selected interest rate, minus the initial investment. This method allows the valuation of income flows that may exhibit variation between years. A firm can determine its minimum acceptable rate of return; if the net present value is positive, the investment is then feasible. If the firm is comparing mutually exclusive projects, the project with the higher net present value is preferred. A critical assumption in the present value method is the interest rate utilized. The equation for net present value (NPV) is:

$$\text{NPV} = \sum_{t=1}^{N} \frac{Rt}{(1+i)t} - I$$

where Rt = cash flow in year t, I = the amount of the initial investment, N = years in analysis, and i is interest rate.

The internal rate of return method is the interest rate that equates the present value of the expected cash flows to the investment outlay. The internal rate of return is calculated through a series of iterations in which an interest rate is selected and applied to the cash flow and then the resulting present value is compared with the investment outlay. This is repeated until the present value is equated to the investment outlay by the appropriate interest rate. Once the rate of return is determined for several alternative investments, the firm selects the investments that yield a rate of return above a predetermined threshold level and within the constraints of their capital budget. The equation for determining the internal rate of return (r) is:

$$I = \sum_{t=1}^{N} \frac{Rt}{(1+r)t}$$

The benefit-cost ratio is often used to evaluate public projects. It is the present value of the future cash flow divided by the required investment outlay. Under most circumstances the latter three methods (net present value, internal rate of return, modified benefit cost ratio) will give identical rankings to mutually exclusive projects. They may give different answers when (1) the cash flow of one project increases over time while that of the other decreases, (2) the projects have significantly different expected lives, and (3) the cost of one project is substantially larger than that of the other [8].

Implementing the Feasibility Study. If the feasibility study was designed and initiated with an objective in mind, implementation is facilitated. It is questionable whether the feasibility study should have been undertaken at all without a clear-cut objective in the first place. However, during the course of the feasibility study, new, alternative uses may be discovered for it. Perhaps in the process of obtaining information on a particular industry through interviewing firms, a firm becomes interested in the study and a "live" prospect that had previously been unknown evolves.

All too often, universities or other research groups do a thorough, professional job of completing a comprehensive feasibility study only to have it gather dust on a shelf. Implementation should be a primary consideration in a comprehensive study design. Implementation should be so closely tied to the well-conceived study that it is an integral part of the objective. All too often, studies are executed without consideration of the simple requirements that they have meaning and can be implemented. The most prestigious methodology and model building become relevant only when application is made to a specific study.

The combining of efforts by a development group and a research organization can increase implementation effectiveness. A price requisite for a true feasibility study is objectivity. If the research is performed by an organization (such as a university) other than the soliciting group, there tends to be an increased sense of impartiality.

The era of a multitude of shallow studies purporting to identify industrial opportunities, either through increased utilization of raw materials or labor resources or of the market potential of a given region, is drawing to a close. The prospective firm, the community, and the developer "matchmaker" are all becoming more sophisticated. Not only must economic aspects be thoroughly considered in a feasibility study, but sociological, political, and environmental impacts can no longer be mentioned only in passing. Clearly, an interdisciplinary research approach is imperative.

The ability of research organizations to respond rapidly can be critical in many instances. The prospect of waiting to integrate a feasibility study into a university department's research plans in another year is discouraging to developers and prospects alike. If universities are to play a meaningful role in rural development feasibility studies, the response time must be minimized. Specialized research centers or institutes and other organizational forms may offer a mechanism for such timely response.

Tefertiller, discussing rural development, noted: "It is possible that the USDA and the state universities are getting their last chance to produce. It is essential that we be successful in this effort" [6, p. 777].

Rural development leaders need a well-grounded research base to fully understand the complex, highly interrelated variables in rural America. It is impossible to achieve development of a relevant set of strategies without a research base to draw on. This is possible if we make the commitment.

REFERENCES

1. Cassell, Robert B. 1972. Research for industrial development. *Guide to Industrial Development*. Englewood Cliffs, N.J.: Prentice Hall, p. 125.
2. Current research on priority rural development topics. 1974. (Mimeo.) U.S. Senate Comm. on Agric. Forestry.
3. Hightower, Jim. 1972. *Hard Tomatoes, Hard Times*. Washington, D.C.: Agribusiness Accountability Project, pp. 95–96.
4. Polopolus, Leo. 1964. Economic feasibility research—An aid to area development planning. *J. Farm Econ. (*46): 989.
5. Smith, Gerald W. 1968. *Engineering Economy: Analysis of Capital Expenditures*. Ames: Iowa State Univ. Press, p. 551.
6. Tefertiller, Kenneth R. 1973. Rural development in an urban age. *Am. J. Agric. Econ.* 55 (5).
7. U.S. Senate, Committee on Agriculture and Forestry. 1972. The rural development act of 1972: Analysis and explanation of Public Law 92–419, p. 1.
8. Weston, J. Fred, and Eugene F. Brigham. 1975. *Managerial Finance*, 5th ed. Hinsdale, Ill.: Dryden Press, pp. 257–308.

CHAPTER FOURTEEN

PUBLIC OPINION SURVEYS

RALPH M. BROOKS

CITIZEN FEEDBACK is not only useful but extremely necessary in developing public policy. Obtaining the reactions of local residents to decisions that have been made (or suggested to be implemented) in their communities is considered a vital input for public policy. Public opinion surveys are a means to that end.

Traditional forms of survey research (e.g., personal interviewing) may be inappropriate for current policy issues. In a recent report by the American Statistical Association, low completion rates in survey research (primarily from personal interviews) experienced in the last few years, interviewee skepticism concerning the purpose of the interview, and invasion of privacy when faced with a personal interview situation all contributed to a need for discussing alternative methods of data acquisition from publics [1]. Furthermore, the recent rise in costs for social research plus the decrease in budgets that traditionally have allotted monies for social research, coupled with the decrease in foundation support for social research, may further contribute to the need to look for alternative methods and cheaper approaches [29].

OBJECTIVES OF THE WORKSHOP. The purpose of the workshop was not to gain proficiency with respect to public opinion surveys, but rather to learn the possibilities and potentials, as well as where to go for additional help. With that in mind, and under the

RALPH M. BROOKS is Assistant Professor, Department of Agricultural Economics, and Assistant Professor, Department of Sociology, Purdue University.

The author would like to express appreciation to Lionel Beaulieu, David Hill, and David Taylor for their help in acquiring many of the materials utilized in this chapter. Appreciation is also expressed to Mrs. Lynn Lewis for preparation of the manuscript.

suggestion of the Conference Planning Committee, the material for the workshop was organized around four major areas:

1. *State of the art of public opinion surveys.* Particular attention was given to some of the early organizations involved in public opinion polling, plus the proliferation of polling organizations during the recent ten years.

2. *The applied and academic ability of public opinion surveys.* Some examples of public opinion surveys were presented, with a discussion of the precision and rigor necessary in public opinion polling.

3. *Identification of persons, organizations, or places currently using the techniques of public opinion surveys.* This was accomplished, again, by focusing on some specific examples throughout the United States of individual researchers involved in public opinion surveys.

4. *Identification of sources of information for those wanting to learn more about public opinion surveys.* It is anticipated that individuals will look to the sources cited and the examples given and contact those individuals, organizations and institutions for further information.

OVERVIEW AND STATE OF THE ART. It is almost impossible to sort through the literature on public opinion surveys without coming across a tremendous amount of literature on public opinion polling. In fact, one cannot help but be impressed with the amount of work over a period of years that has been devoted to assessing public opinion. Presented here briefly are the origin, purpose, and types of public opinion surveys undertaken by the major early polling organizations.

History and Trends of Public Opinion Polling. It would be impossible to present a detailed list of all polling organizations currently existing in the United States. In fact, precise numbers of pollsters and their locations are unknown. However, the organizations that do exist can be classified into four categories:

1. National public opinion organizations that publish the results of their findings. Examples: American Institute of Public Opinion (Gallup Poll) and Louis Harris and Associates (Harris Survey).

2. National concerns that survey public opinion for the private use of political clients. Examples: John F. Kraft, Oliver A. Quayle and Co., Inc., and Opinion Research Corporation.

3. Regional firms specializing in one state or a group of states. Example: Mid-South Opinion Surveys of Little Rock, Arkansas.

4. Local pollsters, one-man operations, and postcard polltakers.

The origins of the public opinion polls go back to the early 1900s. These polls were generally conducted by newspaper editors attempting to poll opinions concerning candidates or issues to provide material for their newspapers. Oftentimes, these issues were selected in order to insure a high degree of reader interest. On a national scale, the *Farm Journal* was the pioneer in public opinion polls, having engaged in polling as early as 1912. Between 1915 and 1936, a most popular polling forum was the *Literary Digest*. It had been drawing up its list of potential respondents from such sources as automobile registrations and telephone books. Hence the sample from the very beginning had an obvious bias from the standpoint of economic status. The final *Digest* poll was conducted in 1936 and proved so disastrous in political polling as to set the stage for the development of organizations using more scientific polling techniques.

About the time the *Literary Digest* was starting its decline in terms of public acceptance of its methods and techniques for polling public opinion, three men had become convinced that by using a small but carefully selected sample of the population, a picture of the whole could be projected not only on a regional but also on a national scale. These three men were George Gallup, Archibald Crossley, and Elmo Roper. In the year the *Literary Digest* missed the national election, predicting that Roosevelt would lose, these three individuals, using scientific methods of sampling, predicted that Roosevelt would win by a substantial margin. Roper was extremely accurate, largely due to luck. The others were correct, even though their percentages were a little off. Thus modern polling was on its way to general acceptance.

One of the larger firms is the Roper Poll; the central aims of the Roper Public Opinion Research Center are to serve in every way possible to stimulate cross national primary and secondary research; to increase the amount of research being done, with the data included in their library; to facilitate access to these materials and, on an international scale, to enrich both substantively and quantitatively the resource of survey data available to social scientists and others working in the public interest. Roper's first public opinion poll was taken in the spring of 1935, with the results published in *Fortune* magazine. In the early stages, Roper was concerned primarily with measuring national sentiment on an issue or a candidate. The organization presently has basic data on 7,730 public opinion surveys. These data from 1936 to the present cover studies completed by 100 cooperating research organizations located in 44 countries. Each data set is prepared in such a way as to facilitate its use by interested researchers.

Currently, the Roper studies are categorized in the following manner: (1) Public Affairs—50 percent (race relations, juvenile delinquency, international relations, welfare); (2) Mass Media of Communications—20 percent (attitudes toward exposure to mass media, etc.); (3) Domestic Political Behavior and Attitudes—15 percent (vote intention and recall, party preference, campaign issues, etc.); and (4) Market Research—15 percent (consumer attitudes and behavior, product ownership, preference, etc.).

Other national opinion polling organizations include the Harris Poll, the Gallup Poll, and Crossley. Each of these differ in the manner in which their samples are selected. However, their ultimate sample size is generally between 1,400 and 1,700 people drawn from across the United States. Their methods also vary as to the specific techniques they employ in getting the individual to serve as a respondent. It is difficult to say how useful these national firms are to public policy in rural America.

In the last twenty years, we have seen a proliferation of polling organizations throughout the United States. The majority serve the interest of politicians in terms of polling their constituents. Furthermore, the politicians make use of the polls in terms of predicting their relative success in upcoming elections.

Market research firms have obviously utilized public opinion polling at great length. Their interest in consumer behavior and the acceptance of new products has been one major use in terms of public opinion polling. Many organizations come under this category, Daniel Yankelovitch and Abt Associates representing two of the better known firms.

Survey research and public opinion polling conducted by researchers located in universities across the nation have increased tremendously. Immediately, various survey research centers, located at the universities of Michigan, Wisconsin, California, Missouri, etc., come to mind. In fact, it may be difficult to find a state where there is not some kind of university-based institute for social research. These organizations conduct ongoing research in various areas of public concern, financed by grants or through contracts.

Strengths and Weaknesses of Opinion Surveys. It is probably not necessary to document the potential use of survey data by policymakers involved in decisions affecting rural America. The real problem is getting the information at the appropriate time and in such a form that it can be used to make decisions. However, some general advantages and disadvantages of opinion surveys ought to be considered. One main source of information covering this area extremely well is the work of Webb and Hatry [30]. They cite a number of uses and misuses of public opinion surveys, and although they are referring primarily to citizen surveys utilized by local governments, their work could also be applied to rural America.

STRENGTHS. 1. *Provide citizen perceptions of the effectiveness of public services, including the identification of problem areas.* In the whole area of delivery of public services, it is important to know whether or not the local residents are receiving any benefit from such services. Periodic assessment of public opinion with respect to services not only provides an opportunity whereby citizen feedback can be obtained, but in addition establishes a framework for gathering longitudinal data. This can serve as a check on problem areas and provide information whereby services can be improved.

2. *Provide selected factual data.* Often we rely on census data to provide particular kinds of information in a given geographic area. These data, however, are often outdated by the time we obtain access to them. Therefore, citizen surveys of public opinion can provide us with data to be used in decisions affecting public policy on a more regular basis. Unreported crimes and unreported citizen complaints can be obtained through this type of procedure.

3. *Help identify reasons for dislike or nonuse of services.* Frequently services can be designed and presented to publics without a complete knowledge as to the potential acceptance of those services. In a study of social services in one county in Indiana, Brooks et al. found that day care centers were not utilized by low-income families because of inadequate transportation to and from the center [6].

4. *Pretests of citizen demand for new services.* This is a difficult area to assess in terms of future policy; however, it is useful to obtain information from local residents concerning anticipated services they may be needing in the near future. This information alone can be useful in making plans for the future rather than immediately starting delivery of a new service. It will also allow several new services to be considered jointly in a long-range planning package.

5. *Provide data on citizen awareness of local government programs.* Many of the programs prepared at the local level depend on voluntary citizen participation for success. There needs to be some way whereby an awareness of these programs can be identified. It might also help to find out how residents learned about various programs and activities at the local level to help with packaging and publicizing activities in the future. This source of awareness can probably be obtained only through survey questions.

6. *Provide a means for increased citizen participation in government planning and policy formulation, thus reducing isolation or alienation from the government.* If we rely on public hearings to allow citizens to vent their feelings, more likely than not we get a

biased opinion of vested interest groups. The public opinion survey is one means whereby local residents have an opportunity to express their opinion with respect to programs, activities, and policies at the local level. Whether or not local officials act on the findings from the surveys is another matter. However, "without prejudging whether that will, in fact, occur, at least a first step is presenting to public officials certain basic informations about people's preferences and experiences that have not previously been available" [30, p. 27].

WEAKNESSES. Thus far, we seem to paint a rosy picture for the use of public opinion surveys in the development of public policy. Some weaknesses exist, and ought to be considered by anybody prior to conducting public opinion survey.

1. *Beware of opinion polls on complex issues about which citizens lack information.* Presenting local people with an issue and then asking what should be done about it may result in a superficial response from these publics. This will probably be so if they lack the necessary information as a basis to make any kind of decision. The feelings expressed by residents, however, can serve as guides to decision makers.

2. *Beware of citizen response reflecting short-run considerations to the neglect of long-term problems.* Many times we do not know what the secondary and tertiary consequences are going to be as a result of some short-run decision. We may find strong support for short-run decisions that have implications in the long run.

3. *Beware of using surveys to hide from controversy and responsibility.* Using surveys to justify actions on behalf of a majority while neglecting minority needs and rights is most likely to occur if surveys are applied as quasi-voting devices.

4. *Beware of question wording—what is said or not said can be misleading.* This is an obvious area of concern. At the present, many of the national polling organizations devote much of their energies to validating questionnaires and checking for ambiguity. The important point here is that the answer you get may not be what you intended. It may reflect the improper wording in your question.

5. *Beware of sensitive issues and questions that tend to elicit silence or a misleading answer.* The respondent may be reluctant to explore his behavior with you; therefore a "no response" or a "don't know" answer may reflect on how you ask the question rather than on the respondent's inability to provide the answer.

6. *Beware of nonrepresentative results if inadequate procedures are used.* This pertains primarily to the manner in which samples are drawn. Telephone directories have the bias of underrepresenting the more affluent citizens, who tend to have unlisted numbers. It also

excludes some of these from the lower-income groups, who are more transient in nature.

In many public opinion surveys, the purpose is to obtain a particular insight that can only be elicited through some assessment of public attitudes. Occasionally, however, the data received may be so biased that one could question their usefulness to decision makers. Here are two of many examples that illustrate this point:

A. In a study of Midland County, Michigan, the purpose was to provide data on resident attitudes which would be taken into account by the County Planning Commission in giving guidance and direction in the county. A sample of 1,100 households was selected from sixteen townships. Only 224 questionnaires were returned for a response rate of 21 percent [18].

B. To assess public attitude toward the development of the Mississippi River in Minnesota, a sample of 5,000 households in the counties bordering the river was selected from motor vehicle registrations. With no follow-ups to the mail questionnaire, the response rate was 20 percent [2].

In both examples, the researchers appear to have identified the right population to provide the data. Also, the sample size seems adequate for making an assessment of attitudes in the study area. However, the response rate was not only extremely low, but probably biased. The author's own work in mail questionnaire response suggests that those responding in the first wave are more likely to be male, better educated, upper income, and from the professional groups. The biases tend to be less as the nonrespondents receive follow-up inquiries. The point is, the biased results do not provide the representative data needed by the policymakers. Hence it is little wonder that many of the research results from mail questionnaires fail to be utilized.

7. *Beware of antagonizing citizens who consider interviews an invasion of privacy.* Much evidence in the last few years suggests that personal face-to-face interviews are no longer being received as well as they were eight to ten years ago. The whole question of invasion of privacy is becoming more and more critical in social science research. Therefore we have seen rise in the last few years (in terms of "resurrecting") the mail questionnaire as a technique for surveying large populations of publics. No doubt the several follow-ups utilized in mail questionnaire research may represent a source of annoyance to many people. Nevertheless, they have the opportunity of responding or not responding without undergoing any undue pressure from an interviewer.

8. *Beware that dissemination of survey findings may be a two-edged sword, raising false hopes among citizens and providing politi-*

cal fodder to candidates. The question of how these findings are to be used is an important one. Obviously, it can be used to defend the status quo or promote social change.

These advantages and disadvantages of public opinion surveys may not be all that could be presented. However, most of these may be encountered in public policy research and should be given consideration in any public opinion survey.

ESSENTIAL INGREDIENTS IN PUBLIC OPINION SURVEYS. The purpose here is not to demonstrate how one goes about designing a public opinion survey. Nevertheless, some general areas should be considered in the development of any kind of public opinion survey. Knowledge in each of the areas is thought to be necessary prior to the implementation of the actual survey.

1. *Selection of topics.* In many public opinion surveys, the main focus is some specific problem or topic. The question arises, however, as to how these topics emerge. Do researchers provide them? Do mass media "expose" the topic? Or does some state or local committee bring it to the public? The next question is whether or not the publics in the area are knowledgeable enough with respect to the given problem area to provide their own opinions relative to a program of action or state their own preferences. Some prior information may be available on the topic or problem area to help in the further specification of the topic to be included in the public opinion survey.

2. *Sample characteristics.* Delineating the particular group within the general population expected to be impacted by the policy may help in specifying the population to sample. Often we survey large populations of people for two reasons: we are not really sure what particular subpopulation we want to sample and it is difficult to obtain lists of any specific population (e.g., minorities, aged, or those with a given marital status). Some knowledge of the sample characteristics can also help in the next step; that is, type of procedure to use to obtain the necessary data.

3. *Methodology.* Given the topic and some information concerning the population one wants to survey, a next step is to decide on the appropriate technique to employ in obtaining that data. This chapter has a major section devoted to mail questionnaires and mail methodology. Although mail questionnaires can be the least costly technique of public opinion surveys, one ought to consider the methodology in light of the other items mentioned.

Personal interviewing should not be ruled out strictly because of the associated costs. Depending on the topic and the sample, the personal interview may be the only feasible way of obtaining the data. Telephone interviewing is becoming more and more attractive as one means of polling public sentiments concerning various issues. For example, Washington State University has had a telephone research component within their Rural Sociology Department in operation for about five years. A recent telephone survey conducted in the state of Washington by Dillman and Wardwell reported a response rate of 87 percent [20]. Wisconsin has the capabilities of conducting extensive telephone interviews throughout the state; other states may have the same capabilities.

Whether one uses any one of these three procedures or a combination of all of them, the important point is to know enough about the population being sampled to know whether or not a given technique can reach that particular population. If not, it may require a combination of the three and some creative thinking in the area of public opinion surveys—at least in the area of methodology.

4. *Development of instrument.* Since most of us may be more interested in the policy implications of our research rather than the methodological rigor required, perhaps we ought to utilize more extensively the services offered by some of the large polling organizations.

5. *Analysis.* Although the analysis is going to depend on the type of questions asked and the data gathered, the form in which that analysis is presented may depend upon the type of audience sought. If the audience is another colleague, then the utilization of multistage models and factor analysis plus regression techniques, linear programming, and perhaps canonical correlation conveys a certain meaning to that individual. If, on the other hand, the results are to be disseminated primarily to policymakers or those in state government, the output ought to take a different form. It certainly will be different from the form that will be presented to the general public. In this sense, we have almost an inverse relationship between the length of time it takes to disseminate the results of the survey with the audiences just mentioned.

Frequently, local citizens can look at a sample tabulation of survey results and begin to get a feel for how others in their area view local problems and situations. The policymaker, on the other hand, may want something more than just a simple tabulation; in fact, a series of cross-tabulations with some simple measures of association and even some tests of significance may be appropriate for him to understand and relate to the data. Finally, there may be a more rigorous analysis of the data in terms of generating additional findings. Yet they must be interpreted for the other two groups to be of any use.

We might be able to decrease the length of time from the initiation of a project to its completion if we were to divide the project output in terms of the publics, the policymakers, and our colleagues rather than have it in the reverse order. There is a danger, however, in doing this. Those who have been involved in research can point out that once one produces some simple tabulations and descriptive kinds of information it is often difficult to get on to the more rigorous type of analysis. On the other hand, starting with the rigorous analysis frequently takes a great deal of time. Hence the data become old, and you lose the relevance for the general public and, perhaps, the policymaker in terms of using that data for a decision.

Probably many other essential ingredients could be considered in this discussion. These can best be illustrated by suggesting some examples from across the United States. Let us draw, primarily, on one procedure that has had some notoriety in recent years. This is by no means the only approach to public opinion surveys but one that appears to have great potential in the future.

We have not addressed the issue of when to use and when not to use a public opinion survey. Most of us can probably make that distinction. More likely than not, the decision to use a public opinion survey has already been made. The dialogue may go something like this: "I want a public survey but cannot afford personal interviews. Besides, they cannot adequately cover my population. Therefore, I am left with a mail questionnaire or telephone interviewing. Mail questionnaires have traditionally had low response rates and telephone interviewing is relatively new. Now what?"

A NEW METHOD OF PUBLIC OPINION SURVEY: AN OLD TECHNIQUE REVISITED. During the last five years, a number of researchers across the United States have experimented with a modification of mail questionnaire techniques used in survey research. The purpose of this section is to introduce examples from these researchers and present the basic methodology. This technique in no way is presented as the answer to public opinion surveys. It is given, however, as a potentially useful tool with an unusually fast turn-around time associated with low costs using sophisticated techniques and appears to be appealing to policymakers and researchers alike. This methodology has been reported extensively in other sources [5, 7, 8, 16].

It is safe to say that the work basically originated with Dillman's study on public values and concerns of Washington residents [17]. This was later followed up by Dillman and Dobash in their work on preferences for community living and their implications for population redistribution [18]. Basically, the procedure includes an initial mailing that contains a cover letter to legitimize the work and express the policy ramifications of the study. This is followed by a postcard send to each individual one week after the initial mailing. Approximately two weeks later, a replacement questionnaire is sent to the nonrespondents with a cover letter asking them to respond if they have not yet done so. Three weeks later a second replacement questionnaire is sent to all nonrespondents by certified mail.

Using this method has resulted in high response rates from samplings of the general public. Dillman has reported response rates in excess of 70 percent. This is significant in that most survey research textbooks will point out that mail questionnaires have extremely low response rates. Returnable postcards or letters mailed to individuals selected in a predetermined order from voter registration rolls or telephone directories usually have response rates lower than 30 percent [25]. Indeed, a recent publication by Webb and Hatry suggests that mail surveys often result in response rates of less than 10 percent [30]. They cite an example in Charlotte, North Carolina, during 1970 when a recreation survey was included in 70,000 water bills. The replies did not exceed 7 percent. Therefore, we are suggesting that if a more workable procedure were developed that could provide policymakers with adequate data upon which to make their decisions, then that procedure would be relevant to public policy formulation in rural America.

Four-State Study. The methodology modified and developed by Dillman was applied in at least three other states, using similar questionnaires. In another state (Wisconsin), a similar procedure was used with exceptionally high response rates.[1] Table 14.1 demonstrates the variability of population characteristics in the Washington, Arizona, Indiana, and North Carolina studies. These four states represent a wide variation in median school years completed, ranging from Washington ranking 2nd in the nation to North Carolina ranking 46th. In addition, although the median family income does not show

1. This study, however, was conducted among a homogeneous (with respect to occupation and race) population of respondents. The studies on community preference, conducted in Indiana and Arizona, were basically replications of an earlier study conducted in the state of Washington. The North Carolina study on public values was also a replication of one of the studies conducted in the state of Washington. Many of the questionnaire items in all four states overlapped sufficiently to allow a comparison of procedures and research findings across the four states. These are referred to extensively in Dillman et al. [21]. Although the studies were not designed as a cross-sectional study looking at the same research problem in all four states, they do represent different regions of the United States as well as different population characteristics. This procedure provided us with an opportunity to look at the basic methodology of a mail questionnaire with successive follow-ups in varying regions of the United States.

Table 14.1. Interstate variations of population characteristics

State	Median School Years Completed* (persons 25 and over)	Median Family Income†	Percent Rural‡	Percent Nonwhite‡
Washington	12.4	$10,404	27.4	4.4
Arizona	12.3	9,185	20.5	8.9
Indiana	12.1	9,966	35.1	7.1
North Carolina	10.6	7,770	55.0	23.1
Average for the United States	12.1	9,586	26.5	13.0

Source: *County and City Data Book* [15].
  * Data from 1970 p. 3.
  † Data from 1969, p. 5.
  ‡ Data from 1970, p. 2.

as great a variability, it does range from 12th highest in the nation with Washington to 41st for North Carolina. The percent urban ranges from Arizona ranking 12th in the nation to North Carolina ranking 45th. Finally, the percent white does not show as much variation as the other three variables; nevertheless, it does range from 18th with Washington to 44th for North Carolina. With respect to Arizona and Indiana, ranking is very similar on percent white.

The Arizona study further examined the applicability of sending multiple questionnaires to a household to get both male and female responses. Also, varying degrees of personalization were attempted in an effort to determine to what extent personalization influences rate of response. These are all reported in Carpenter [8]. These four states also provided an opportunity to look at different ways of obtaining samples of a large population. In their studies, Washington and North Carolina utilized extensively the development of lists from telephone directories. The Arizona and Indiana studies utilized preprinted lists available from automobile registrations. Both studies suggest different biases.[2]

2. A problem such as this was encountered in conducting statewide community preference studies in Indiana, Washington, Arizona, and North Carolina. Drawing samples from telephone directories (in Washington and North Carolina) and automobile registrations (in Indiana and Arizona) did not allow the researchers any degree of confidence as to the proportion of Blacks included in the sample. As a result, a low response rate among minorities in these state studies was found. The question is whether or not they were in the sample to begin with. When conducting a study in Bartholomew County, Indiana, we had representatives from the CAP Agency and the Retirement Foundation approach us, wanting to make sure their clients were included in the list generated from automobile registrations. We had previously drawn a sample of 2,000 households representing one out of every eight households in the county. The Retirement

One of the purposes of these four studies was to develop a benchmark of attitudes and opinions across residents in each of the states. In Indiana, aside from the explanation of the method used and characteristics of respondents over time of response by Brooks et al. [5], the remaining publications deal with specific details of the survey results.

Gordon et al. attempted to answer the questions: "What size of community do Indiana residents prefer?" "What community services are considered essential?" "How does the preferred community differ from the existing community?" "What type of community do Indiana residents dislike?" [24]. Ryan et al., on the other hand, looked at the implications communities would experience resulting from a population redistribution and population composition, should people move to the community of their choice [27]. The findings show that migration to a community of preferred size would lead to less people living in large cities and more in middle-sized communities, while the smallest communities would remain virtually unchanged. Furthermore, if residents were allowed to act out their preferences, migration to a community of preferred size would only lower the educational and income levels of the present smallest communities. Blake et al. attempted to determine the processes underlying residents' orientations to the characteristics of the desired community [3]. Finally, Blake et al. also looked at reported dissatisfactions as a useful guide for the development of remedial programs in community development efforts [4].

The North Carolina study was undertaken to provide the Extension Service, along with other local and state leaders, planners, and policymakers, with an assessment of the public's perceptions of needs, problems, and goals in North Carolina [9, 10, 11, 12, 13, 14]. This study has yielded several volumes of short analyses entitled "Through Our Eyes," to give an idea of the preferences, goals, rural-urban problems, public concerns, and, in general, who wants what in North Carolina.

The studies conducted in each of the four states were primarily interested in assessing public opinion of residents within the respective states. It is almost safe to say that they represent the first statewide studies conducted in each of these states. The potential is present whereby each of these individual state studies can contribute

Foundation and the CAP Agency provided us with lists of their clients to supplement the survey. In checking their lists against our master list, we found exactly one-eighth of the CAP Agency clients, as well as one-eighth of the Retirement clientele, were included in our master sample. Therefore, we now were certain that minorities, as well as the aged, were included in the original sample. However, getting them to respond is another matter.

immensely to public policymakers. The output from Washington and North Carolina has more readily found its way into the hands of policymakers, decision makers, and planners in those two states than has taken place in Arizona and Indiana. Other states are also taking this approach. Iowa just completed its study and Kentucky is initiating one on public values and priorities, using a similar mailing procedure.

Issue Specific. Thus far, the discussion has focused on these very broad benchmark studies conducted in four states. Also, some evidence suggests that the basic procedure employed in the mail questionnaire in the Washington, Indiana, Arizona, and North Carolina studies is also applicable when dealing with specific issue areas. The examples cited next are only two of many that could be mentioned.

Let us recall the energy problems facing the United States during the latter part of 1973 and the early part of 1974. It is safe to say that the information provided local people concerning levels of fuel and other energy resources available was somewhat less than adequate. Many decisions were made by policymakers with respect to closing gasoline stations one day a week—suggesting that people get into car pools—and alterations of the same with respect to installation of storm windows, insulation, and so on. Other suggestions were to turn the thermostat down and use mass transit systems to get to and from employment. In essence, we knew little about the behavioral implications resulting from the energy crisis.

A mail questionnaire study subsequently was conducted in the state of Indiana by Doering et al. [22]. They utilized the same methodology in terms of the mail questionnaire concept; however, they deleted one of the stages in the process (postcard). From the first week of April 1974 to mid-May, a sample of 1,000 residents, whose names were obtained through auto registrations, received a series of mailouts. In less than two months, the data had been collected and were in the process of being tabulated. The results of this particular study were then made available to policymakers through open meetings and special symposiums throughout the state. The response rate was 75 percent.

Another example is research undertaken by Ryan and Justice [26]. Their work concerned national health insurance; the data were obtained by asking a random sample of Indiana residents to evaluate their present health services. Again, this study was conducted among 1,000 Indiana residents whose names were obtained from automobile registrations. The study represents a quick turnaround time from initial questionnaire to completion, with a publication that can be utilized by decision makers and others involved in health care policy. Further, analysis of the data demonstrates the impact of health insurance on the poor, the middle-income, and the upper-income people as specific subgroups of the population. In spite of current dissatisfaction, "most of the respondents did not support the national health insurance concept. Fear was expressed that such a program would not effectively keep costs down while, at the same time, resulting in too much government control" [26, p. 1].

Local County Level. The final two examples included here illustrate how the mail questionnaire technique can be put to use at the local level. The first example is the Pierce County study conducted in the state of Washington. This study was an outgrowth of a growth policy conference held in the state during 1974. The purpose was to identify desirable directions for Pierce County's future. The questionnaire was based upon the assumptions, conclusions, and recommendations of the conference; the hoped-for result is some indication of where the general public stands on the many issues that seem vital in determining directions of that county [19]. Local response to the mail questionnaire was 80 percent.

A number of issues were presented, ranging from the "loss of good agricultural land to other uses" to "inadequate planning throughout the county." In addition, a number of problems stemming from the issues were presented to get some kind of ranking by the residents of the county. These problems included raising property taxes, suburban sewage, public transit, lack of civic pride, and others. Local sentiment was obtained with respect to the services residents receive, given the tax dollars they contribute, plus some assessment of the overlap of services offered by other agencies within the county. Finally, a series of goals developed by local citizen boards was presented to get some feel as to what the county should do in the near future.

The other example of utilizing the mail questionnaire in research at the county level is exemplified in the Bartholomew County United Way Services Project [6, 28]. This project was an attempt to aid a local United Way agency and its member agencies in the decision-making process of allocating resources among member agencies. Local people were involved in preparation of the proposal, selection of the sample, development of the research instrument, personal interviewing, and final write-up of some of the project outputs.

The results of the study were used to supplement a number of secondary sources to prepare a Community Service Profile. Each profile area (e.g., Community Health Maintenance Services) contained a definition of the field with the problems and conditions, objectives, and programs offered in that area. In addition, the nature and extent of need covering clientele and the estimate of current need were presented, along with an analysis of the present delivery of services. These are the agencies providing services in the area of Community Health Maintenance.

The data obtained from the mail questionnaire, of which a sample of 2,000 households was selected from auto registrations, were utilized in the development of city and township maps to point out the area of need for services throughout the county. In essence then, a handbook for agencies in the county was developed to help in the decision-making process pertaining to the utilization of current services and the need for future services in the county in the next few years.

The Bartholomew County Project also had local sponsorship in that all mailings came out under the direction of the United Way of Bartholomew County. The mail questionnaire in this particular project, which followed the procedure described previously in this chapter, yielded a response rate of 62 percent. Although the response rate was lower in this project than in any of the projects reported in this chapter, it is important to release this information because it demonstrates what we might expect under situations where local people design and operate their own public opinion survey.

INTERPLAY BETWEEN RESEARCHERS AND POLICYMAKERS. All the examples cited thus far have varying degrees of input to policymakers. Of the studies conducted in Indiana, Washington, Arizona, and North Carolina, reported in Dillman et al. [21], the Washington and North Carolina studies have had the greatest exposure to public policymakers and decision makers at the state level. This conclusion is based on the manner in which project inputs have been packaged and prepared for dissemination among potential decision makers as well as public meetings held throughout the state.

An example of one study which appears to have had extensive involvement and interplay between researchers and policymakers is the Alternatives for Washington survey by Dillman and Wardwell [20]. This survey had sponsorship by the governor of the state. In fact, the questionnaires were returned to the state legislature under the guidance of the governor; approximately 26,000 completed questionnaires were returned. In addition, television time was purchased, experimenting with the technique of allowing television viewers to complete a questionnaire and return it, in much the same way the Safety Council Citizen Driver Test was conducted in the United States about ten years ago.

An important point here is to have early involvement between researchers and policymakers with respect to the problem area. In fact, what is needed is a better interplay between researchers (providers of information), policymakers (users of the information), and the impact group (local citizens). This interchange is somewhat evident in the suggestions by Fowler concerning how information generated by researchers can be utilized [23]:

1. Those considering policy or making decisions must want such information (citizen and decision maker).

2. The information available must be relevant to the policies or decisions being considered (researcher and decision maker).

3. The data must be available where issues are being considered (researcher and decision maker).

4. The research findings must be in a usable form (researcher, policymaker, and local citizen).

5. The policy implications of the findings must be feasible to accomplish (researcher and policymaker).

Confidence in the researcher's ability to deliver quality work must be gained by the policymaker, as well as by those in the impact group. Also, the time it takes to deliver the work must be shortened. The findings may be simplified, but they must be based on sound research.

It is a rare individual indeed, whether he be in research, in extension, a planner, or an organizational leader interested in rural America, who feels adequate to cover all areas of the research process. In other words, the ability to conceptualize, operationalize concepts, adequately define the problem, and then conduct the research, analyze the findings, write up the project results, and have them easily transmittable to a wide range of potential recipients requires input from several people and disciplines. Generally, researchers write for one audience, whether that be their own colleagues or the consumer. Somehow, we have to acquire the skills or the teamwork to put this whole thing together.

In addition, it is regrettable that in the case of numerous studies the information would have been more useful had it been obtained yesterday. Somehow, in the development of our skills, we need to be able to demonstrate a quicker turnaround from the inception of the research project to its conclusion. The presentation of the mail questionnaire procedure and the many examples is a step in that direction.

CONCLUSIONS AND QUESTIONS FOR DISCUSSION. We have now covered the waterfront from early opinion surveys, public opinion survey organization, advantages and disadvantages of public surveys, and some specific examples using mail questionnaires. Furthermore, an attempt was made to raise some issues concerning the interplay between providers, users, and publics. In essence, the real question is how the whole thing can be put together so that public opinion surveys can be used in policy formation. Rural America has not been addressed per se, and perhaps it should be. That is, do we approach public opinion surveys any differently in rural than in urban America?

The mail questionnaire, used in several public opinion surveys, is presented as one way to poll publics (when that approach is deemed useful) and place some faith in the results based on the higher response rates. Many of the studies had significant integration between policymakers, researchers, and local people.

If this approach appears to be one way of obtaining public opinion data, how relevant is it to your situation, be it university, public agency, extension program, USDA, or planning organization? What model can you suggest to "put it all together"? Would it be advisable, feasible, and worthwhile to develop a public polling organization within your state to handle broad issues for input to policy? Many of you have undoubtedly participated in public opinion surveys, either as designer of the study, analyst of the data, preparer of project findings, provider of information, respondent, policymaker, planner, or concerned citizen trying to make decisions on the findings. How useful have public opinion surveys been to your work, and how can they be made more relevant to public policy? Suppose we were interested in some topic or concern in which we felt a public opinion survey was appropriate. What kind of commonality of interest, if any, would you expect to find among planners, agency personnel, policymakers, researchers, and extension workers? Of what use are the national polls to you? Can they help set policy for rural America?

REFERENCES

1. American Statistical Association. 1974. Report on the ASA conference on surveys of human populations. *Am. Stat.* 28:30–34.
2. Baron, Norman J., E. James Cecil, Phil L. Tideman, and James P. Ludwig. 1972. A survey of attitudes towards the Mississippi River as a total resource in Minnesota. Minn. Water Resour. Res. Cent. Bull. 55.
3. Blake, Brian F., Vernon D. Ryan, Ralph M. Brooks, and John R. Gordon. 1974. Residents' orientations to community attributes: An exploratory study. Purdue Univ. Agric. Exp. Stn. Bull. 58.
4. Blake, Brian F., Ralph M. Brooks, Vernon D. Ryan, and John R. Gordon. 1974. Some implications of citizens' reactions to their communities: Monitoring versus remediation in community development efforts. Purdue Univ. Agric. Exp. Stn. Bull. 62.
5. Brooks, Ralph M., Vernon D. Ryan, Brian F. Blake, and John R. Gordon. 1974. An explanation and appraisal of the methodology used in the 1973 Indiana community preference study: A mail survey. Purdue Univ. Agric. Exp. Stn. Bull. 53.

6. Brooks, Ralph M., Dale L. Graff, and Mark B. Triplett. 1974. United Way services evaluation: A survey of the opinions and needs of Bartholomew County residents. Department of Agricultural Economics, Purdue University.

7. Buse, R. C. 1973. Increasing response rates in mailed questionnaires. *Am. J. Agric. Econ.* 55 (Aug.): 503–8.

8. Carpenter, Edwin H. 1975. Personalizing mail surveys: A replication and reassessment. *Public Opin. Quart.* 38:614–20.

9. Christenson, James A. 1973. Through our eyes. Vol. 1, People's goals and needs in North Carolina. N.C. Agric. Ext. Serv. Misc. Publ. 106.

10. ———. 1973. Through our eyes. Vol. 2, People's goals and needs in North Carolina—Summary. N.C. Agric. Ext. Serv. Misc. Publ. 107.

11. ———. 1974. Through our eyes. Vol. 3, Who wants what in North Carolina? N.C. Agric. Ext. Serv. Misc. Publ. 111.

12. ———. 1974. Through our eyes. Vol. 4, Community preferences and population distribution. N.C. Agric. Ext. Serv. Misc. Publ. 112.

13. ———. 1974. Through our eyes. Vol. 5, Rural-urban problems in North Carolina. N.C. Agric. Ext. Serv. Misc. Publ. 113.

14. ———. 1974. Through our eyes. Vol. 6, Public concerns in Guilford County. N.C. Agric. Ext. Serv. Misc. Publ. 114.

15. *County and City Data Book.* 1972. Washington, D.C.: U.S. Government Printing Office.

16. Dillman, Don A. 1972. Increasing mail questionnaire response in large samples of the general public. *Public Opin. Quart.* 36 (Summer): 253–57.

17. ———. 1971. Public values and concerns of Washington residents: Priorities for spending public funds. Wash. State Univ. Agric. Exp. Stn. Bull. 748.

18. Dillman, Don A., and Russell P. Dobash. 1972. Preferences for community living and their implications for population redistribution. Wash. State Univ. Exp. Stn. Bull. 764.

19. Dillman, Don A., and Deanna Rankos. 1974. The future of the Pierce County area. Department of Rural Sociology, Washington State University.

20. Dillman, Don A., and John Wardwell. 1975. Final results: Alternatives for Washington surveys. Department of Rural Sociology, Washington State University.

21. Dillman, Don A., James A. Christenson, Edwin H. Carpenter, and Ralph M. Brooks. 1974. Increasing mail questionnaire response: A four state comparison. *Am. Sociol. Rev.* 39 (Oct.): 744–56.

22. Doering, Otto C. III, Jerry Fezi, Dave Gauker, Mike Michaud, and Steve Pell. 1974. Indiana's views on the energy crisis. Purdue Univ. Coop. Ext. Serv. Pap. 6.

23. Fowler, Floyd J., Jr. 1974. *Citizen Attitudes toward Local Government, Services and Taxes.* Cambridge, Mass.: Ballinger.

24. Gordon, John R., Brian F. Blake, Ralph M. Brooks, and Vernon D. Ryan. Preferences for community living: A 1973 statewide opinion of Indiana residents. Purdue Univ. Coop. Ext. Circ. 435.

25. Public polls: Variance in accuracy, reliability. 1971. *Congr. Quart. Wkly. Rep.* 29 (July): 1927–36.

26. Ryan, Vernon D., and Valerie Justice. 1975. What Indiana people say about health care. Purdue Univ. Coop. Ext. Serv. Circ. 443.

27. Ryan, Vernon D., Brian F. Blake, Ralph M. Brooks, and John R. Gordon. 1974. Community size preference patterns among Indiana resi-

dents: Implications for population redistribution policies. Purdue Univ. Agric. Exp. Stn. Bull. 55.
28. Triplett, Mark B., Dale L. Graff, and Ralph M. Brooks. 1974. Bartholomew County community service profiles: A report of the United Way services evaluation project. Department of Agricultural Economics, Purdue University.
29. Walsh, John. 1974. The budget of the United States government. *Science* 183:635–36.
30. Webb, Kenneth, and Harry P. Hatry. 1973. *Obtaining Citizen Feedback: The Application of Citizen Surveys to Local Governments.* Washington, D.C.: Urban Institute.

CHAPTER FIFTEEN

SUGGESTIONS FOR INTEGRATION OF INFORMATION GENERATORS AND INFORMATION CONSUMERS: AN OVERVIEW AND SUMMARY

DAVID L. ROGERS

UNIVERSITIES have a great problem-solving potential, but are often prisons for new ideas [1]. Although information is generated through elaborate programs of research, it often is held within the scientific community because of a lack of incentive to transmit it to nonscientific audiences or because mechanisms for disseminating ideas to nontechnical groups are inadequate. Clark proposes that the utilization of knowledge has two main facets: knowledge building (i.e., integrating research and theory into forms that can be used by lay audiences) and institutionalization of knowledge (creating networks to introduce knowledge to consumers) [1]. In this summary chapter, some of the recommendations found in the preceding chapters will be reviewed within two contexts—the integration of theory, research, and application and the development of linkages between information-generating and information-using institutions.

The focus here will be on both "what is" and "what ought to be" in the conduct of policy research. The chapter will emphasize answers to the question: "Where should we go from here?"

INSTITUTIONAL ARRANGEMENTS FOR EFFECTIVE POL-ICY RESEARCH. The generation, transmission, and consumption of policy research occurs within an institutional context. Policy research is conducted in universities, private research institutes, and government agencies; it is transmitted through the press, through educational institutions, and through formal training programs. Finally, it is consumed by public decision-making institutions located at local,

DAVID L. ROGERS is Associate Professor of Sociology, Iowa State University.

county, state, regional, and federal levels. Three important questions in analyzing any public policy research are: "Who are the sponsoring units?" "Who are the research units?" "Who are the consuming units?"

The relevant institutions in policy research often are defined in a narrow manner. Daft (Chap. 1) and Moe (Chap. 5) both point out, however, that the scope of groups relevant to policy research is very wide. Examples of clients for policy research on rural development go well beyond the agricultural institutions and especially beyond the U.S. Department of Agriculture. Daft argues that new linkages should be developed with federal agencies such as the Health Services Administration, the Manpower Administration, the National Institute for Education, the Advisory Commission on Intergovernmental Relations, the Office of Revenue Sharing, and the Social and Rehabilitation Service. Moe recommends extending the list of relevant groups to those in legislative branches of government and to private groups including the Coalition for Rural Development, the Rural Caucus, the National Association of Regional Councils, the Rural Educational Association, the Rural Housing Alliance, the Housing Assistance Council, and the American Bankers Association. As the number of relevant groups increases, the need for improved communication between research and consuming units also increases. Identification and knowledge of these groups could be critical in conducting policy research; many of these organizations will likely support, use, or be impacted by the results of such research.

Both limits and strengths are associated with the present set of institutional arrangements for conducting policy research. The limits of present arrangements could be modified to reduce their negative effects. Strengths of the present institutions, on the other hand, may suggest points for the potential expansion and development of institutions.

Limits of the current institutional arrangements can be classified into three categories; two relate to the boundaries between research and policy-making units and one involves the internal design of the research institution itself. Moe observes that research institutions often lack formal procedures for exchanging information. He comments that information releases and publications for user audiences have not been adequate. Not only is there a lack of mass media techniques, but research institutions often lack systematic arrangements for bringing researchers, transmitters, and users together. In the past, this has led to suspicion or distrust among these various groups. The absence of systematic linkages among relevant groups also reduces the potential user's awareness about what information is available and, furthermore, makes it more difficult for the research community to determine the needs of different groups of users.

A second category of limits is the rather narrow definition of institutional domain often held by research institutions. Ordinarily, institutions expand their domain beyond what they may be capable of delivering. It could be argued, however, that many research institutions hold a very narrow definition of their responsibility, that is, it ends with the creation of information. This may lead to some of the problems mentioned by Moe: the failure to provide technical and educational assistance to users, the failure to increase public literacy on public issues and policy alternatives, the failure to respond to requests from users, and the failure to devote research monies to strategical variables that can be manipulated. This limited definition of domain or responsibility also precludes the use of inputs from relevant user groups, that is, the position may be taken that "it is not our task to go out and solicit inputs from the public or from interested agencies."

Finally, the third category of limits relates to the organization of research institutions. A critical factor in organizing tasks is how to motivate the actors. As Daft points out, universities reward originality and sophistication of techniques more than synthesis, application, and conceptualization. Incentives presently being used appear to be misplaced and make it difficult to conduct policy research.

The strengths of the present research institutions include those related to the general research setting and to specific techniques being used. At a general level, Daft suggests that comparative advantages for policy research in universities include: (1) an environment conducive to study and reflection, (2) greater freedom to evaluate programs, (3) the opportunity to bring several disciplines into the analysis, and (4) institutional flexibility.

A set of specific institutional arrangements that might be further strengthened are described by Moe. Among characteristics that could be improved are the present researcher-user contacts. Some extensive contacts already occur between researchers and clients in selected areas (e.g., agricultural production) but more extensive contacts should be developed around social and economic policy issues. Some efforts are presently being made by universities to interpret data or information about issues and alternatives for users. Books and newsletters published through rural development regional centers are examples of this activity. Several individual state universities also have similar programs for disseminating information. These programs could be expanded, especially those that aid in the interpretation of data.

One of the more important strengths that could be further developed is the current effort to secure user inputs in identifying policy issues and researchable problems. Recent developments associated with Title V of the Rural Development Act of 1972 have made important strides in requiring public involvement in identifying problems, alternatives, and types of information reported. Presently the users of rural development research are being brought to meet researchers to help clarify research issues and to participate in direct exchanges with research personnel. Initiatives are being developed within universities to create linkages with new groups, including municipal, county, and state officials. Some of these linkages involve the development of overlapping boards of directors (as with Title V), others involve shared data banks, and still others involve the transfer of resources and information between universities and public agencies.

In addition to building on these current strengths, three other innovations in policy research should be adopted, according to contributors to this book. The first of these innovations relates to techniques for increasing user involvement. Eberts and Sismondo (Chap. 4) propose the development of governing boards for policy research units. Such boards would be composed of members representing a cross-section of local residents (including low-income residents) and university and nonuniversity specialists. User involvement also might be increased through other forms of citizen participation where research units coordinate their activities more closely with established agencies such as social planning councils. In Moe's terms this represents a commitment that goes beyond the traditional research-extension relationship because it involves the participation of the public in the discovery and use of ideas.

A second innovative theme relates to the management of projects and to providing institutional support for (1) interdisciplinary research, (2) long-run vs. short-run programs, (3) joint research-extension activity, (4) policy planning, and (5) improved techniques for distribution of information. Huie (Chap. 2) suggests that additional support and encouragement to researchers needs to be provided through the reward system. Incentives must be provided to induce researchers to participate in joint multidisciplinary research. Those who have been involved in such research know that it is difficult to develop, conduct, and complete and, therefore, is not attractive to a large number of scientists. Multidisciplinary research is achieved in some institutions through multidisciplinary faculties in research institutes, departments, or regional projects, but little evidence is available to suggest the "best" procedure for achieving research broad enough in scope to be useful to planners.

Huie also suggests the need for a mix of commitment to long-run and short-run types of research. Institutions must decide which mix of research is appropriate for their situation. Should the institution focus on development of nontheoretical and applied techniques? Does the institution provide a climate favorable for researching local interests? Do local decision makers have direct access to researchers? Do researchers expect their research outputs to be used? If the answers to these questions are positive, the institutional climate may suggest a favorable commitment to policy research. If the answers are negative, institutional changes will have to be made before policy research receives appropriate attention.

Third, improvements in existing techniques for disseminating information are needed. Huie suggests that at the present time the system rewards researchers for disseminating results to other scholars and peers and the extension service is defined as responsible for disseminating information to local publics. If these role definitions remain unchanged, improved methods of communication between research and extension will be imperative. A much needed innovation, therefore, in policy research is the involvement of local decision makers, extension personnel, and researchers throughout the life of the project, including the dissemination phase.

PROJECT ORGANIZATION FOR EFFECTIVE POLICY RESEARCH.

This section will be developed within the context of proactive research as described by Eberts and Sismondo. It also will draw from suggestions and comments made by other chapter authors.

A critical element in designing policy research is identifying the potential users or the audience. Moe recommends, for example, that research publications be identified in terms of the specific audiences for which they are being prepared. Furthermore, attempts should be made to relate research information to specific classes of users on a continuing basis. Daft and Moe have both outlined the range of potential users. Daft's outline is in general categories (research/scientific through judicial) and Moe's list of users is fairly specific. They both argue that our present knowledge of potential audiences is inadequate.

In addition to knowing something about the audience, however, the policy researcher also must know and understand the local situation or context in which the research occurs (Huie). In addition to identifying users, techniques must be developed to involve these groups in the design and transmission of knowledge itself. Moe and Eberts and Sismondo describe how citizens might participate in identifying problems for research and in exploring alternative strategies to be researched.

Finally, it is important when considering the specific audience for whom research is being conducted that the function and character of the information be clarified (Huie). Researchers need to be clear about what the research is supposed to show and what type of information will be needed to answer relevant policy questions. Because policymakers are not a homogeneous group and do not have the same information needs, attention must be given by policy researchers to the different types of user needs and to which research designs will help acquire the necessary information.

A second major area of concern in designing policy research is the design of projects themselves. Research projects should focus on specific problems or issues (Daft). These may be developed from suggestions and requests by local policymakers, local residents, or local interest groups. As problem or issue specification proceeds it is important that a design be developed in which basic elements (i.e., concepts, hypothesis, data collection techniques, and analysis) are understood and clearly defined.

Policy research, according to several of the authors, is similar to basic research because it uses the same methods, instruments, and rigor (Eberts and Sismondo). It also is similar in that it uses theory, concepts, and hypotheses and involves data collection (Eberts and Sismondo). Moe argues, for example, that project objectives should be developed within the context of a specific problem area, should facilitate analysis of issues, should allow for the testing of alternative solutions, and should involve the testing of instruments. All these activities are common to both policy and basic research.

Some important differences between policy and basic research include: (1) policy research contains an overlap in democratic and research values (Eberts and Sismondo); (2) the boundaries of policy research are defined in terms of goals and means specified by policymakers rather than by researchers; (3) the central foci in policy research of strategic or manipulatable variables are those that have direct or indirect causal impacts on public needs (Daft; Eberts and Sismondo); (4) the predominately macroorientation in policy research (Daft; Eberts and Sismondo); and (5) feedback as an integral component of policy research (Eberts and Sismondo).

The proactive research paradigm posits that institutions and the research process itself are structures that can and should be modified through feedback and as such should be investigated and understood. Policy options and alternatives should be reassessed, negotiated, and modified as a result of information about the research process itself.

A third concern in the design of research involves the role of values (Daft). As Brown (Chap. 3) and Moe point out, all choices made in the research act (whether in policy or basic research), from selecting the problem to be studied to decisions on publishing results, involve value decisions. Policy researchers are counseled to meet the needs of users or clients. This means, presumably, using client values in problem identification, developing alternative solutions, then using scientific values in the design and operation of the research but returning to client preferences in the dissemination of research findings. One of the many problems associated with this recommendation is whether the information collected is public and available to all or is private and, therefore, restricted to the relevant clients only. Agreements must be reached about who will receive the information early in the project. This one problem illustrates one of a series of potential conflicts between the values of scholars and those of clients. If analysis is conducted for power holders, should those outside the power system have access to the information?

In addition to determining the relevant audiences for policy research, recognization should be given to the fact that consumers are not a homogeneous group. It is important to understand the character of information needed by different groups. Huie agrees that most decision makers prefer to make choices among alternatives rather than "yes" or "no" choices on a single solution. Some groups may want to know what has occurred in their own community, others may want to know what to expect in the future, and still others may wish to know the probabilities of success associated with specific programs.

EFFECTIVE USE OF POLICY RESEARCH IN PLANNING. Recommendations involving planning per se are few in number and not well developed in this collection of writings. Most of those preparing chapters either conduct research or transmit information to policymakers. However, several points can be identified that could be useful in conceptualizing and organizing the planning process.

One of the major problems in planning is the complexity of the process (Daft). This complexity is especially obvious in the wide range of variables and issues encountered and are relevant in any given situation. For example, often numerous units are participating, and of these, some have more decision-making power than others. The decisions made are often serial and incremental, and many of them involve long-run trade-offs. Finally, in considering direct and indirect effects of variables and the problem of identifying what is a "strategic variable," a broad framework and familiarity with previous empirical research can be valuable assets in the planning process.

A second important activity in the planning process is the need to clarify the problem and understand its source. Huie comments that local decision makers can make better use of plans when (1) the problem is stated clearly, (2) there are major alternatives to be considered, and (3) the consequences of each alternative are known, including the social, political, economical, legal, physical, and technical impacts. Unless local planning officials are associated with professional associations or publications, their ability to develop alternatives or, more importantly, anticipate even the first-order consequences may be limited. Involving the policy researcher at an early point in the planning activity, therefore, could bring additional skills to bear on the problem.

Third, those involved in the planning process need an appreciation for the various functions, roles, and interrelatedness of the system parts. Angell et al. (Chap. 10) comment on the need for modeling as part of the planning process. Modeling, they argue, should help to improve an understanding of the functions, roles, and interdependencies within the system. Structural-functional planning models are given as an example of a technique for delineating the relevant elements in planning for housing.

Associated with the need to clarify the problem and alternative solutions and to understand the interrelatedness of strategic variables is the importance of identifying who benefits and who pays the costs associated with the alternatives. Huie identifies several types of costs (e.g., social, political, and economic) that should be identified and their distribution in the population made known. Researchers and planners working together are more apt to ask the question: "Who benefits?" and at the same time be able to design a method for getting an answer.

A second theme in the effective use of policy research relates to the strategy described by Brown. He argues that the forensic model used in courts is a viable alternative to our present system of linking research and policy. This model involves an adversary system for each policy alternative that possesses both research and information-generating capacity. In this model, the value commitments of policy-makers and researchers are recognized and given visibility as each side attempts to present its case. A potential problem with this approach, however, is whether all sides to an issue have the same capacity to generate information in support of their position. Where all parties do not have equal information, generating strength considerations other than "facts" might influence the final decision. In spite of this potential limit, the forensic model is currently being used extensively in court cases in which each party mobilizes expert testimony to win its case. Recent court decisions on the impacts of reservoirs, military bases, and mining are examples of situations in which this alternative has been used.

A third set of recommendations on this topic relates to the better integration of researchers, planners, and users in the planning process. Eberts and Sismondo's proactive model proposes that researchers and policymakers both be involved throughout the entire process. The capacity of planners to deal with questions of multiple and circular causation, manipulatable variables, and levels of evidence and their associated costs should be increased through interactions with researchers who deal with multivariate models and tests.

Finally, it appears that access to policy research might improve the potential and the structure for short-run (fast turn-around) projects conducted by planners (Libby and Shelton, Chap. 8). Planning agencies make decisions with whatever information is available. This often is done on very short notice; therefore information must be made available very rapidly. The typical university research unit has difficulty responding to requests with fast turn-around demands. A closer working relationship between researchers (those engaged in policy research) and planners could improve the turn-around time on projects. Dialogue between planners and researchers would improve problem identification, the level of confidence associated with a particular question would be better understood, and, therefore, the research design would reflect the minimal requirements of planners.

POTENTIAL TECHNIQUES FOR POLICY RESEARCH. Following is a review of potential techniques that could be used in policy research. This discussion is not meant to be exhaustive but, rather, alerts the reader to places in the book where these selected tools are discussed in greater detail and where other tools might be located. These potential tools are grouped into two categories: those relating to data collection and those relating to data analysis.

Data Collection. Within this category are those tools or issues that relate to the type of variable and unit being studied, to data collection techniques, and to the evaluation of these techniques.

The authors in this book uniformly call for aggregated variables (i.e., index formation), macrovariables (e.g., data on groups or higher level variables rather than on individuals), and manipulatable variables (properties that are subject to manipulation by decision makers). Data collection techniques described in the chapters range from situations in which researchers are assumed to have access to secondary data through the use of mail and telephone questionnaires to a fairly novel procedure for collecting data as subjects interact with the computer (Richards et al., Chap. 7).

An important consideration in any data collection process is the cost involved. These costs vary with the amount, kind, and frequency of data collection efforts (Hickman and Warren, Chap. 12). If planners and researchers were to set up a full-scale proactive research project involving repeated measurement (as a result of monitoring and evaluation processes) it would be very costly. Both researchers and planners should know what costs are associated with selected designs.

Data Analysis. A major emphasis throughout these chapters is on multivariate analysis. One encounters this emphasis in Angell et al. and in Eberts and Sismondo's discussion of a system model, especially in their recognition that both the problems being researched and the process of conducting this research are complex systems of interrelated parts. Angell et al. describe the interrelationship of the several components of the housing system in detail.

Two specific statistical techniques used in multivariate analysis are regression analysis and simulation. Both require high speed computers, but each technique is designed to answer a different set of questions. Regression analysis is used by Richards et al. to identify growth centers and combine social, economic, and physical variables in the same mathematical model. Eberts and Sismondo use regression analysis to identify the independent effects of one variable on another in their matrix. These coefficients become weights that are useful in exploring policy alternatives.

Three types of simulation are described by Maki et al. (Chap. 11): computer simulation, games, and gaming simulation. The application of each type of simulation is described for areas such as transportation, population and employment, housing, and as a technique for improving planning and decisionmaking skills. Simulation is used in policy analysis by Richards et al. In studying public response to mass transit as a transportation alternative. The computer is used to assist residents in exploring alternative energy conservation practices. Angell et al. characterize simulation efforts in housing as beneficial because they permit the testing of policy variables prior to their implementation.

Many other important recommendations for policy research are presented in this collection of writings. Each should be studied carefully for its implication in conducting policy research. This chapter has identified only ideas most directly related to four topical areas: (1) institutional arrangements, (2) project organization, (3) use of policy research, and (4) potential techniques. In each of these areas, suggestions answering "where do we go from here?" are presented. Not all of these suggestions are new, nor should all of them be implemented in every situation, but taken as a whole, they raise important questions about the present system of policy research and offer some modest proposals improving future research efforts.

REFERENCE
1. Clark, Peter A. 1972. *Action Research and Organizational Change.* New York: Harper & Row, pp. 129–30.

INDEX